IMAGES
of America

LAKE RONKONKOMA

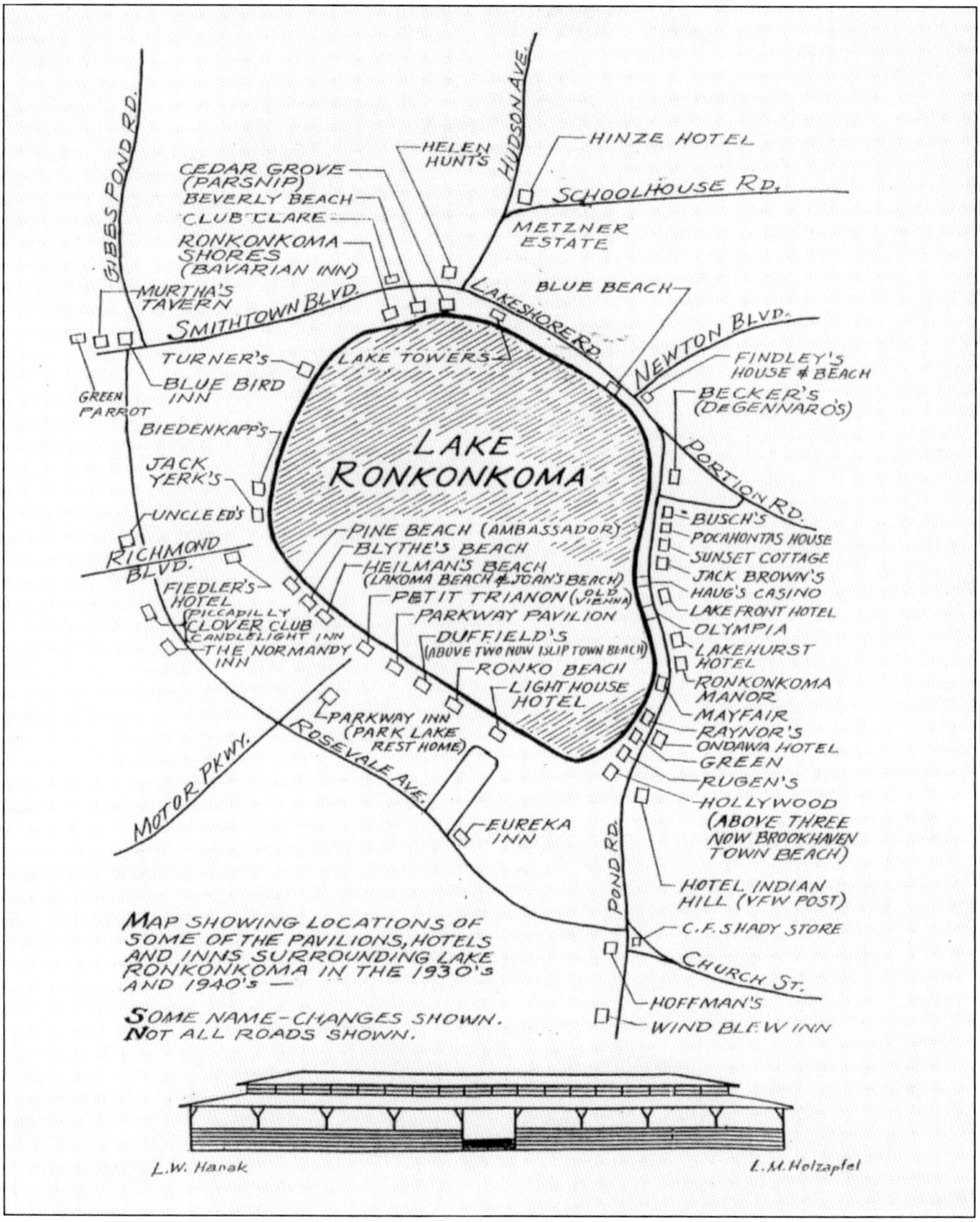

This map of Lake Ronkonkoma shows many locations of the pavilions, inns, and hotels during the 1930s and 1940s. Originally, Les W. Hanak created a map of the area. In 2001, Lawrence M. Holzapfel wrote his memoir of Lake Ronkonkoma, the *Fall of Apple Blossom Time*. Holzapfel decided to create his own version of the map and include it in his book. (Courtesy of Lawrence M. Holzapfel and Les W. Hanak.)

ON THE COVER: This photograph shows Raynor's Beach during the 1930s. The beaches and pavilions had their hands full on summer weekends. Buses, the Long Island Rail Road, and automobiles brought visitors by the thousands to enjoy this magnificent area. The Olympia Pavilion (back center) and the Mayfair Pavilion are clearly visible in this photograph.

IMAGES
of America

LAKE RONKONKOMA

Keith Oswald and Dale Spencer

ARCADIA
PUBLISHING

ISBN 978-0-7385-7656-5

Published by Arcadia Publishing
Charleston, South Carolina

Printed in the United States of America

Library of Congress Control Number: 2011930449

For all general information, please contact Arcadia Publishing:
Telephone 843-853-2070
Fax 843-853-0044
E-mail sales@arcadiapublishing.com
For customer service and orders:
Toll-Free 1-888-313-2665

Visit us on the Internet at www.arcadiapublishing.com

This book is dedicated to our wives, Jami Oswald and Janet Rischbieter, for their love, understanding, and patience.

Contents

ACKNOWLEDGMENTS

We would like to thank the following people for their input with this project: Helen Hethy Mulvihill; James Browne; Lawrence and Dolores Holzapfel; James Mooney; Paul Weber and Agnew and Taylor; Evelyn and Quinn Volgraff; Pat Duffield; Ellyn Okvist; Donna Snow; Debra Schramm; Emma Bruno; Fred Struss; Maria Hansson; Ron Ziel; Kevin and the VFW, Lt. David Cook and the Lake Ronkonkoma Fire Department; and the board, staff, and members of the Lake Ronkonkoma Historical Society.

We would also like to thank Abby Henry, Erin Rocha, Jennifer Pratt, Gervase Kolmos, and the rest of the staff at Arcadia Publishing for making this idea come to life.

Keith would like to thank the following for encouragement and inspiration on this project: my parents, Fred and Diane Oswald; my daughter, Madison; my brother and his wife, Eric and Jackie Oswald; my grandparents, Jean Pennachio, Amelia Pascucci, and Robert Beers; my in-laws, JoAnn and Herman Goetz; my uncle, John Pennachio, and his family; Mike Zanchelli; James Mroz; Keith Ellis; and King Fowley (by the way, the new album is awesome!).

Dale would like to thank Eva Stieberitz-Shutts, Reghan Shutts, and Astrid Spencer for their inspiration. Also, thanks to Josephine Molinari, Paul McInerney, and, of course, Anna P. Spencer for passing on her love for history.

Unless otherwise noted, all images appear courtesy of the Lake Ronkonkoma Historical Society.

INTRODUCTION

Lake Ronkonkoma was formed more than 17,000 years ago, when a massive block of ice separated from the glacial front during the Pleistocene glaciations. As the ice began to retreat, a large crater was left and groundwater began to fill the hole. The hole was so deep that the lake tapped into the underground water table. Lake Ronkonkoma is the largest lake on Long Island and is defined as a kettle hole.

Out of the 13 Indian tribes on Long Island, there were four that shared the shoreline of Lake Ronkonkoma—the Secatogs, Unkechaugs, Setaukets, and Nissequogues. In 1655, the Setauket tribe was the first to sell their land to white settlers.

Patents from the king of England were required since the purchases from the Indians were not lawfully acknowledged. This verified the titles and set boundaries. Patents were granted to William Nicholl (Islip), Richard Bull Smith (Smithtown), and Richard Woodhull and several others for Brookhaven. The three towns formed separate townships, using Lake Ronkonkoma's shoreline as the starting point to purchase land. The settlers not following the lines that were drawn up in England caused boundary disputes between the townships. The land adjacent to the rim of Lake Ronkonkoma in the Brookhaven section originally belonged to the Setauket and Unkechaug tribes; in Smithtown, the Nissequogues; and in Islip, the Secatogs.

The name Ronkonkoma—which was spelled many different ways—was never used, except if it was in reference to the lake itself. Smithtown records show that the land around Spectacle Pond was called the Ronconkomy Plains.

Some of the earliest settlers began buying property on the Smithtown side of the lake during the 1740s. Descendants of the Richard Bull Smith family found their way to the shores of Lake Ronkonkoma. By the 1790s, a survey was done and reported five houses north of Ronkonkomey Pond. Another family who became synonymous with Lake Ronkonkoma was the Smith family—known as the "Mooney Smiths" to distinguish them from the Bull Smith family of Smithtown. Arthur Smith was a Quaker who was expelled from Southold in 1654. Five years later, he was accepted as a townsman in Setauket. From there, the Smiths came to Lake Ronkonkoma.

Shortly after the Township of Brookhaven ordered the construction of Portion Road in 1795, John Woodhull, a descendant of Richard Woodhull (who held the patent for land in Brookhaven), built a house a half-mile east of the lake. One of his sons, Richard, also occupied the house. Later, the house was owned by Richard Woodhull Newton and came to be the homestead of the Newton family. With the expansion of the town during the 1960s, this home has been moved to Division Street in Ronkonkoma. It is the oldest home in Lake Ronkonkoma.

With the advent of the Long Island Rail Road in 1842, people began building homes close to the train station in Lakeland. (The train station would eventually move to its present site in Ronkonkoma in 1883.) An electrical engineer named George Warner had the longtime urge to drive a locomotive. Around 1842, he was given the chance to do so, and he drove a train to the end of the line in Islip. While waiting for a return trip, George Warner went for a walk, which led him to the shore of Lake Ronkonkoma. He was so impressed with the serenity and beauty of the lake that he bought some land on the north side of the lake. He encouraged his brother, an optician, to leave New York City and open an optical shop at Lake Ronkonkoma. The Warner family remained here permanently.

Lake Ronkonkoma became known as a summer resort in the late 19th and early 20th centuries. At the time, the area did not attempt to draw people by the multitudes. Lake Ronkonkoma was becoming a place for the wealthy and famous from New York City.

By the 1920s, the automobile brought dramatic change to Lake Ronkonkoma. Roads began to appear everywhere. Portion Road and Hawkins Avenue would become focal points for Lake Ronkonkoma. Gasoline pumps were installed in and around town. The middle class now had the opportunity to enjoy and to partake on what almost exclusively the wealthy had enjoyed for the previous 25 years. Developers seeking the potential of this new market for homes began to buy up land around the lake.

A man by the name of George Raynor bought some property in 1921. He discovered that people driving out from New York City were using his property for picnics. Every weekend, he would clean up the mess that was left by these visitors. He decided to build a small pavilion and some bathhouses on the beach. On the hill, a large building was transformed into a restaurant where hot meals were served. People would pay 50¢ for parking. Raynor's Beach ran from the lake up to Ronkonkoma Avenue. Raynor's Beach and Pavilion became one of the most popular spots on the lake.

In no time, about two-dozen beaches and pavilions sprang up around the lake, with waterwheels, floats, and slides. Music and dancing could be seen and heard by people passing by the lake. Boats were rented, and on Sunday afternoons a parachute jumper would come down from the sky into the lake. Some of these beaches and pavilions were Duffield's West Park Beach, Beckers, Hollywood Pavilion, Green Pavilion, Jack Yerk's, Turner's Corner Park, Haug's Casino, and many others. Lake Ronkonkoma adjusted to a two-season pattern. The economy of the town depended on a good season. At the end of each summer season, Lake Ronkonkoma returned to being a small town with familiar faces.

By the end of World War II in 1945, Lake Ronkonkoma was changing. The beaches and pavilions were slowly disappearing, and advertising began to suggest that people might want to live here year-round. Men and woman were coming home from the war and wanted to start families. This began the birth of suburbia on Long Island and in Lake Ronkonkoma. Age-old woodlands were disappearing. Homes and shopping centers began to dot the area.

In the 1950s, many of the original owners began selling their beaches to others. Many of the pavilions were left unattended and eventually burned down. These sections of the lake began to deteriorate. Garbage and dumping over the banks of the lake killed many trees and ruined the pristine beauty of the lake. During the 1970s, Suffolk County was to acquire the lake and the adjacent lands for the creation of a Shore Front Park. This was designed to clean up the lake and its surrounding areas. A deep recession hit in the 1970s, which put a halt on any plans for a cleanup or a county park.

There have been many attempts to revitalize Lake Ronkonkoma—some good, some bad. The town of Brookhaven has cleaned up Raynor's Park, giving the community a place they can relax, picnic, and for children to play. The town of Islip side of the lake has Ronkonkoma Town Beach. Similar to Raynor's Park, Ronkonkoma Town Beach has tennis courts, a playground, picnic areas, and access to the lake. The town of Smithtown has also, in recent years, cleaned up their side of the lake. Located off Smithtown Boulevard, Lake Ronkonkoma County Park has attracted many families to experience and enjoy the north side of the lake.

One

Beaches, Pavilions, Restaurants, and Inns

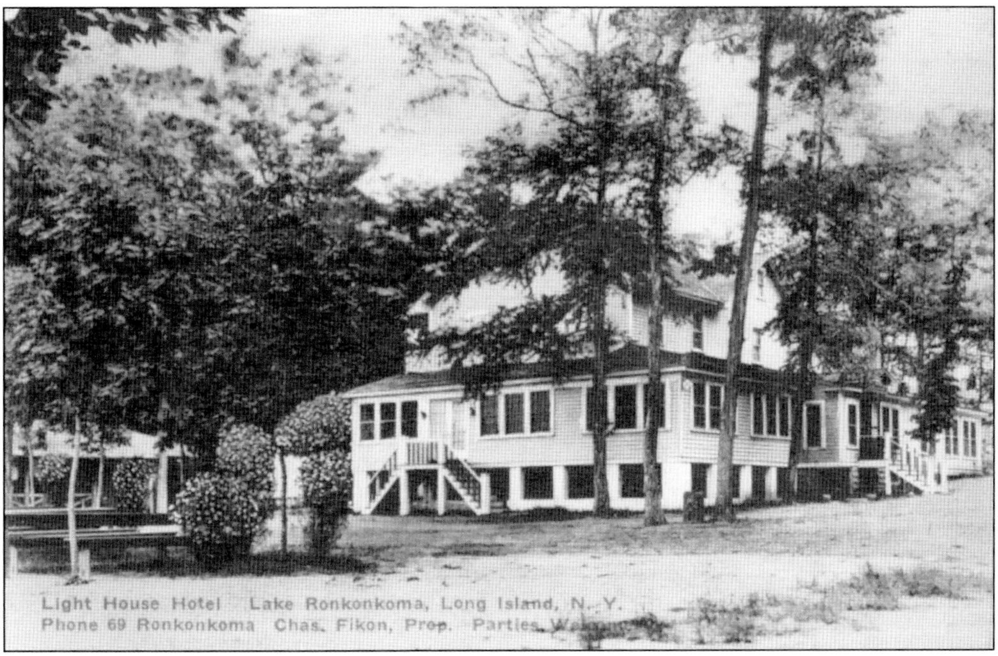

The Lighthouse Hotel is located on the southwest side of the lake. This postcard view shows the rear of the building leading to the lake. Patrons staying at the Lighthouse Hotel could enjoy fine dining, dancing, swimming, and the town's first bowling alley. This postcard dates to 1916.

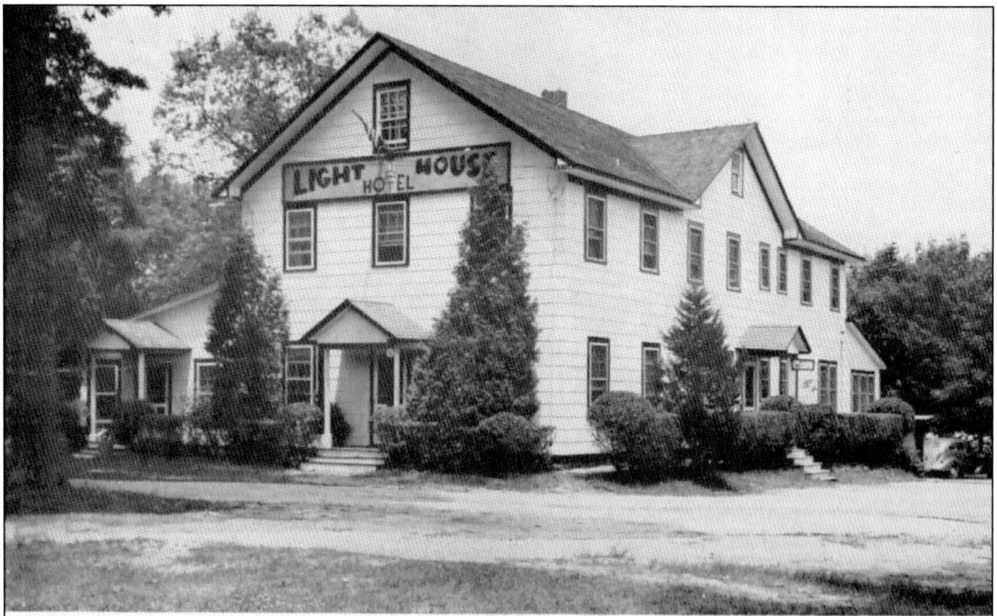

LIGHTHOUSE HOTEL, FINEST AND MOST REASONABLE DINNERS-OUTINGS ACCOMMODATION-FISHING-BATHING BOATING & DANCING. — W. RICHERT, PROP. - TEL. RONKONKOMA 8569 — LAKE RONKONKOMA, L. I.

This picture shows the front of the Lighthouse Hotel during the 1940s. Shortly after World War II, many hotels and inns began to disappear. The Lighthouse Hotel never became a casualty of modernization in Lake Ronkonkoma. From 1984 to 1996, the nightclub KISS occupied the building, until issues arose with neighbors in the surrounding area. Currently, the Beach Club Estate occupies the building.

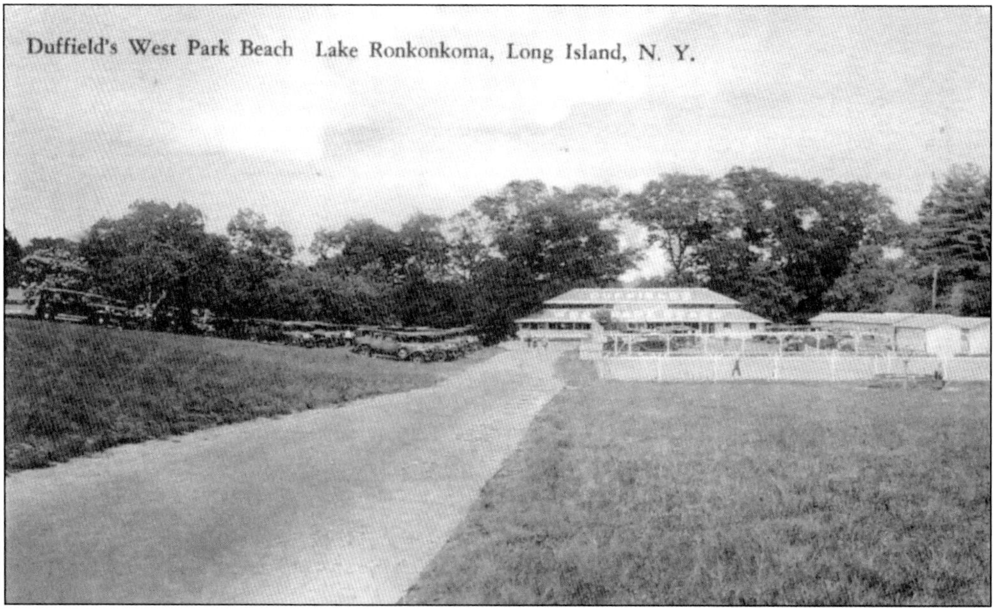

Duffield's West Park Beach is seen here during the 1930s. Ray and May Duffield constructed their pavilion and property in 1922. They offered numerous activities and had a parking field that could accommodate about 400 cars and numerous buses. The same layout seen in this postcard is visible today, entering the Ronkonkoma Town Beach off Rosevale Avenue.

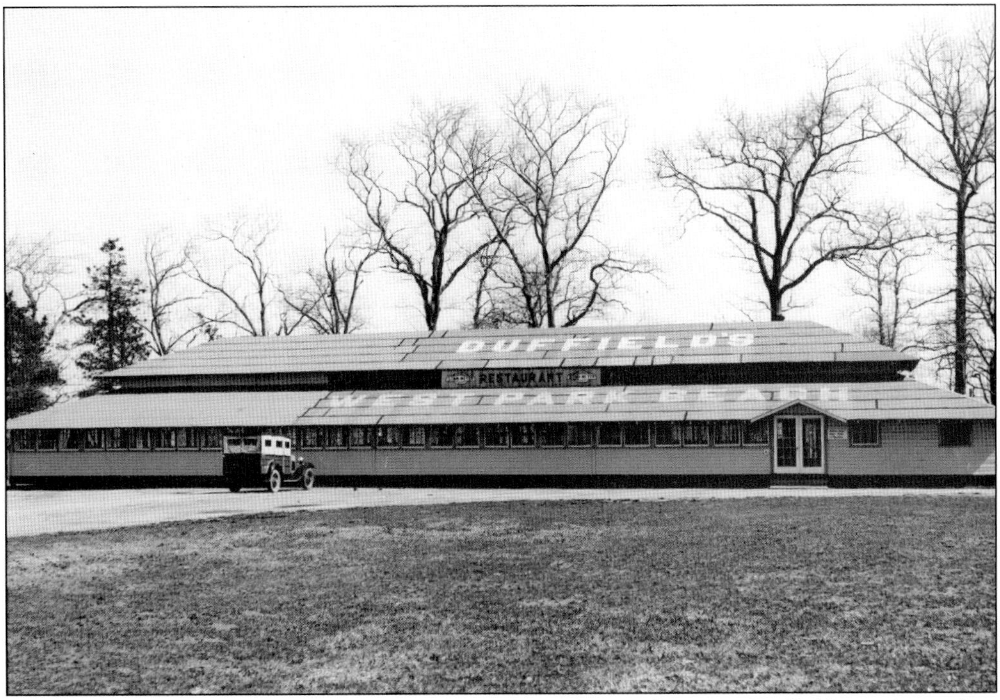

This is an impressive photograph of Duffield's pavilion taken in the 1930s. Duffield's was located on the west side of the lake; the site is now the Ronkonkoma Town Beach. During summer weekends, 100–200 hot meals were served every day at the restaurant located in the pavilion.

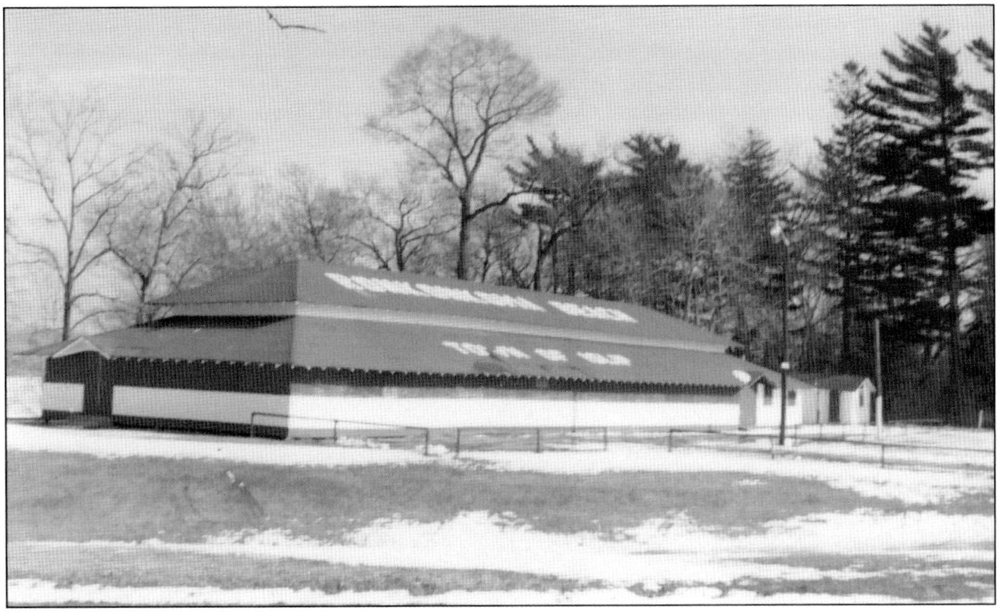

In 1953, Ray Duffield sold Duffield's West Park Beach. This photograph, taken in 1969, shows Ronkonkoma Town Beach (once Duffield's pavilion) in the town of Islip. During the 1970s, this pavilion would be demolished, and new facilities would be assembled on this site. As the 1980s were in full swing, Ronkonkoma Town Beach was the place to go for picnicking, swimming, and outdoor activities.

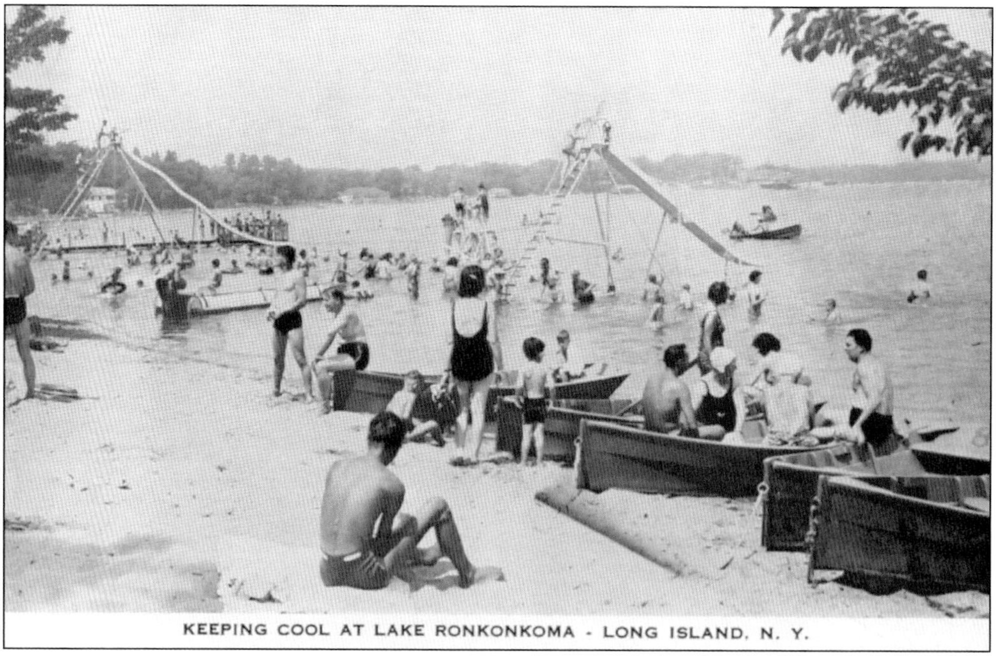

An action shot shows families at Duffield's West Park Beach during the 1940s. Like many beaches at the time, Duffield's had two large slides, 20 rowboats, a waterwheel, a diving platform, and a motorboat used for sightseeing. (Motorboats were banned on the lake by 1934.) Note the pavilion to the far right is Turner's and the one towards the back center of the picture is Jack Yerk's.

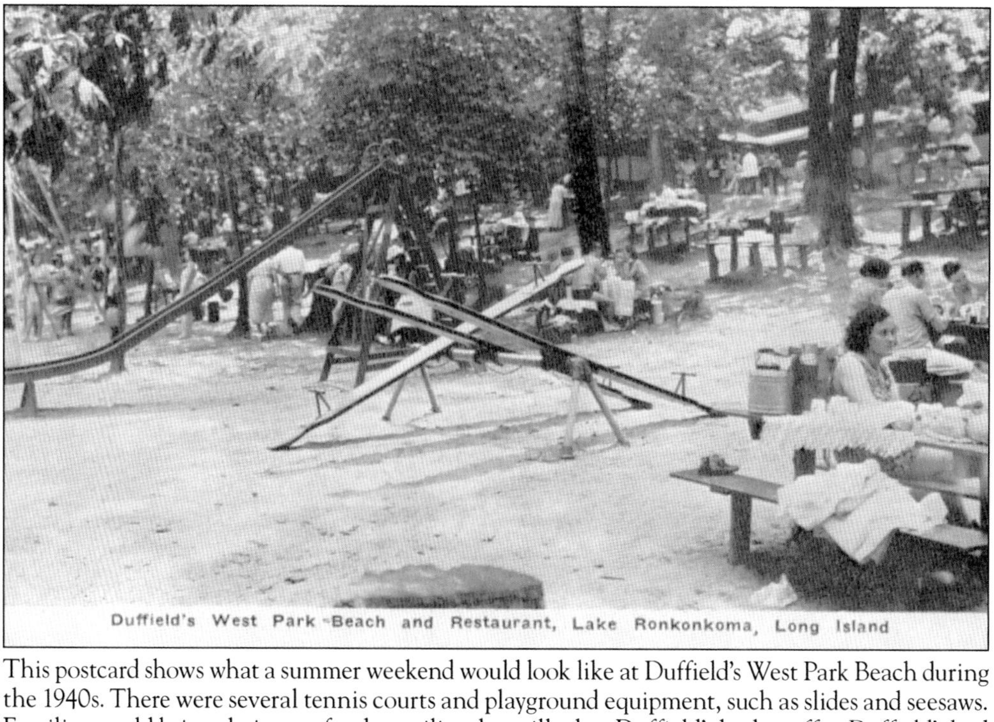

This postcard shows what a summer weekend would look like at Duffield's West Park Beach during the 1940s. There were several tennis courts and playground equipment, such as slides and seesaws. Families would bring their own food or utilize the grills that Duffield's had to offer. Duffield's had one of the largest picnic grounds on the lake.

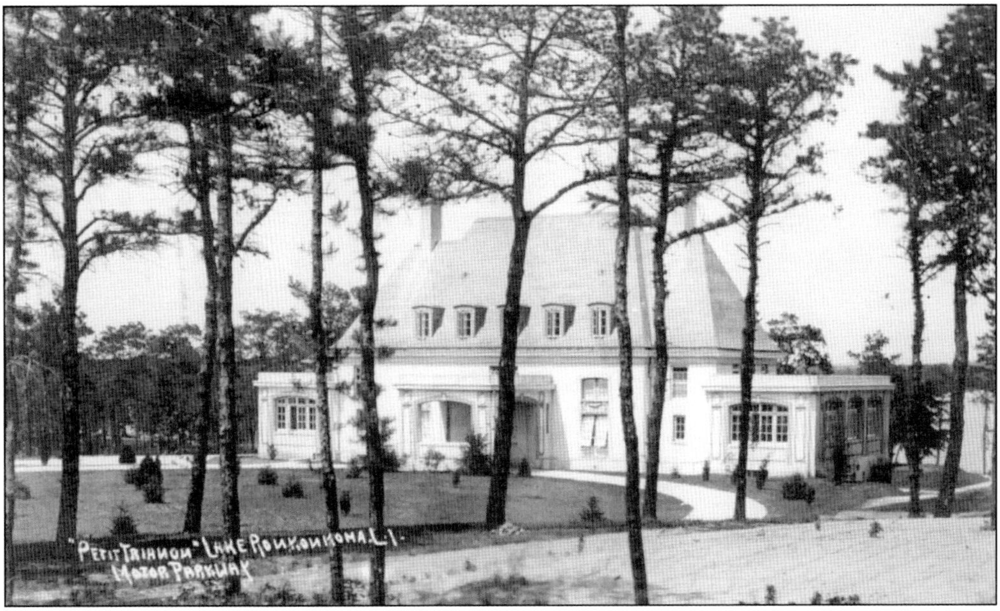

In 1911, the Long Island Motor Parkway reached Lake Ronkonkoma. Parkway officials decided to build a high-class inn for dining and a halfway stop for travelers. William K. Vanderbilt Jr. commissioned John Russell Pope to design the building. It was named the Petit Trianon, after one of the buildings on the grounds of Versailles Palace near Paris. The inn was under the Long Island Motor Parkway's ownership until 1926.

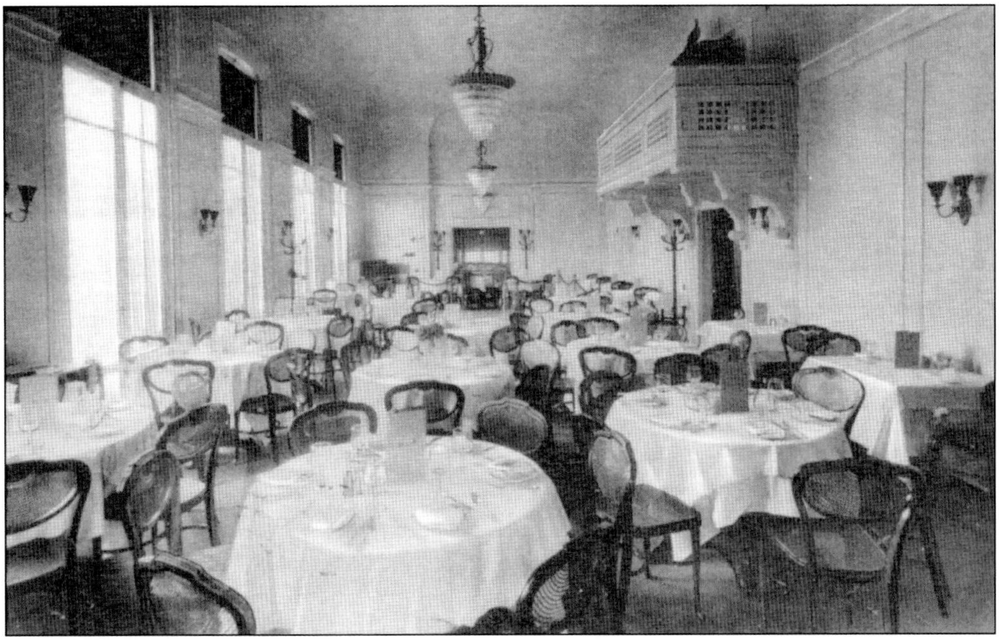

Pictured is the main dining room of the Petit Trianon. Many weddings, balls, and special events were held in this room. The interior of the inn also featured a lounge area in the south wing of the building. This postcard dates to c. 1916. Later on, the inn became a club and restaurant under various owners. On January 11, 1958, the Petit Trianon caught fire. The building burned for five hours. (Courtesy of Helen Hethy Mulvihill.)

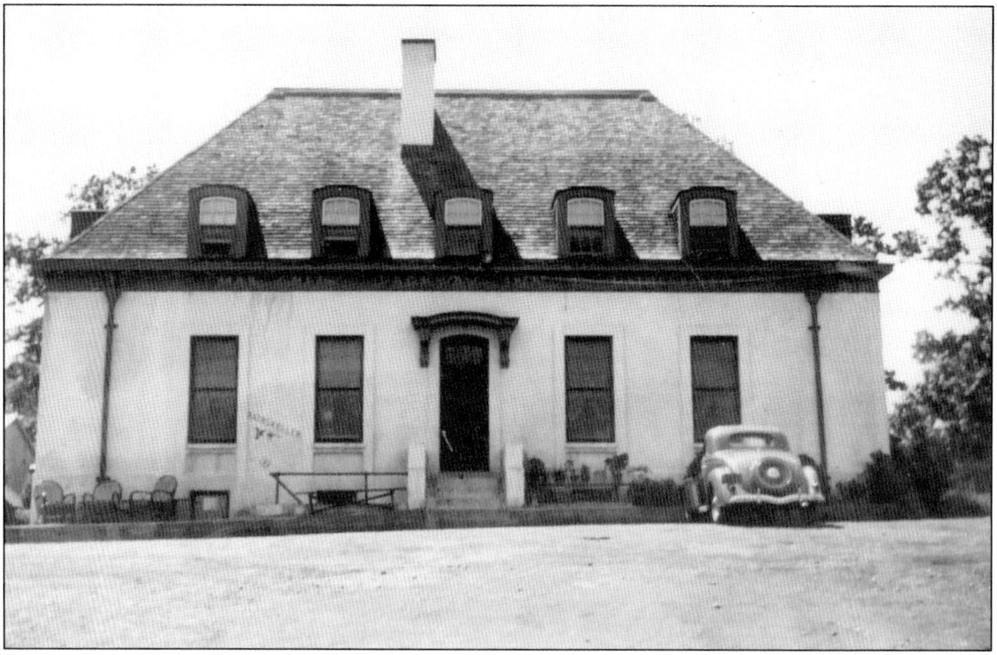

The Max Greis Parkway Inn was originally the servants quarters for the Petit Trianon. By the 1930s, Max Greis turned the building into an inn. The inn featured a German restaurant on the first floor. In the basement was a German tavern called the Rathskeller. Decades later, the inn became the Park-Lake Rest Home. By 2005, the building was destroyed and replaced by residential homes. This photograph was taken in 1937.

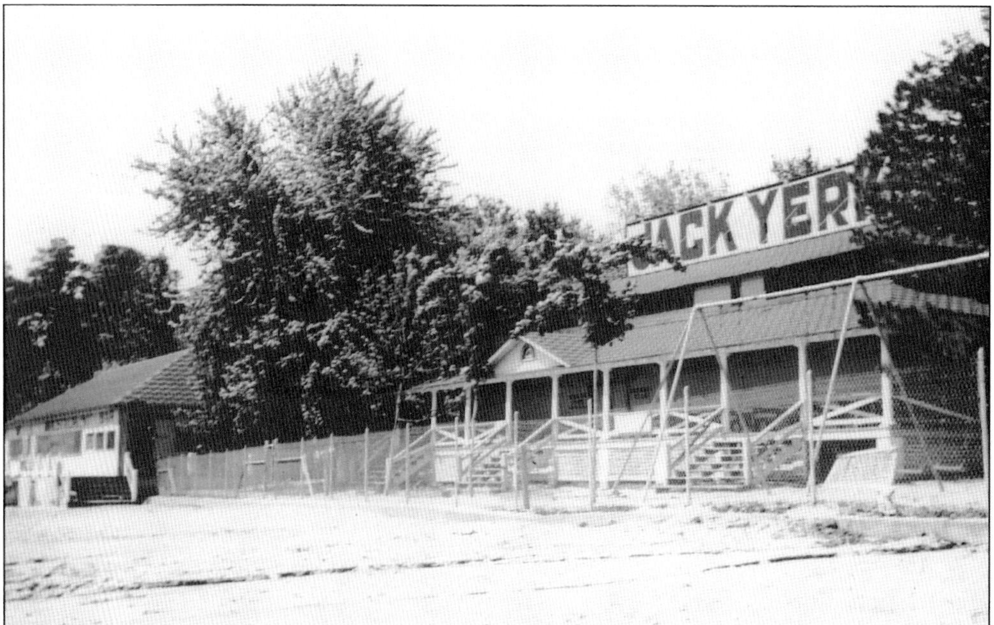

During the 1920s, Jack Yerk opened up a beach and a pavilion on the west side of the lake. Jack Yerk's was a very popular hangout at the time. Liquor was sold, and there was an outdoor bowling alley, which was a first for Lake Ronkonkoma. James Browne Sr. took this photograph in 1937.

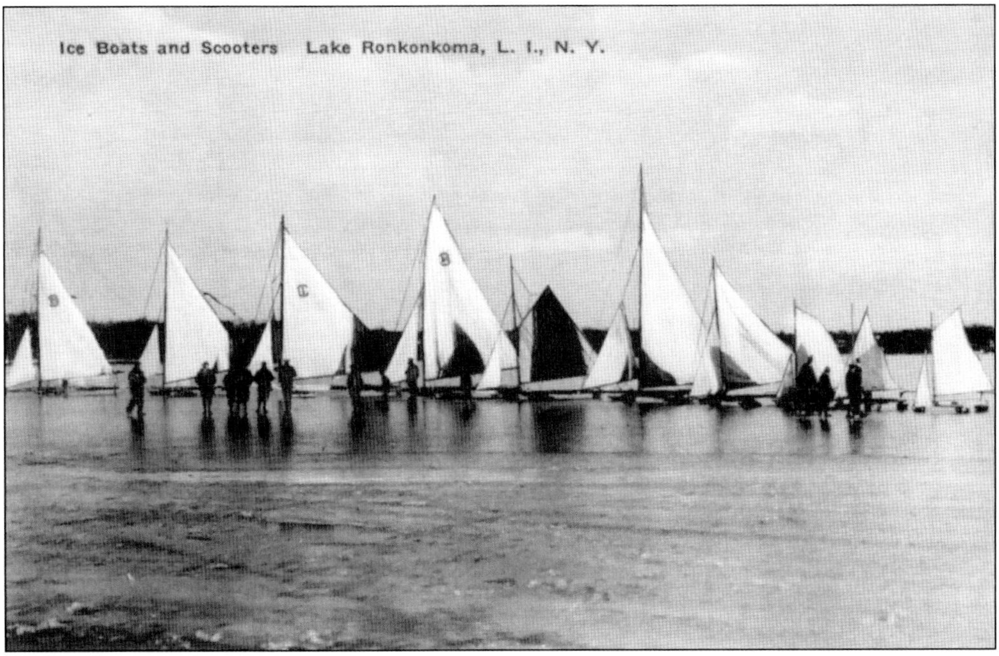

Jack Yerk's was best known as the Pavilion, which stayed open year-round. The Pavilion was the center for winter sports, iceboat races, and scooter races. Almost all the races started at Jack Yerk's, with boats from all over the island competing. Great skating parties were also held at night; floodlights would illuminate the ice until midnight.

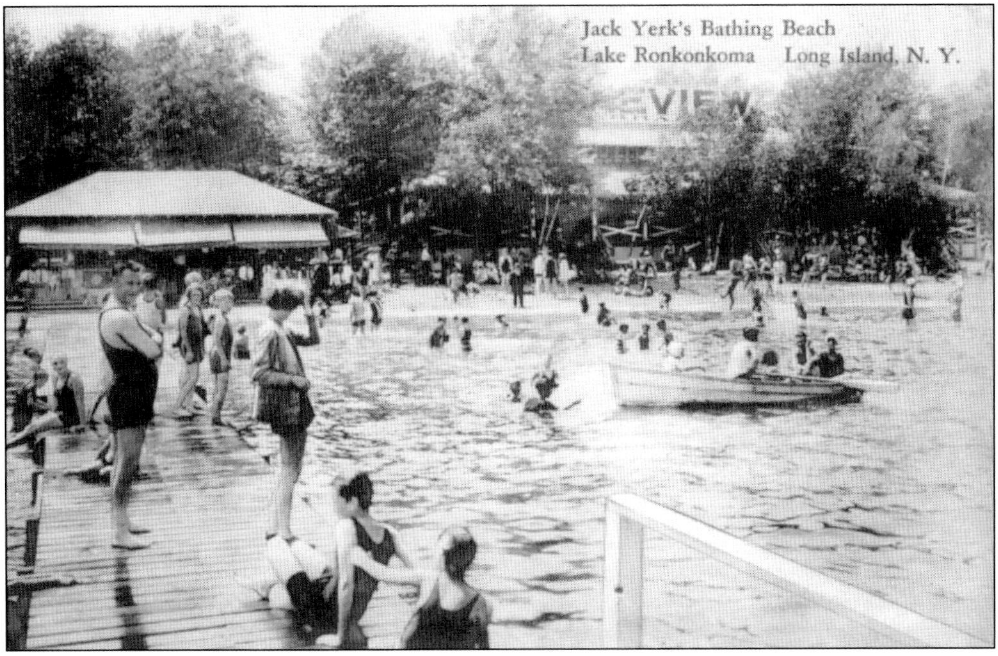

This postcard shows a busy beach scene at Jack Yerk's during the 1930s. As most pavilions were being destroyed or vandalized by the 1950s, Jack Yerk's was still in operation. Then, one night in 1969, a fire broke out and destroyed the Pavilion. Nothing was ever rebuilt, and Jack Yerk's became another casualty of fire.

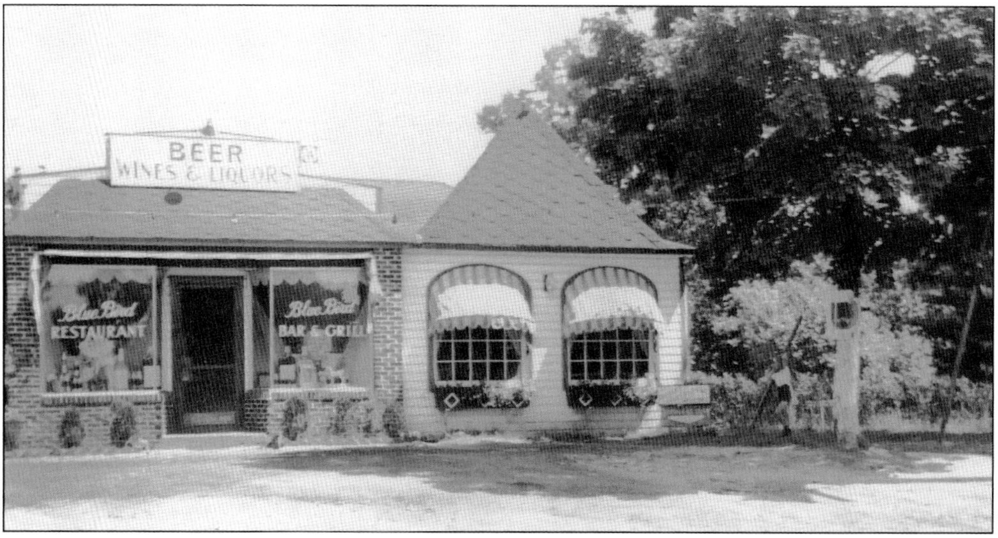

James Browne Sr. took the photograph shown above in 1937. The Blue Bird Inn was located on the corner of Smithtown Boulevard and Gibbs Pond Road. The proprietor was George Shlakis. The Blue Bird Inn was a popular place for duck and chicken dinners. Their slogan (as it states on the advertisement shown below) was "strictly home cooking." During the 1980s, the building became home to General Rental. They sold canopies, tables, and chairs. In the fall of 2008, the town of Smithtown began improvements on the intersection of Smithtown Boulevard and Rosevale Avenue. Unfortunately, this meant the destruction of the Blue Bird Inn.

Page Twenty-nine

Telephone: Ronkonkoma 32

The BLUE BIRD INN

Proprietor, GEORGE SHLAKIS

SMITHTOWN BLVD. & GIBBS POND RD.
LAKE RONKONKOMA

DUCK AND CHICKEN DINNERS

Strictly Home Cooking Soda Fountain

P. O. Box 31 NESCONSET, L. I.

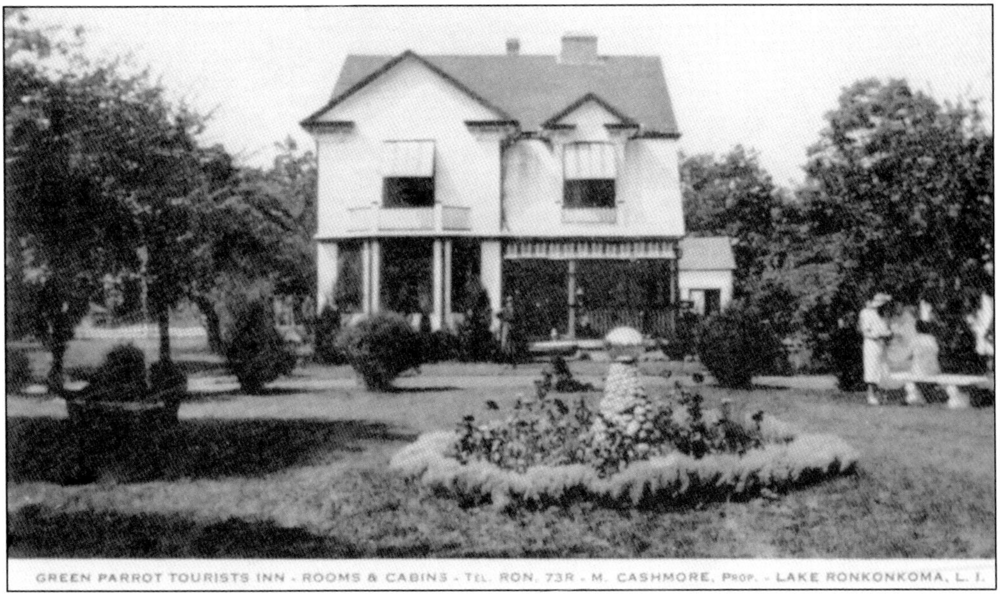

In 1900, Timothy Whitte built this home located on Smithtown Boulevard, just west of Gibbs Pond Road. By the 1920s, the residence became the Green Parrot Tourists Inn, with eight new cabins. Mildred Cashmore was the proprietor, until she sold the Green Parrot in 1961. The Green Parrot became residential rental housing.

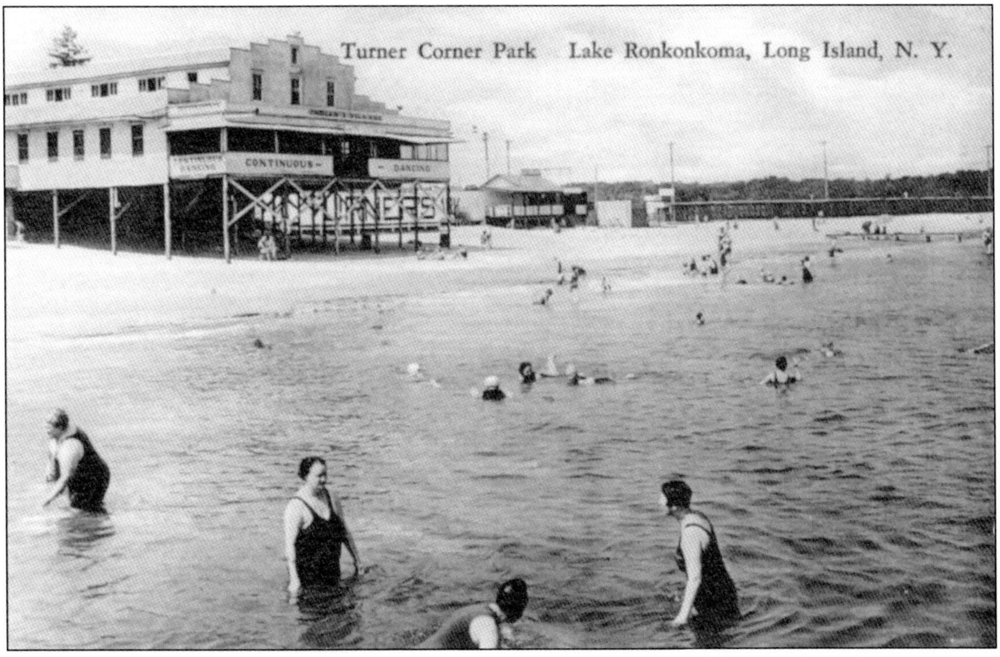

Turner's Corner Park was located on the northwest corner of the lake. Arthur Turner created his pavilion in the 1920s. This postcard shows how impressive Turner's looked around 1930. In 1937, a tornado tore the roof off the pavilion. When World War II began in 1941, Turner's saw a decline in revenue. Necessary maintenance was not done, and deterioration set in. The pavilion at Turner's was eventually declared off limits. By the end of World War II, Turner's was demolished. (Courtesy of Helen Hethy Mulvihill.)

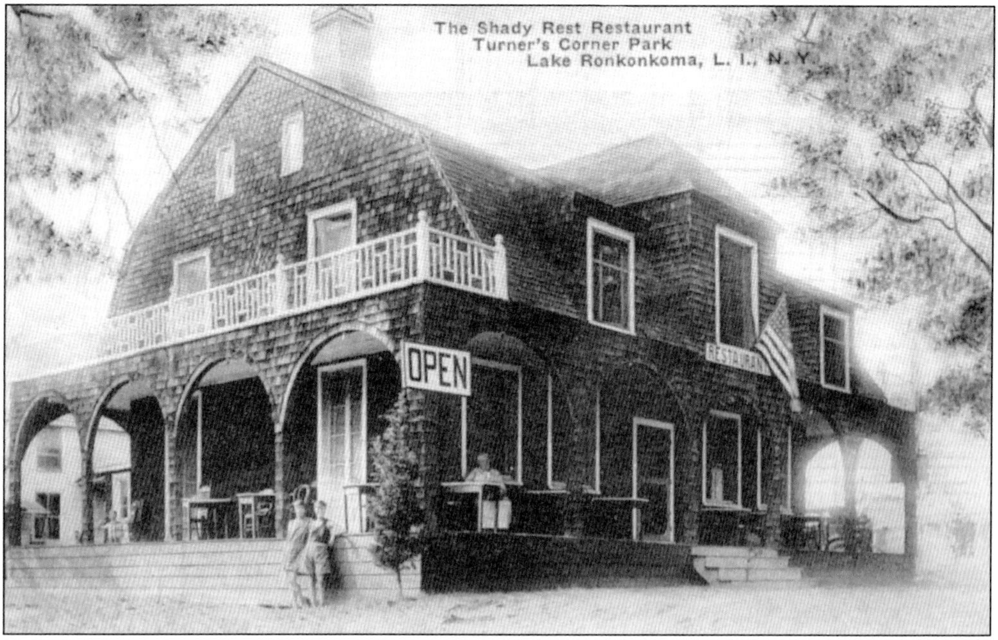

This postcard, c. 1927, shows a private home that was converted into the Shady Rest Restaurant at Turner's Corner Park. Turner's was considered a honky-tonk area around the lake. Prohibition was in full affect, but people from all over would utilize Arthur Turner's bar. Problems would occur when many drinks were consumed, and authorities would be called in to control the disorder at Turner's.

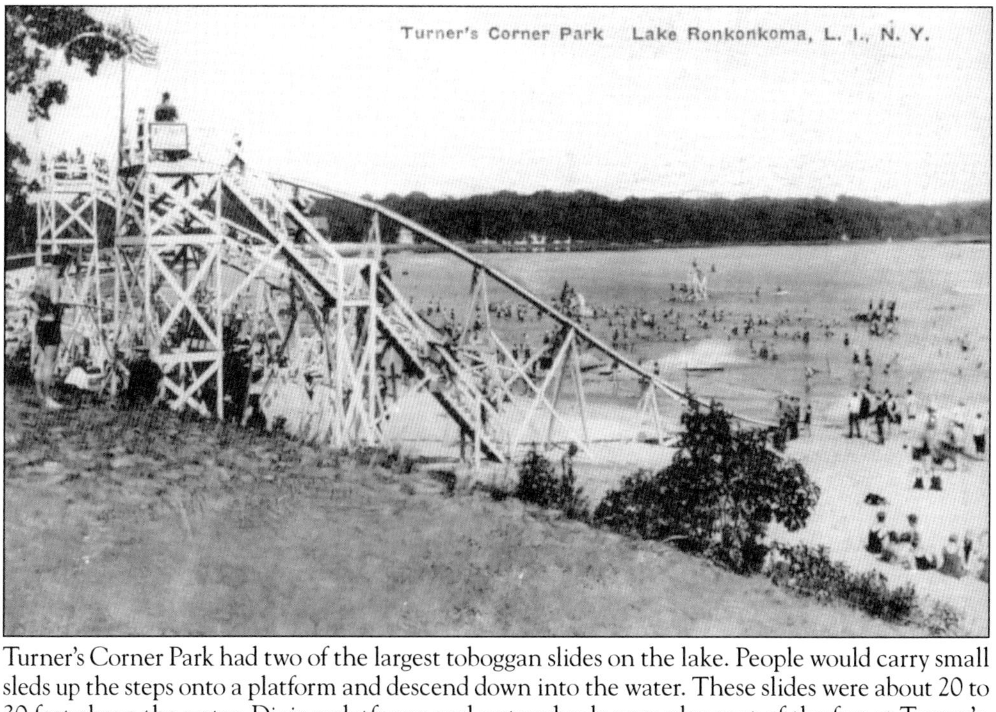

Turner's Corner Park had two of the largest toboggan slides on the lake. People would carry small sleds up the steps onto a platform and descend down into the water. These slides were about 20 to 30 feet above the water. Diving platforms and waterwheels were also part of the fun at Turner's. This postcard is from the early 1930s.

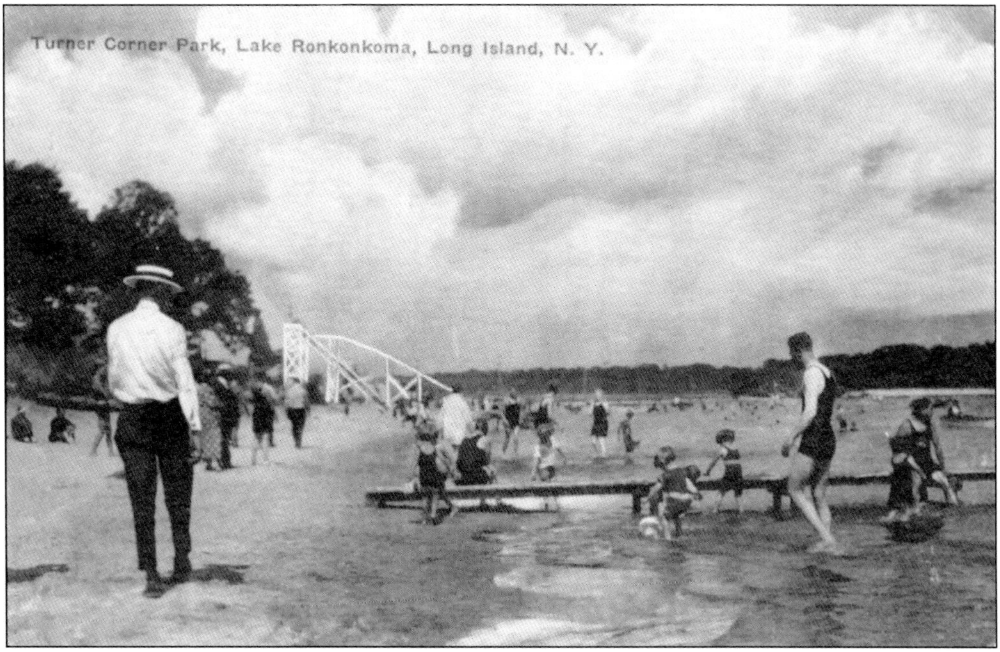

Fun and games were always found at Turner's Corner Park. There was an outdoor merry-go-round, a shooting gallery, and motorcycles racing inside a bowl. Arthur Turner also operated a dance hall where he would bring jazz bands to his pavilion. Occasionally, people would take a rowboat out on the lake and listen to the music.

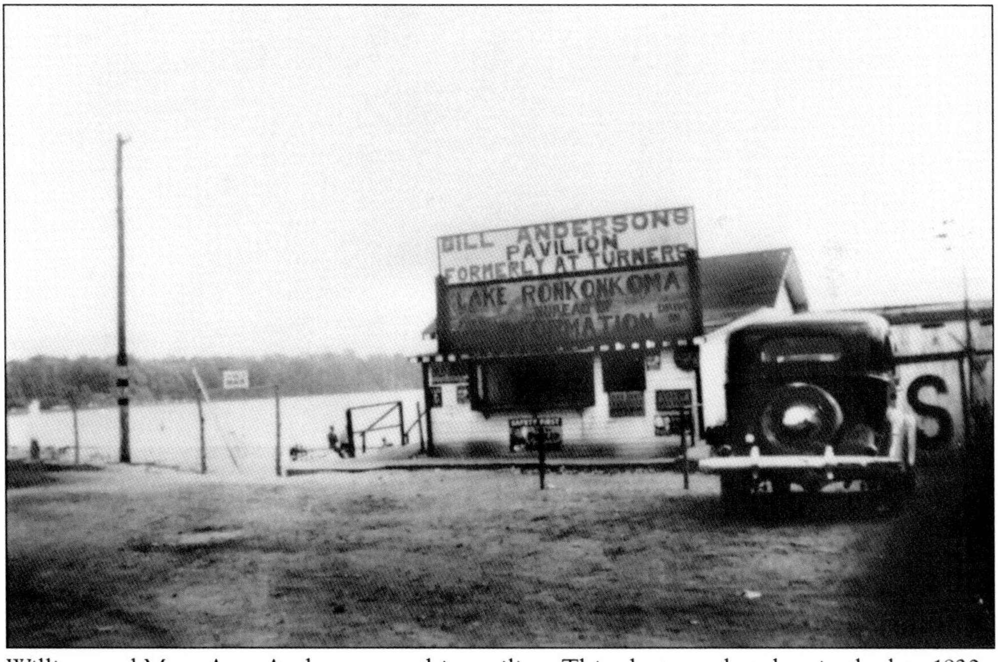

William and Mary Ann Anderson ran this pavilion. This photograph, taken in the late 1930s, shows the front end of the building. The sign reads Bill Anderson's Pavilion Formerly at Turner's. In 1934, a hurricane destroyed the bathhouses visible on the left side of the picture. This pavilion was located just east of Turner's.

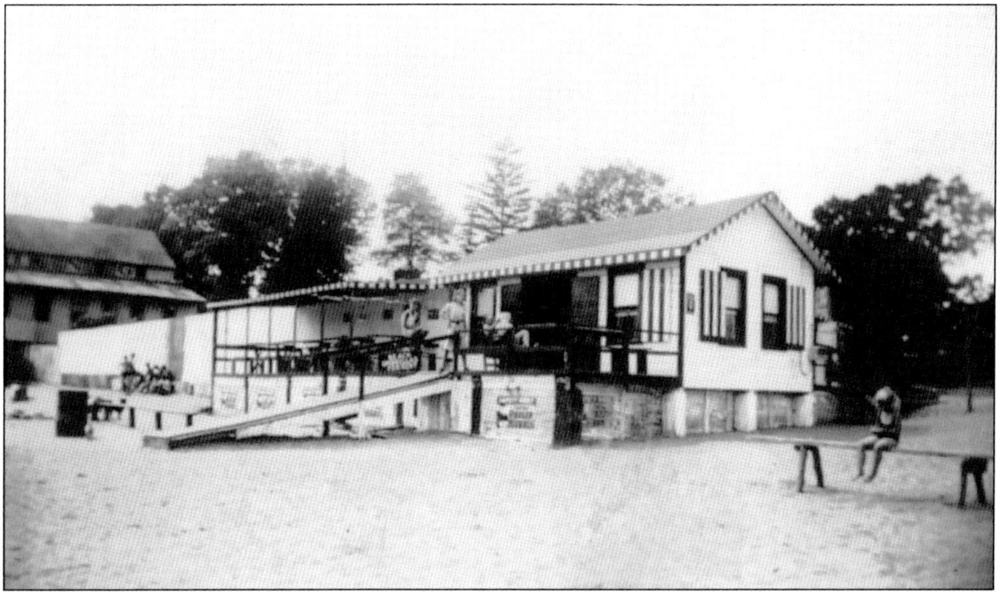

This is a side view of Merkel's refreshment stand, which was located east of Turner's Corner Park, around 1936. William and Mary Ann Anderson ran this stand for a while. The refreshment stand sold cigarettes, chewing tobacco, bubble gum, candy, soda, hot dogs, and ice cream. Umbrellas and chairs were available for rent.

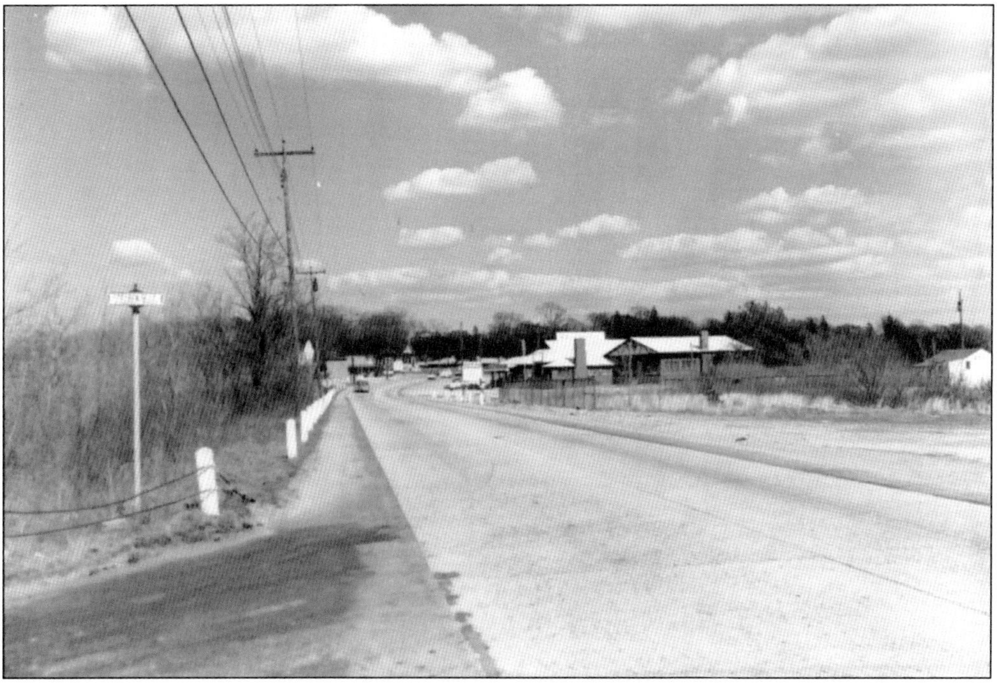

This photograph, taken in 1961, shows Smithtown Boulevard facing east. The street on the left side is Steuben Boulevard. Towards the center of the picture is the Bavarian Inn. Many changes were being made to Lake Ronkonkoma at this time. New residential developments were happening, and shopping centers were making their way into town by the mid-1960s. (Courtesy of James Mooney.)

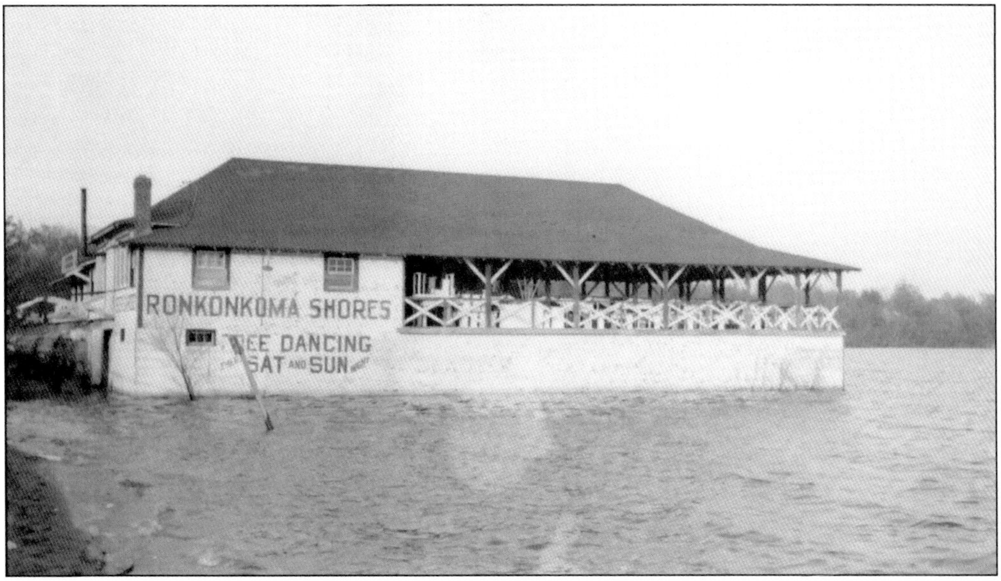

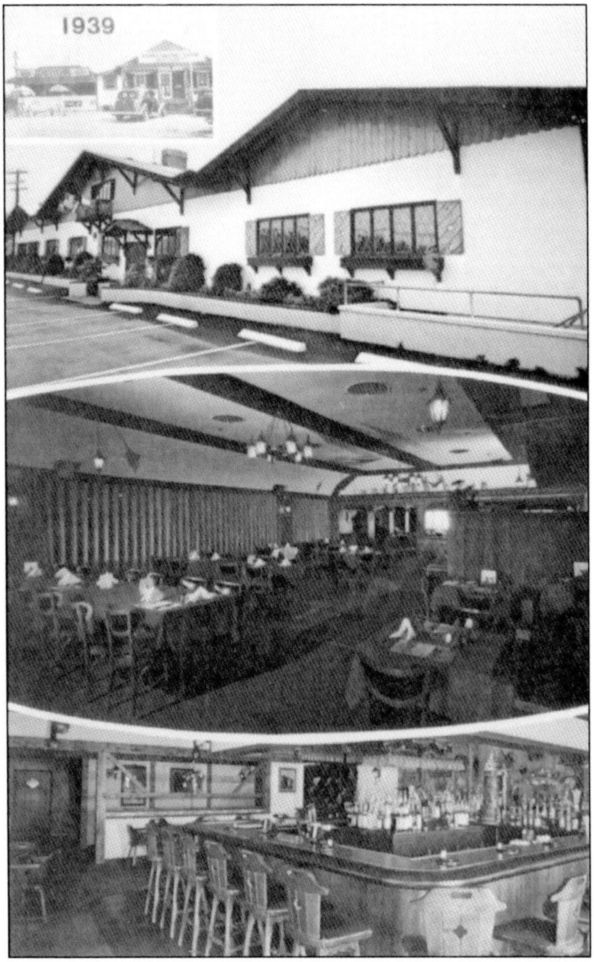

The Ronkonkoma Shores Restaurant opened for business in 1939. The blue-plate special was roast beef, a vegetable, and potato for $1.25. To the left of the restaurant, there was a refreshment stand where hot dogs, ice cream, and sodas were sold. To the right of the restaurant were bathhouses along the creek. The Ronkonkoma Shores charged a total of $1.50 to rent rowboats, park the automobile, and to utilize the bathhouses. In 1955, William Huber converted the Ronkonkoma Shores into the Bavarian Inn. He watched his restaurant go from an outdoors operation to an indoor restaurant with seating for 140 and catering for up to 400. The restaurant expanded in 1967 and 1972. Within the last 20 years, flooding and water damage took its toll on the building. On April 25, 2007, the Bavarian Inn closed its doors forever.

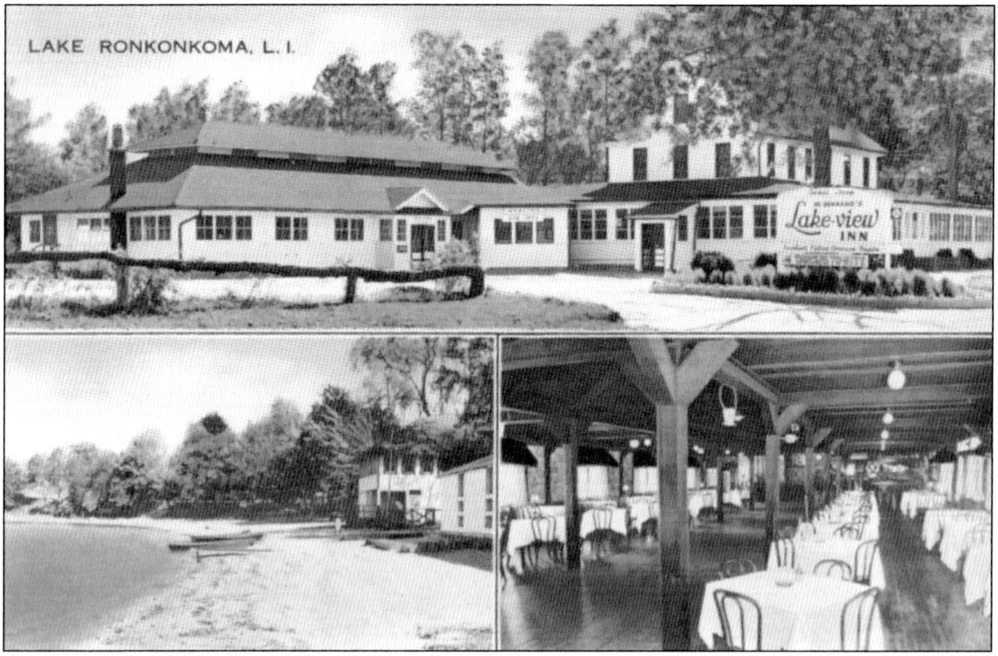

In the 1920s and 1930s, on the corner of Pond Road and Portion Road, sat Becker's Beach. There was a shaded picnic grove on the beach and a large pavilion across the road with a bowling alley. In the 1940s, Becker's became De Gennaro's Lake View Inn. De Gennaro's offered Italian and American cuisine and seafood and catering for weddings, banquets, and outings. This postcard dates to the late 1940s.

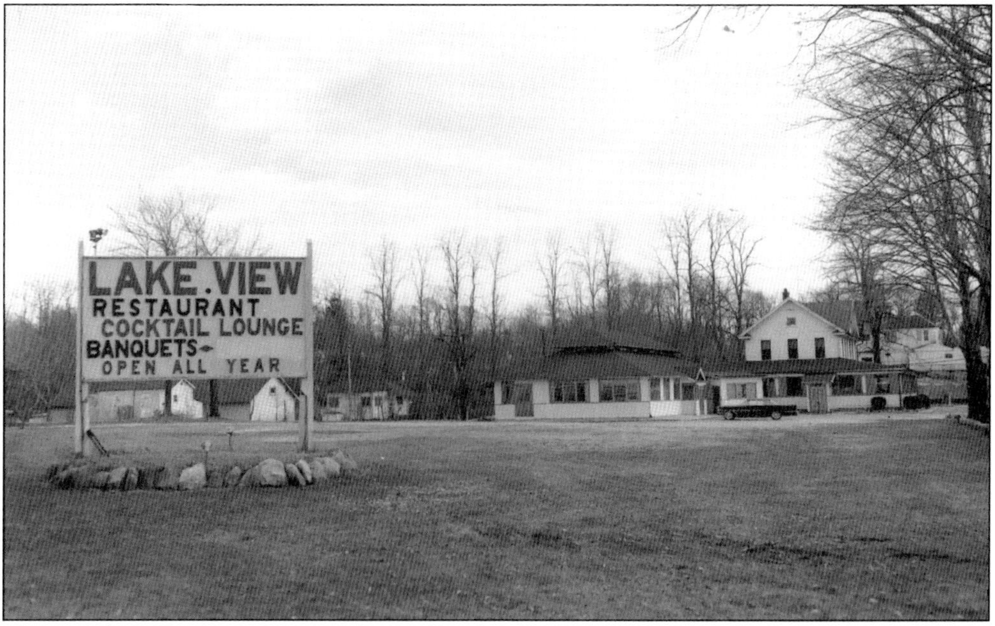

This wonderful James Mooney photograph, taken from Portion Road in 1961, shows a spacious view of the Lake View Restaurant. The Lake View, by the mid-1970s, would be another casualty of neglect and deterioration. A sump currently occupies the site where the Lake View once stood. (Courtesy of James Mooney.)

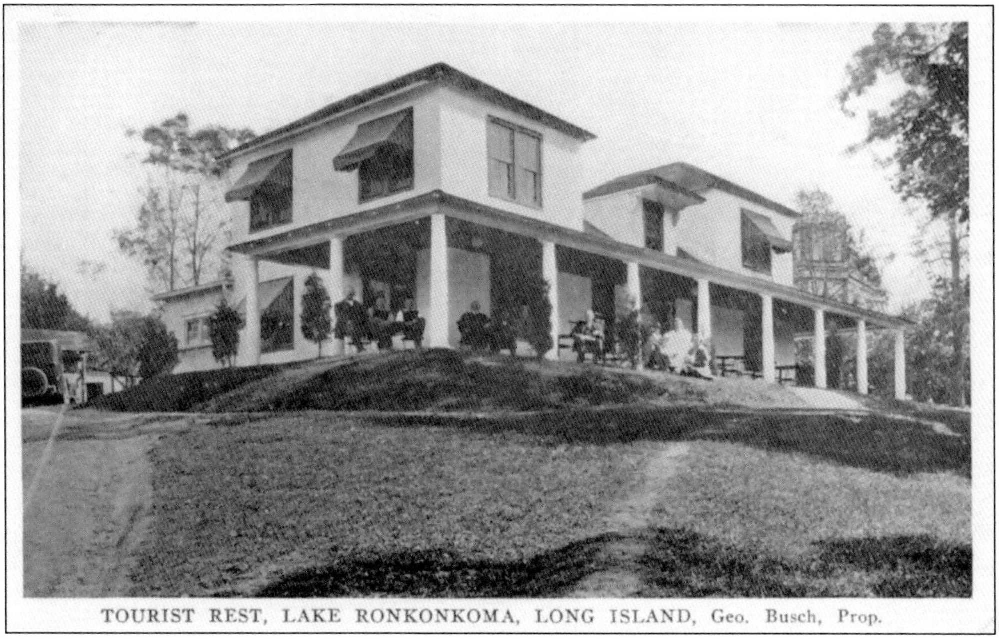

George Busch began a tourist home in the early 20th century. People from New York City would come to Lake Ronkonkoma during the summer months and enjoy the serenity of the area. Home-cooked meals, a beach, and a marvelous lake were across Lake Shore Road. This postcard is dated 1912.

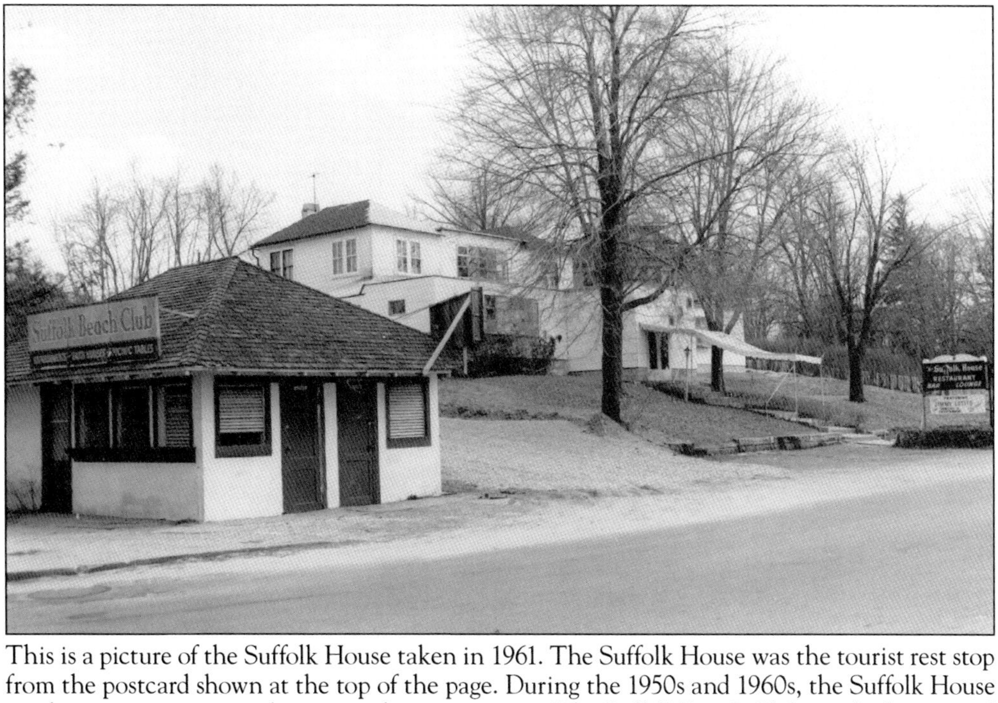

This is a picture of the Suffolk House taken in 1961. The Suffolk House was the tourist rest stop from the postcard shown at the top of the page. During the 1950s and 1960s, the Suffolk House was home to a restaurant, lounge, and entertainment. The Suffolk Beach Club, a refreshment and bathhouse stand, is pictured on the left. By 1993, both buildings would be part of the Windows on the Lake catering facility. (Courtesy of James Mooney.)

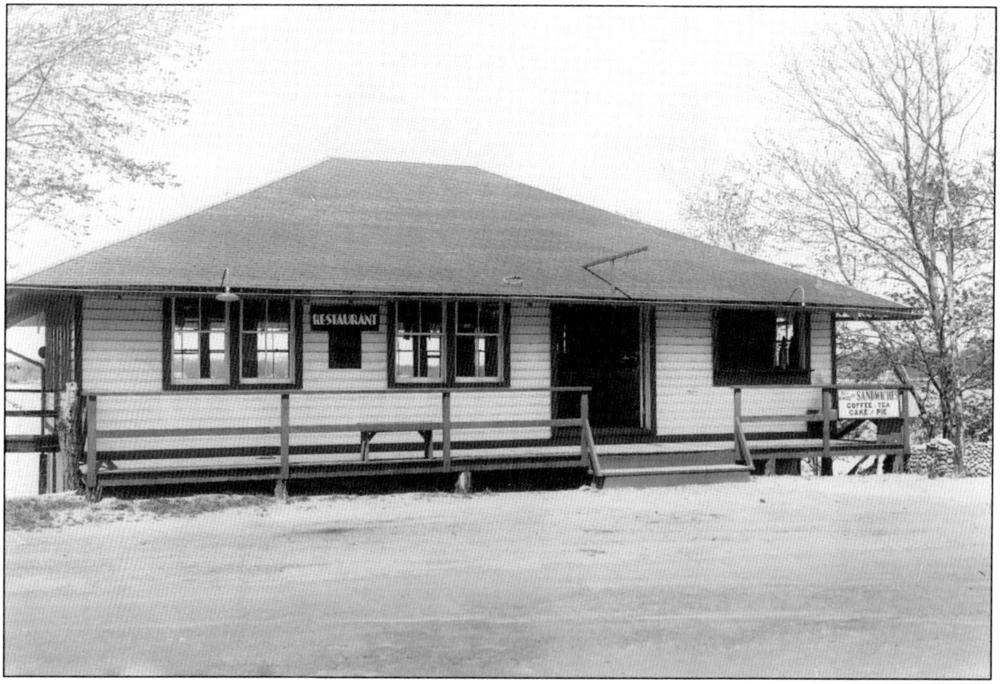

While George Busch was the proprietor of the tourist home that became the Suffolk House, he wanted to be a part of the ongoing trend that was happening around the lake. He bought Max Becker's beach property on the lake. Located on the lakeside of Lake Shore Road just south of Portion Road, Busch's pavilion was finalized in the early 1930s. This impressive close-up of the pavilion was taken c. 1934. Busch created business cards advertising what he had to offer to visitors coming to Lake Ronkonkoma—dinners, fishing, boating, bathing, golfing, and room and board. This business card is from the mid-1930s.

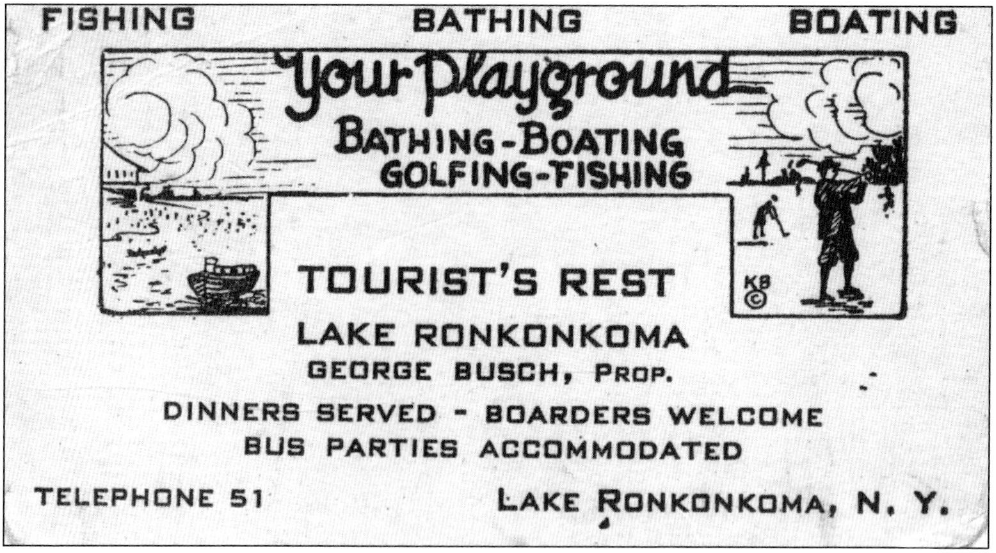

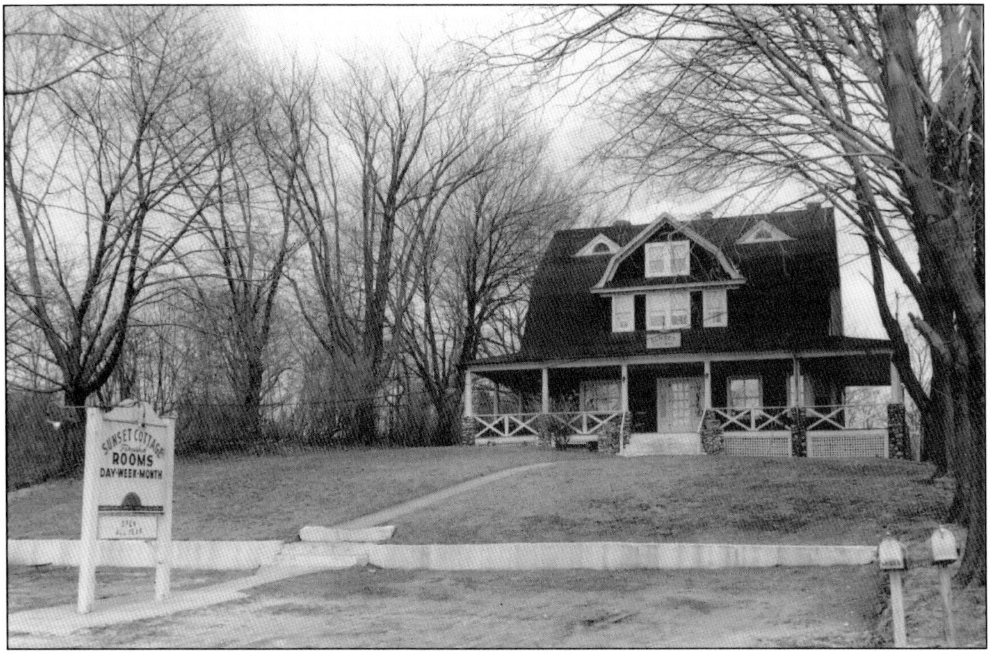

This James Mooney photograph was taken on April 5, 1961. Sunset Cottage was located on Lake Shore Road, just south of the Suffolk House. This quaint, less noticeable cottage did not have a pavilion or bathhouses on the lake. Today, an adult rest home occupies the site. (Courtesy of James Mooney.)

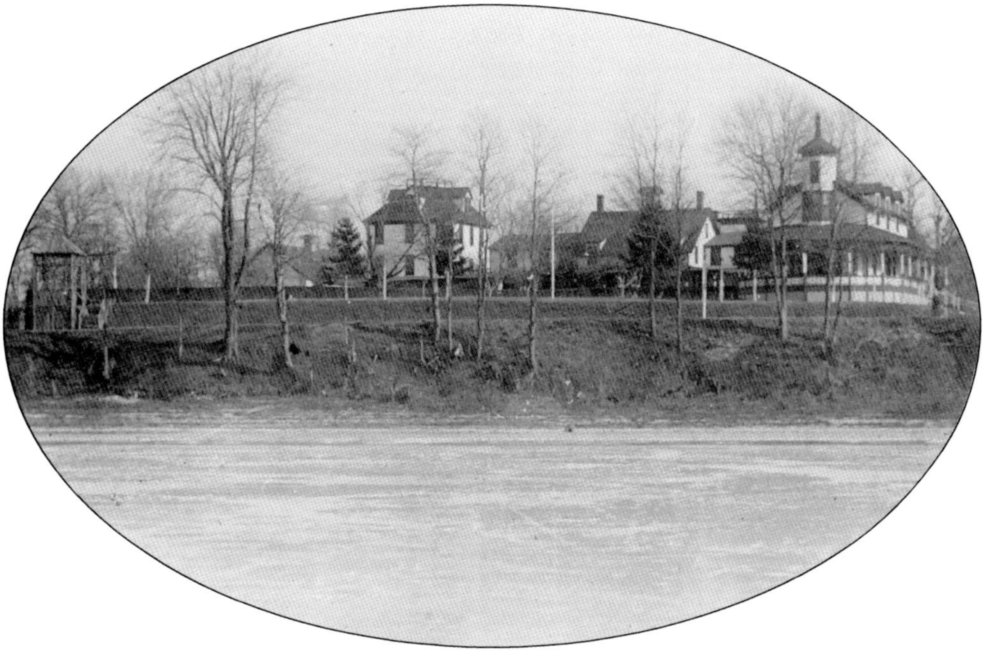

This postcard dates back to the 1890s and shows an impressive view of the Lake Front Hotel. The hotel was located on the east side of Lake Shore Drive. Many guests would stay here for the summer months. Social events were common here, and only the exclusive would be able to stay at a place like this.

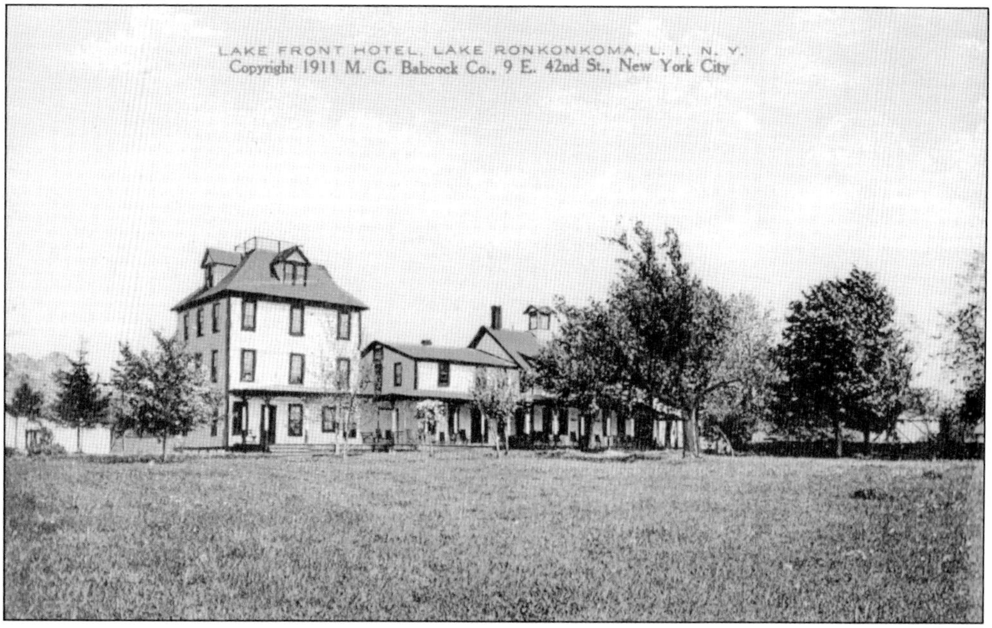

The Lake Front Hotel was on 24 acres of land. The hotel was open from May 1 to January 1 each year. Numerous people, such as Mr. and Mrs. Burnham, the Brown family, and Mrs. McKedrick, operated the hotel. Besides a hotel, carriage house, and stables, there was another building called the Casino. The Casino had three cottages that were available to rent. (Courtesy of Helen Hethy Mulvihill.)

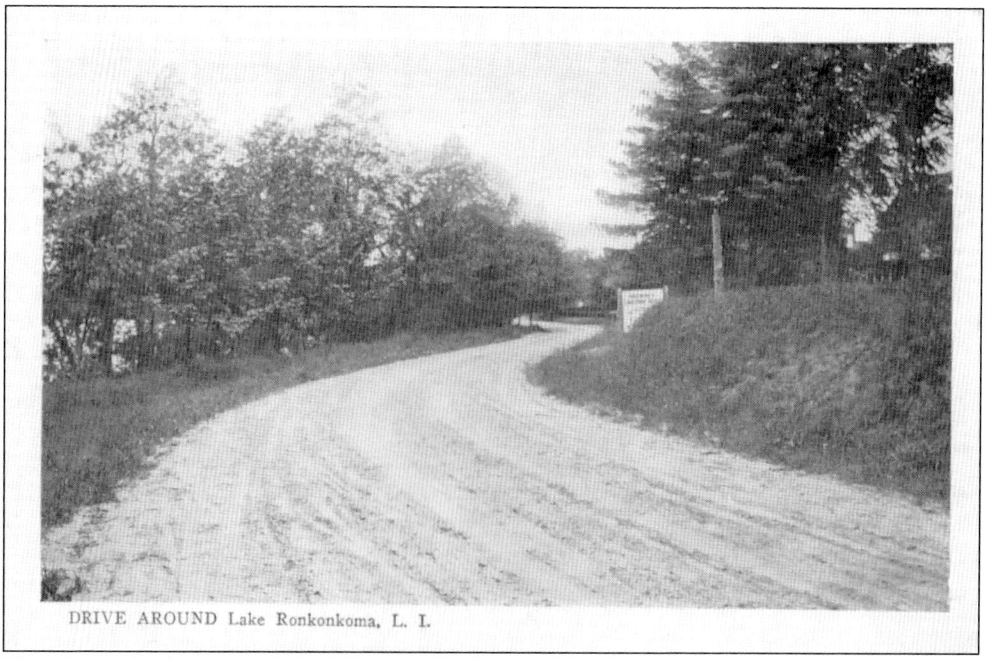

This postcard, taken around 1916, shows Lake Shore Road facing north. The sign says Brown's Lake Front Hotel. Most people spent the day boating, fishing, or swimming on the lake; towards the evening, there were many social activities for the guests. Reading, writing, sewing, conversation, and dancing were among such activities.

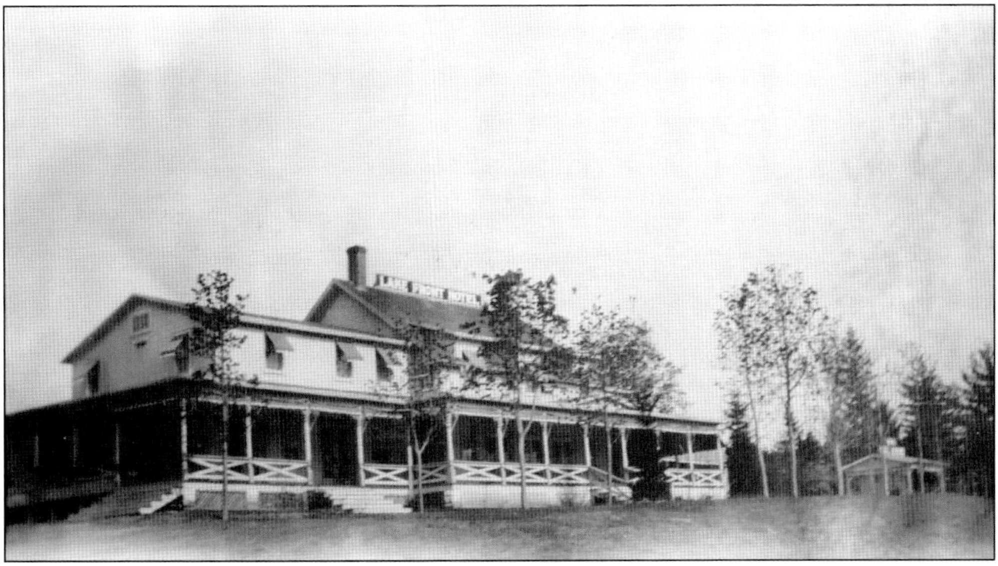

This is a photograph of the Lake Front Hotel in the 1920s. This would be the final decade the hotel would be in operation. Part of the hotel would become Jack Brown's Tavern. The Casino would become a residential home and finally an apartment complex, which still is in existence today.

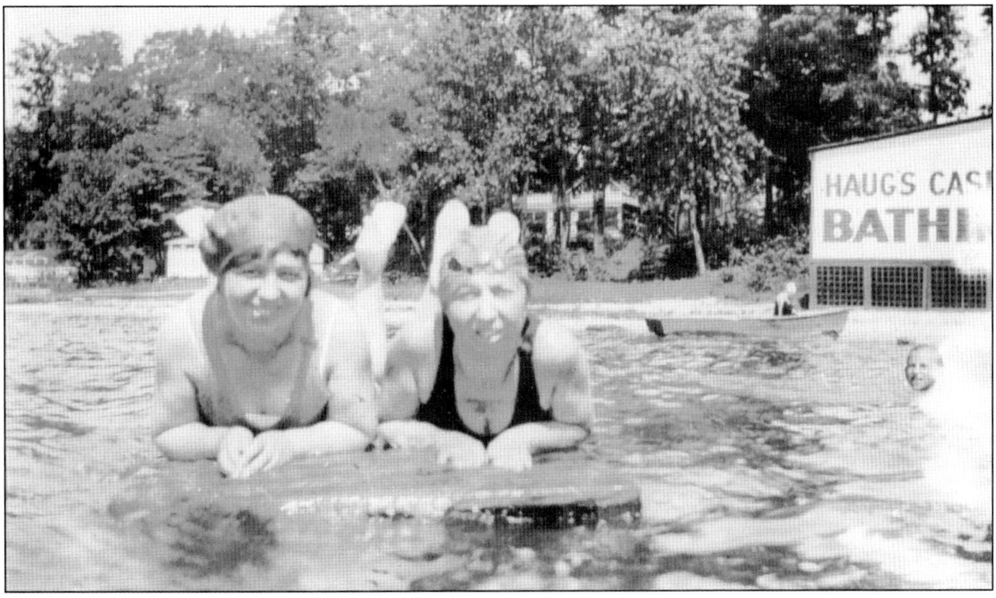

This is a very rare photograph of Haug's Casino in 1932. This pavilion was situated on the shoreline of Lake Shore Road just north of the Olympia. A very small pavilion compared to others, Haug's Casino would be a refreshment stand from the 1940s until 1964. In 1979, Larry Holzapfel opened the Book House, which he ran until 2005. Pictured in the photograph are Eva Lenning (left) and Henrietta Wecht.

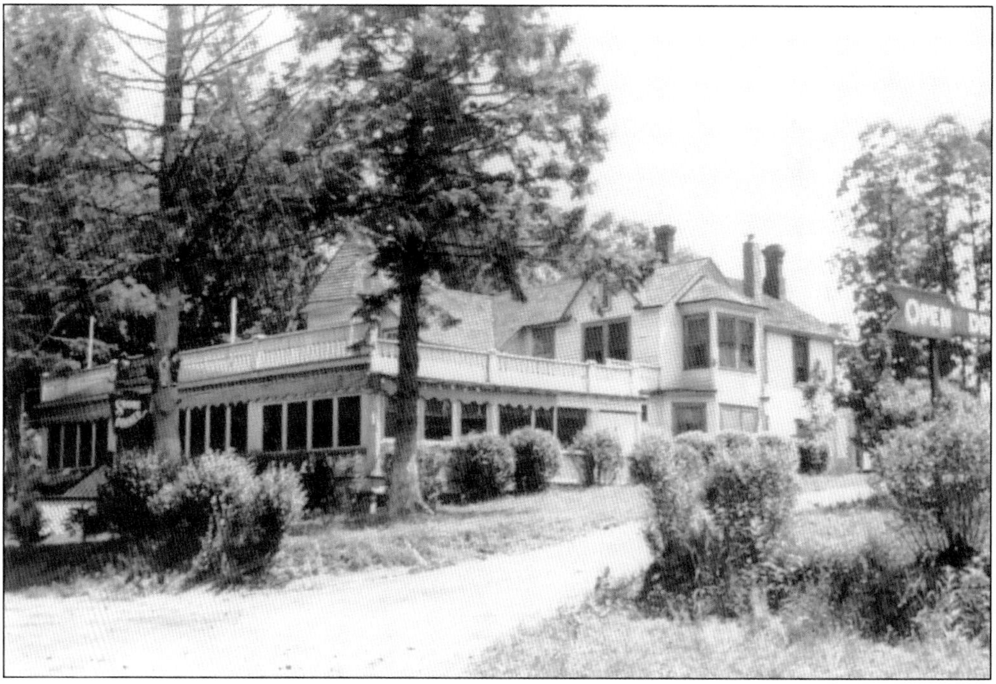

Jack Brown's Tavern was a very popular place among the younger generation. Jack Brown's occupied part of the old Lake Front Hotel. During Prohibition, speakeasies and houses of prostitution were opened in secluded areas in the woods. This would attract the wrong type of people to the area. James Browne Sr. took this photograph in 1937.

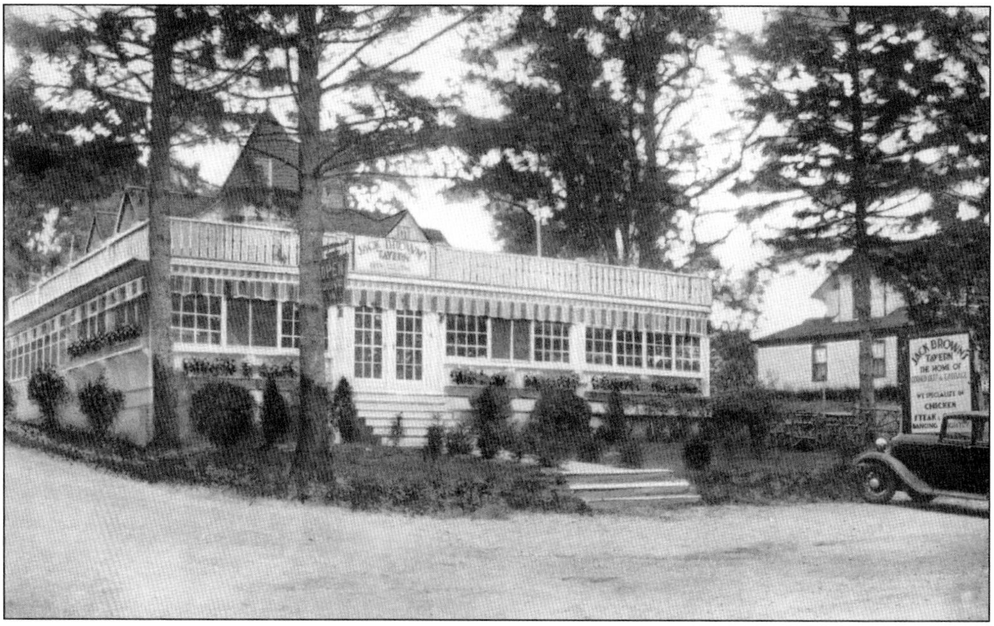

This image of Jack Brown's Tavern in the mid-1930s mentions on the sign (seen on the right) that this was the "Home of Corned Beef and Cabbage." Many visitors, and even the local townspeople of Lake Ronkonkoma, would go to Jack Brown's for this dish. By the 1940s, Cumming's Irish House occupied Jack Brown's Tavern. (Courtesy of Helen Hethy Mulvihill.)

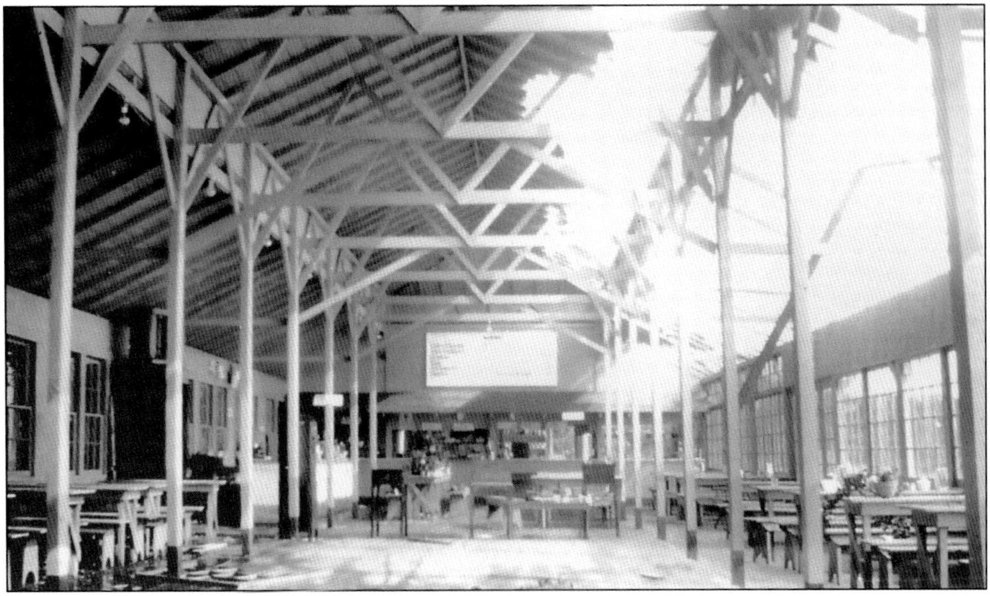

These two remarkable photographs were taken of the Olympia Pavilion after the hurricane of 1938. The photographs show that most of the roof was torn off the pavilion with severe flooding and damage. The Olympia was located on the shoreline of the lake off Lake Shore Road. Built in the late 1920s, M. Andreanopolis was the original proprietor of the Olympia. People who wanted room and board stayed at the Lake Front Hotel. Bathing, dancing, refreshments, hunting, and fishing were the attractions at the Olympia. Mr. and Mrs. Deutsch were the proprietors during the final years of the Olympia Pavilion. After the devastation from the hurricane, the Olympia Pavilion was demolished and never rebuilt.

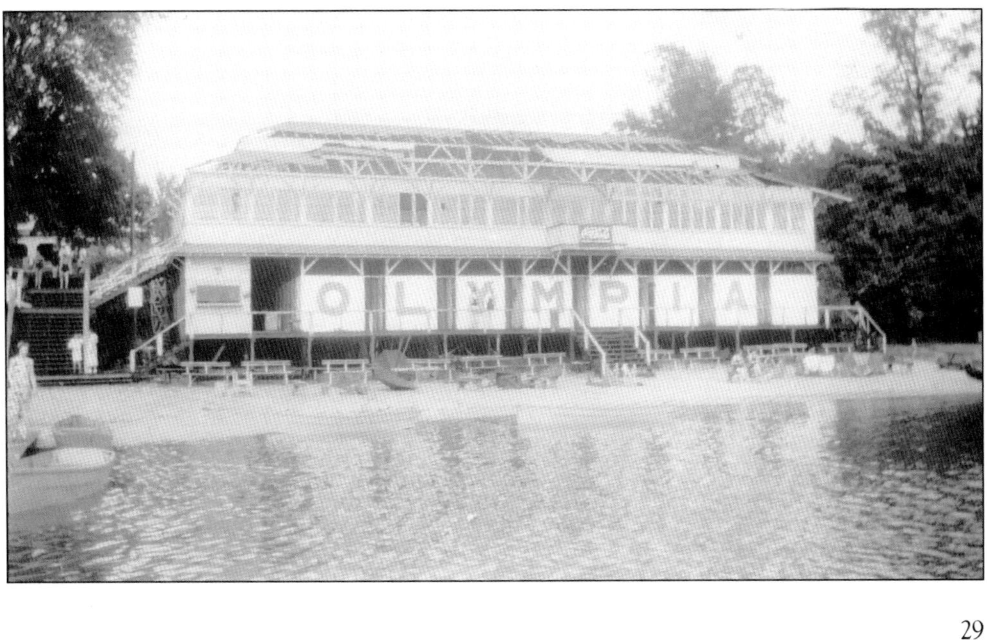

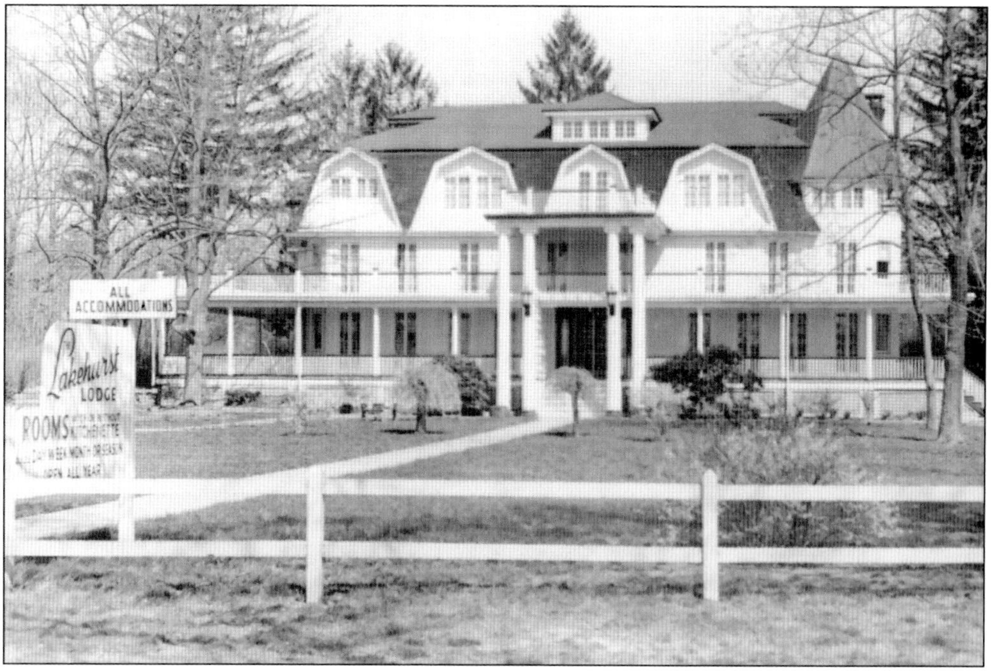

The Lakehurst Lodge is located on Lake Shore Road. Originally, Capt. Frank H. Rohrig, a retired police captain from New York City, owned the home. Captain Rohrig built and lived in this home until his death in 1943. Louis Feiler became the owner from 1943 to 1959. Feiler transformed this home into a lodge by adding a third floor. This photograph was taken in 1945.

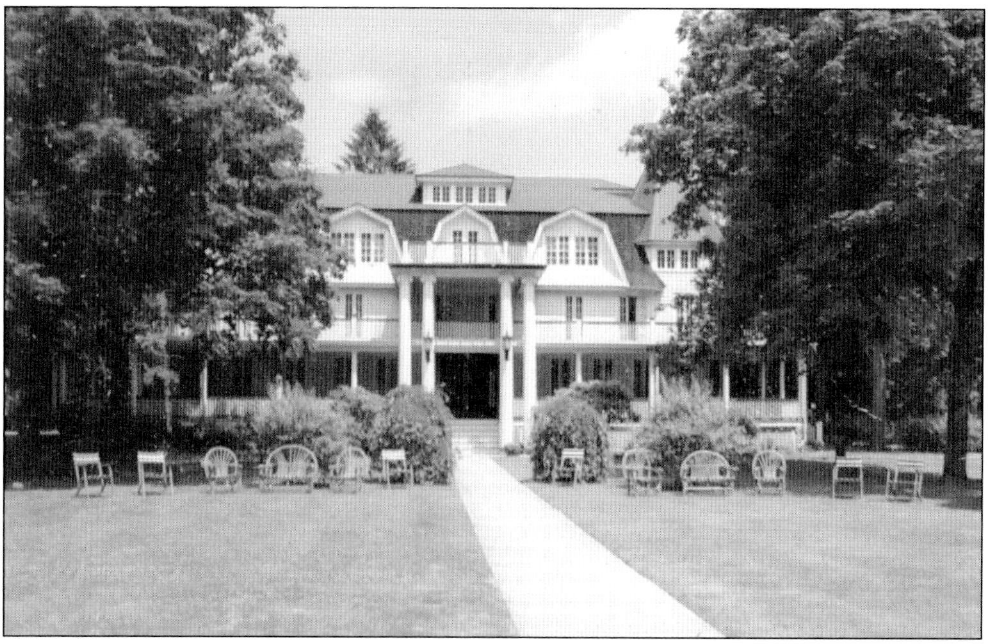

The Lakehurst Lodge was active on through the 1950s and into the early 1980s. By around 1985, Lakehurst Lodge had become home to the Apple Agency drug rehabilitation center. Phoenix House (a substance abuse treatment center) currently resides at the two buildings that once housed the Lakehurst Lodge and the Ronkonkoma Manor.

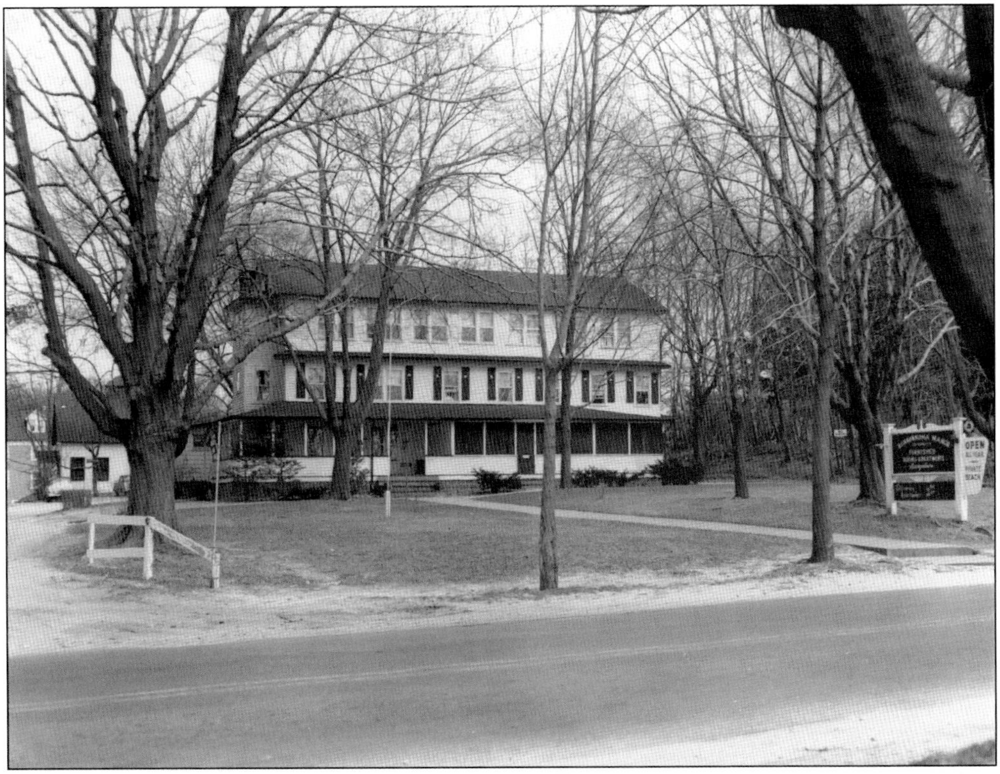

During the 1920s, the Ronkonkoma Manor, located on Lake Shore Road just south of the Lakehurst Lodge, was a very well-known place to stay. The Ronkonkoma Manor was open all year and featured its own private beach, restaurant, and activities at the lake. This photograph was taken April 5, 1961. (Courtesy of James Mooney.)

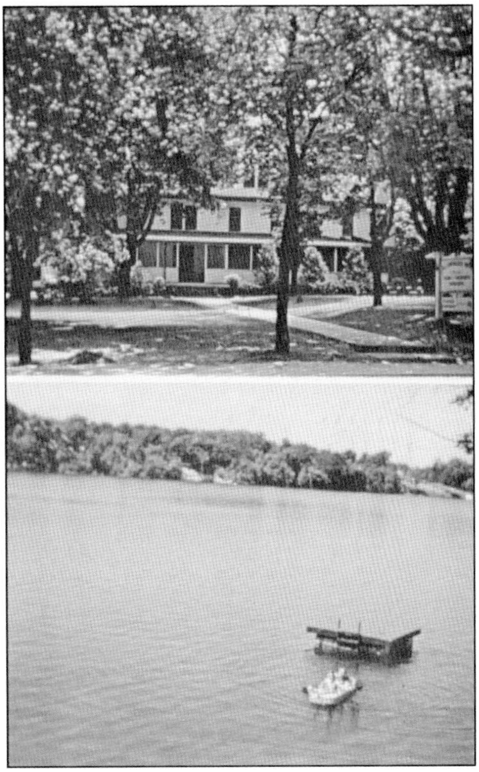

The Ronkonkoma Manor, during the 1960s into the early 1980s, was a place for families to enjoy indoor and outdoor activities while visiting Lake Ronkonkoma. By 1985, owners of Ronkonkoma Manor started doing business with the department of social services, offering rooms for clients needing emergency housing. Within 10 years, the Phoenix House began operation at the Ronkonkoma Manor building.

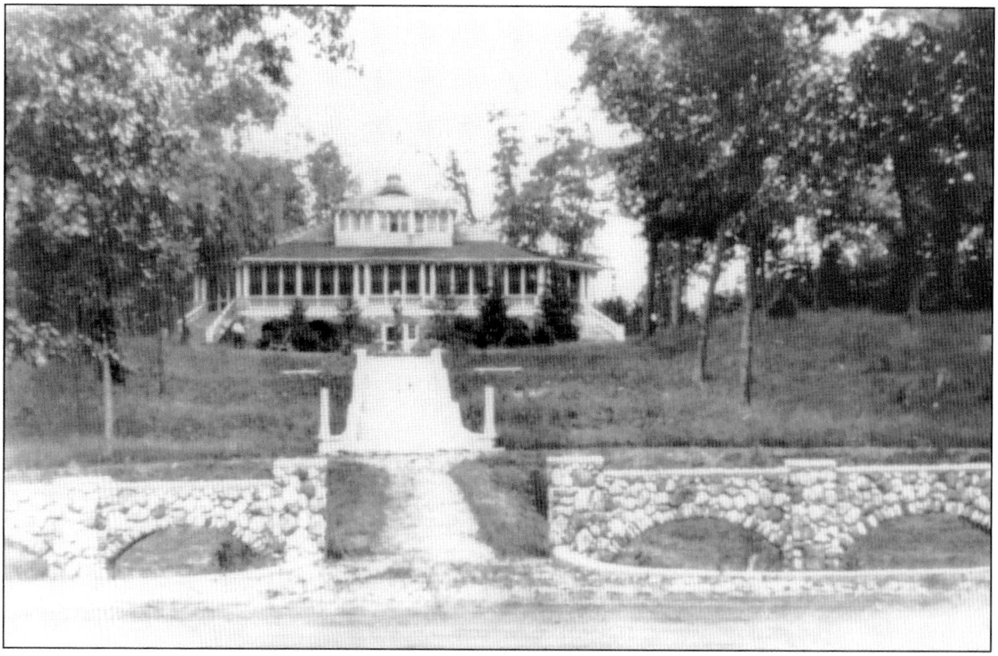

The Ondawa Hotel was located on Lake Shore Road, across the street between Raynor's Beach and the Green Pavilion. Originally, this was an estate owned by Adolph Weichers. By the 1920s, Weichers's daughter Paula Browne owned and lived in the newly created hotel. During the 1940s, the hotel became Club 38. One night in February 1959, the hotel burned mysteriously. The concrete steps leading to the hotel still remain there today.

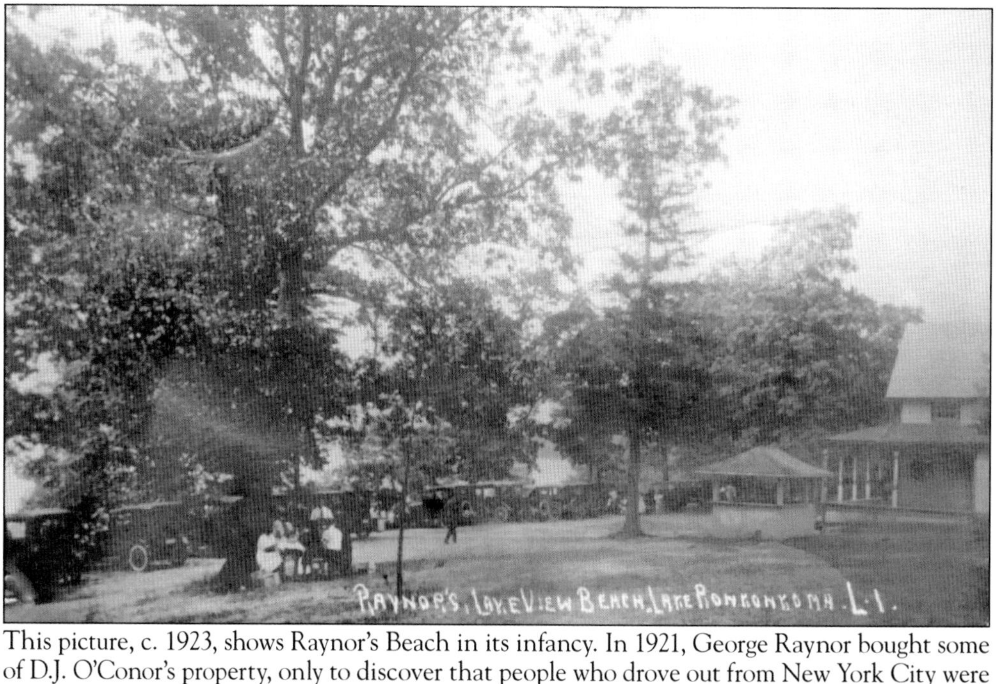

This picture, c. 1923, shows Raynor's Beach in its infancy. In 1921, George Raynor bought some of D.J. O'Conor's property, only to discover that people who drove out from New York City were using his property for picnicking. Raynor decided to make money from this situation. He built a small pavilion and some bathhouses on the beach and charged for their use.

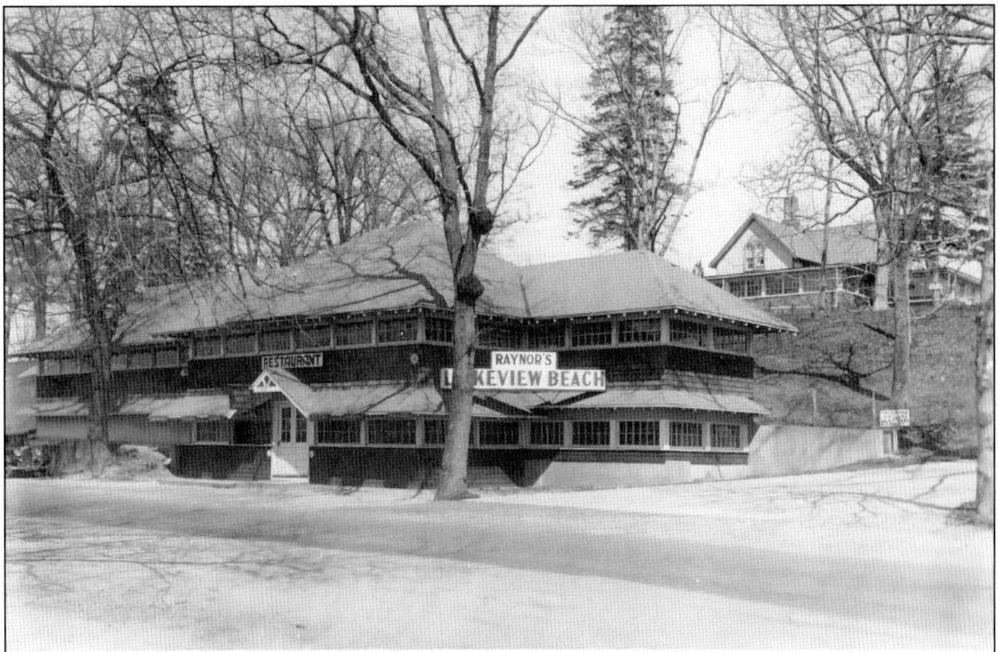

Raynor's Beach Restaurant Lake Ronkonkoma

Here are two photographs of the Raynor's Beach Restaurant. This building's location was on Lake Shore Road, across the street from Raynor's Beach. Originally, when George Raynor opened Raynor's Beach in 1921, there was a large building up on a hill, which was converted into a restaurant serving hot meals. By the late 1920s, the building was taken down for tax purposes, and Raynor's Beach was created. The photograph shown above was taken c. 1930, with only one entrance for patrons. The photograph below, taken in the 1940s, shows that a second entrance has been added. The restaurant would later be named Herby's and Wil's. By 1960, the building would be demolished.

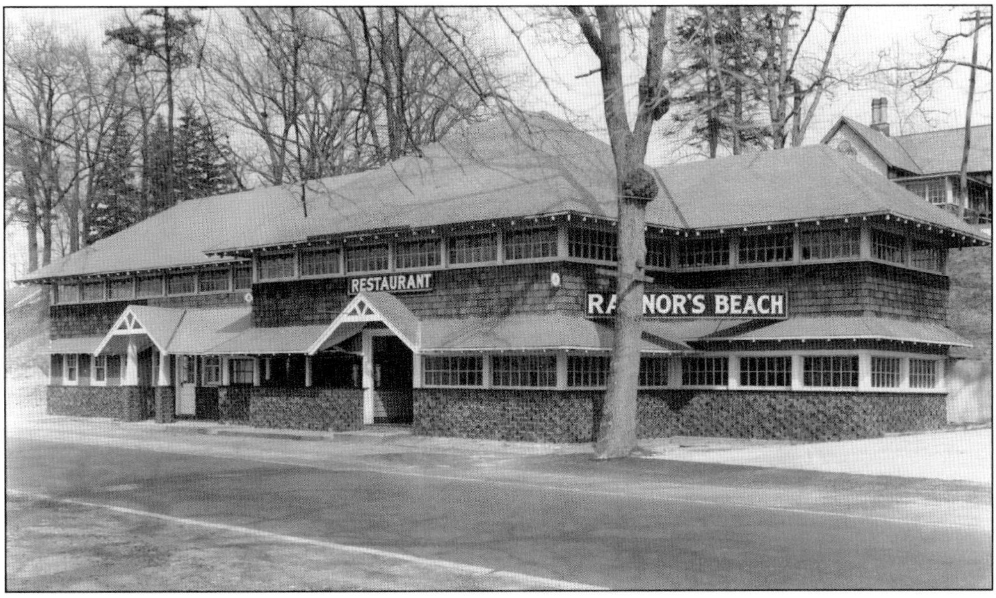

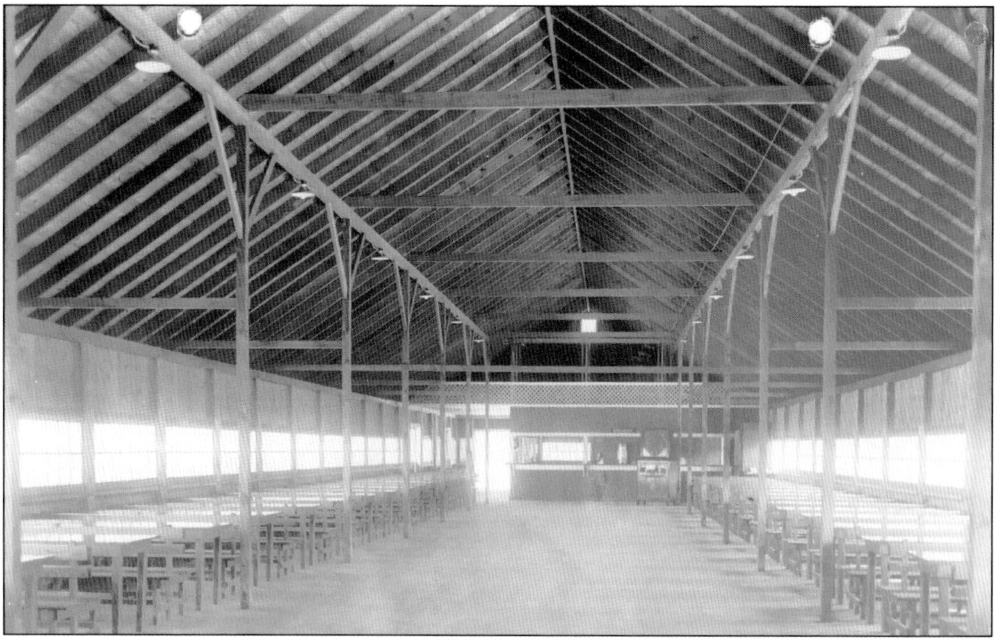

George Raynor had several pavilions throughout the 1920s. Some were larger then others, but Raynor had a vision to create a pavilion that could seat hundreds of people at one time. In 1933, he built a pavilion to accommodate very large crowds. These two photographs show how massive it was. This pavilion was the first to have glass windows and to extend out into the lake. Raynor's Pavilion was used year-round. Barn dances, costumed Halloween parties, graduation ceremonies, and all other forms of celebration were held at Raynor's. Bingo was a very popular game played inside the pavilion. Dried corn kernels were used as bingo markers.

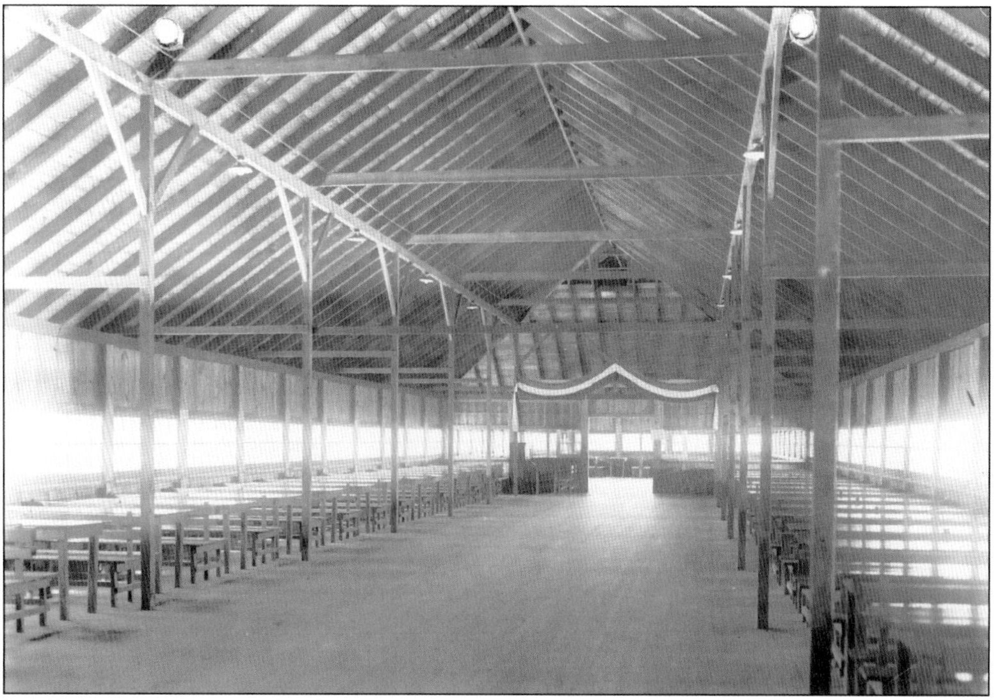

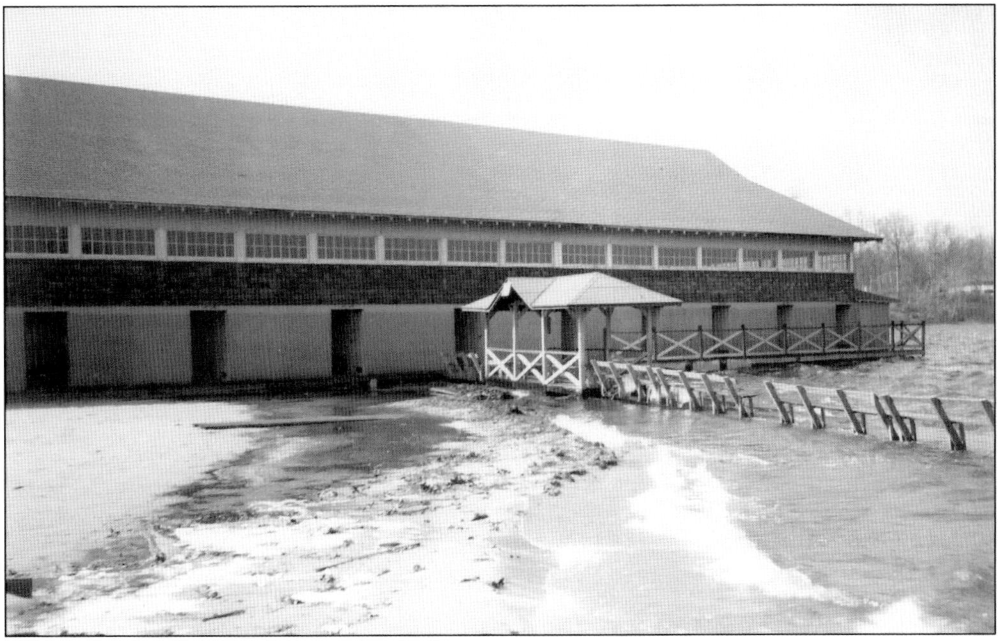

These two marvelous photographs are close-ups of Raynor's Pavilion, taken on March 22, 1939. At this time, locals were dealing with the problem of the lake rising. A year earlier, George Raynor had his pavilion lifted a few feet off the beach to avoid water damage. The lake did not reach the pavilion in 1938. When these photographs were taken, the water was five feet deep at the end of the pavilion. The photograph above shows the benches submerged in the lake. The photograph below shows the Mayfair Pavilion through the door on the far right.

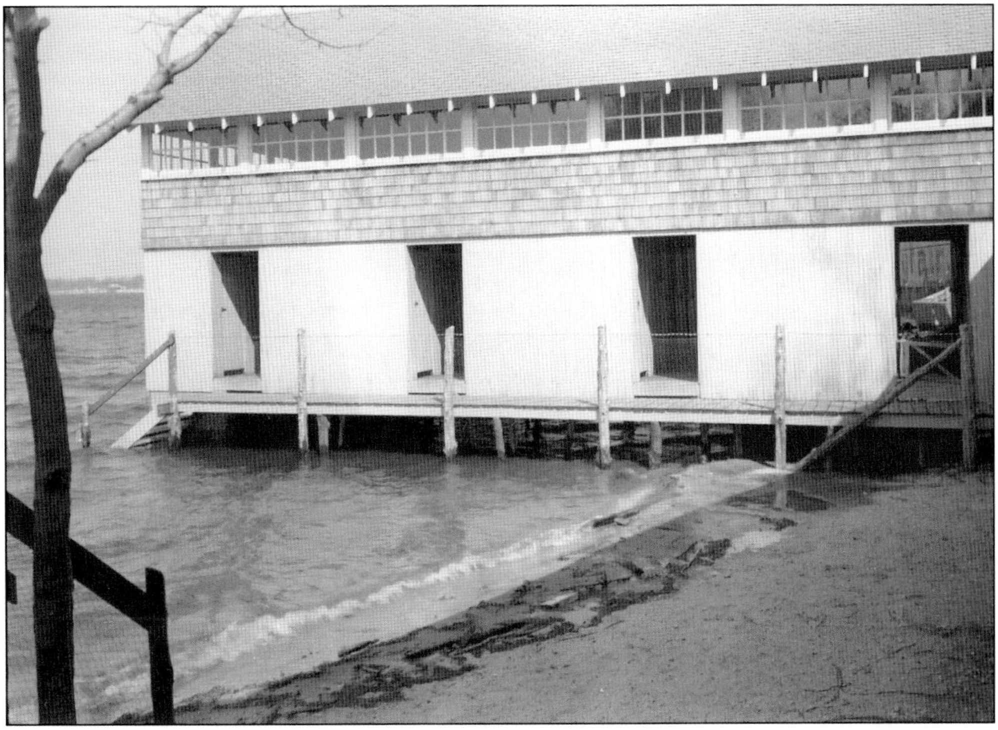

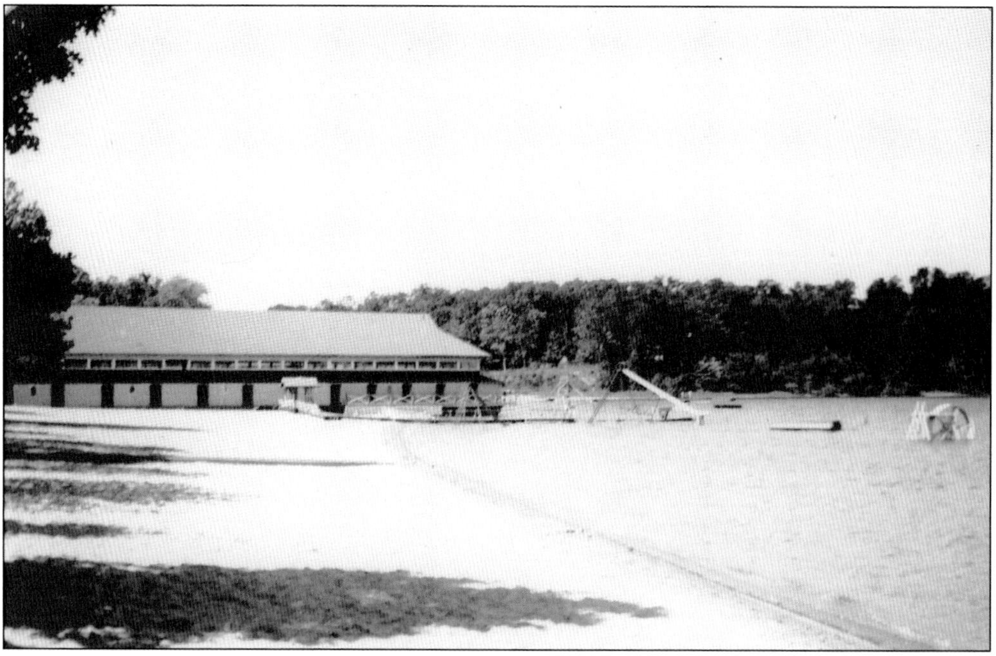

This James Browne Sr. photograph was taken of Raynor's Pavilion facing south in 1937. The photograph shows some of the activities awaiting visitors at the lake—slides, floating docks, waterwheels, and a pavilion with food and activities. The Mayfair Pavilion would be behind the photographer. Note the lake has not risen as shown on the previous page.

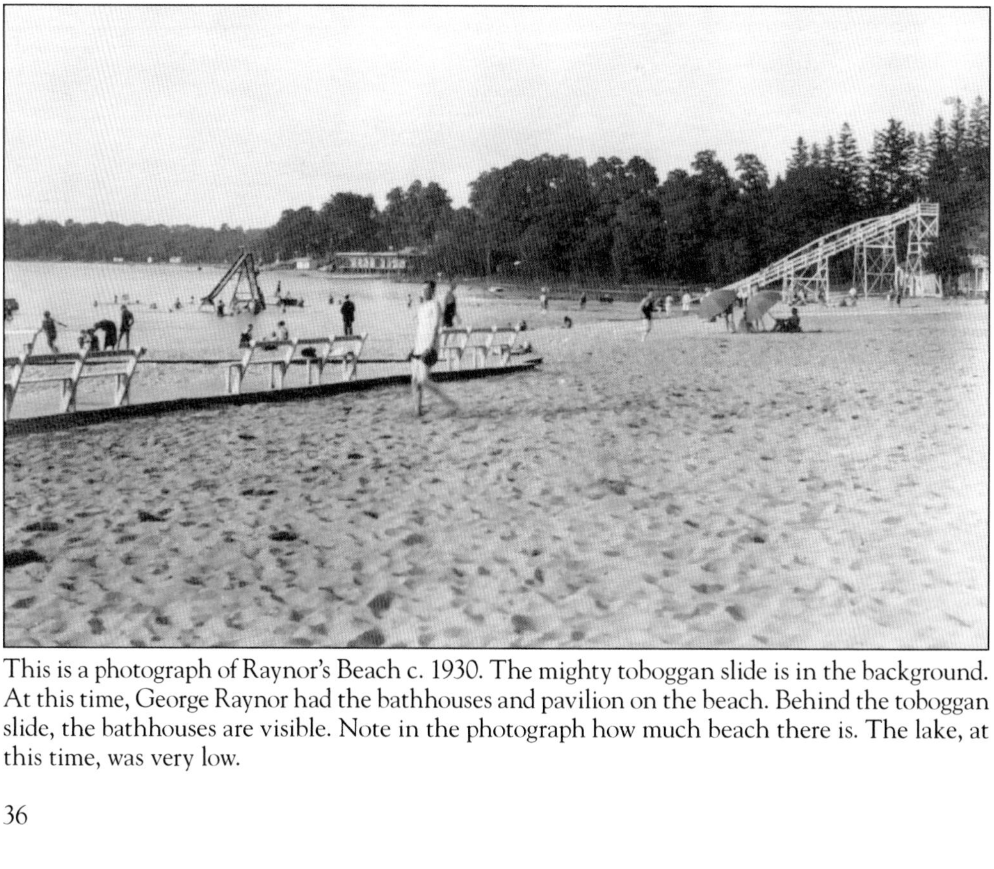

This is a photograph of Raynor's Beach c. 1930. The mighty toboggan slide is in the background. At this time, George Raynor had the bathhouses and pavilion on the beach. Behind the toboggan slide, the bathhouses are visible. Note in the photograph how much beach there is. The lake, at this time, was very low.

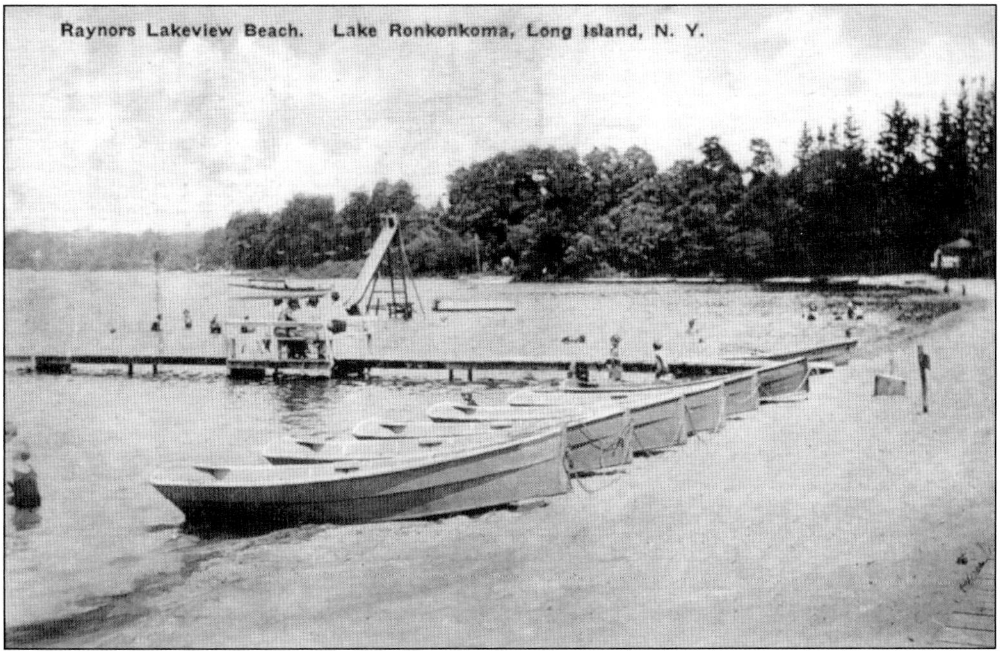

Boating was a very popular activity during the summer months at Lake Ronkonkoma. A summer weekend one may see as many as 50–60 boats out on the lake. This postcard shows Raynor's Beach c. 1923. Note that the Toboggan slide has not been constructed, nor any of the pavilions that would soon decorate the shoreline.

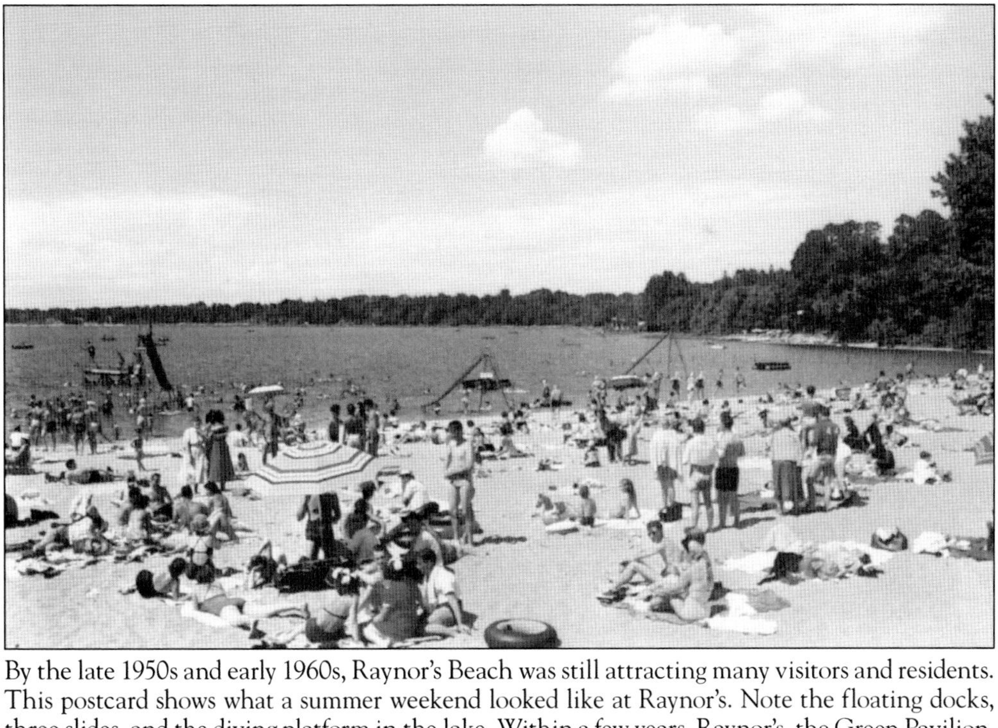

By the late 1950s and early 1960s, Raynor's Beach was still attracting many visitors and residents. This postcard shows what a summer weekend looked like at Raynor's. Note the floating docks, three slides, and the diving platform in the lake. Within a few years, Raynor's, the Green Pavilion, and Hollywood Pavilion would become the property of the Town of Brookhaven.

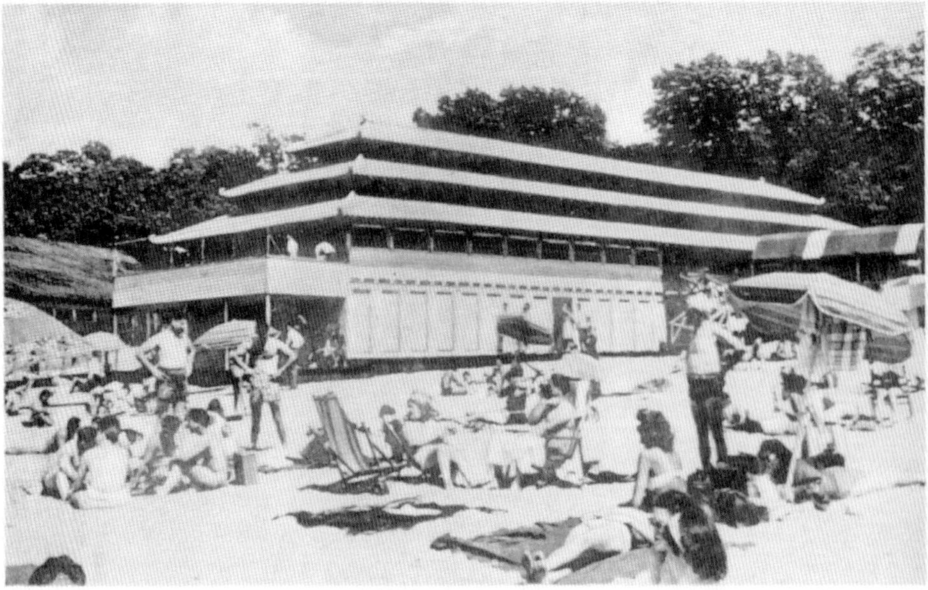

Meet me at "The Green" Lake Ronkonkoma, Long Island, N. Y.

Paula Browne realized that the lake was an attractive place and decided to buy land on both sides of Rugen's Tavern. She built two large pavilions and rows of bathhouses on the beach. The Green Pavilion located next door to Raynor's was built c. 1925. On August 31, 1932, a suspicious fire destroyed the Green Pavilion. No one was hurt or killed. These two postcards, taken c. 1940, show what the rebuilt pavilion looked like. The Green Pavilion became one of the largest on the lake. This three-tier pavilion was used for dancing, parties, and also the Miss Lake Ronkonkoma beauty pageant. The famous saying the Green Pavilion would use in their advertisements was "Meet Me at the Green." (Courtesy of Helen Hethy Mulvihill.)

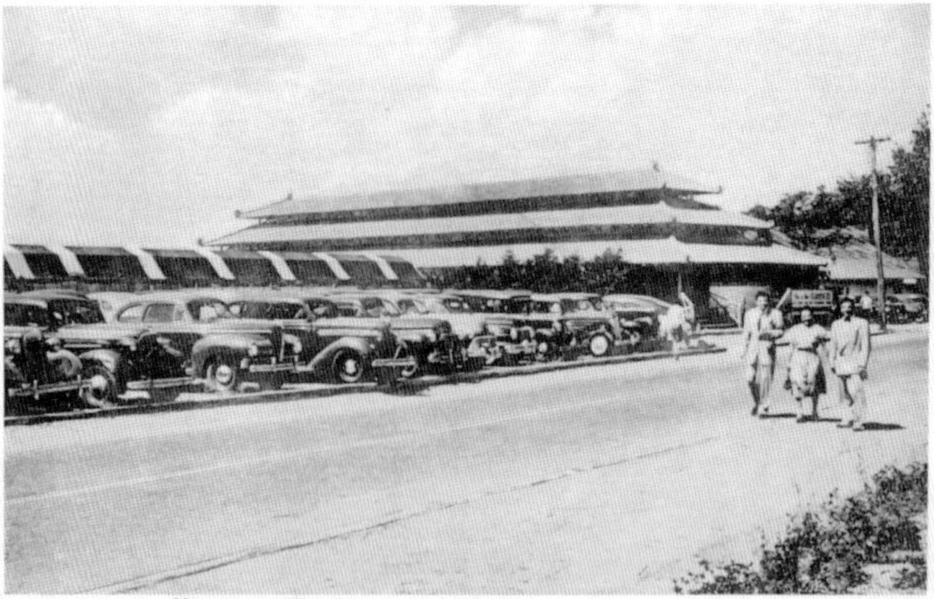

Meet me at "The Green" Lake Ronkonkoma, Long Island, N. Y.

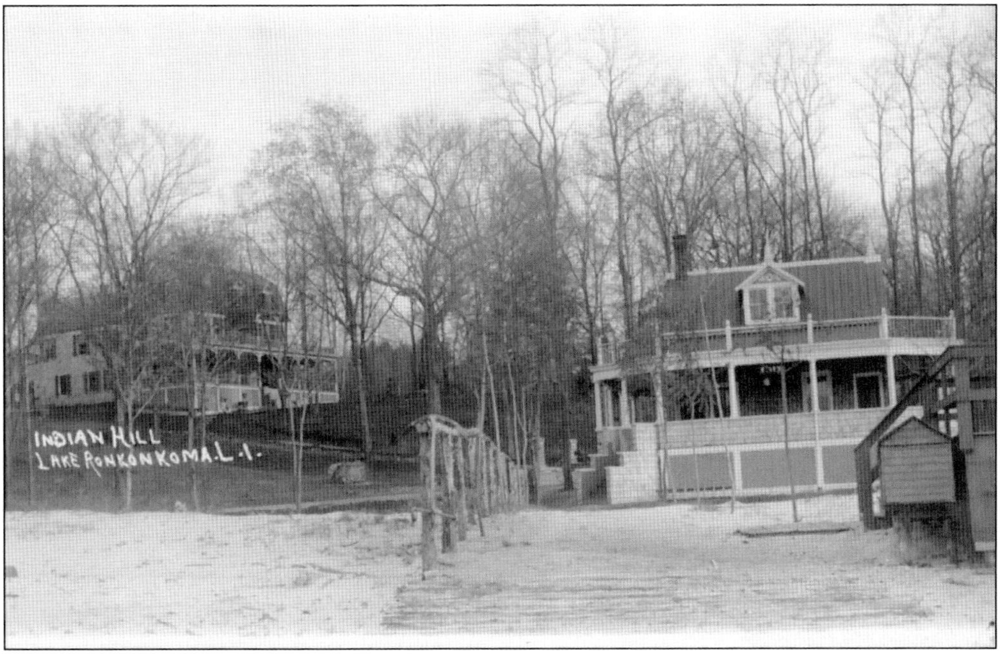

Pictured on the left side of the photograph was the Hoyts' home c. 1900. The building in the foreground was the Indian Hill Café. Pond Road is between both buildings. The Hoyts owned this café and a strip of beach leading to the lake. This was also one of the first cafés built near the lake. (Courtesy of Helen Hethy Mulvihill.)

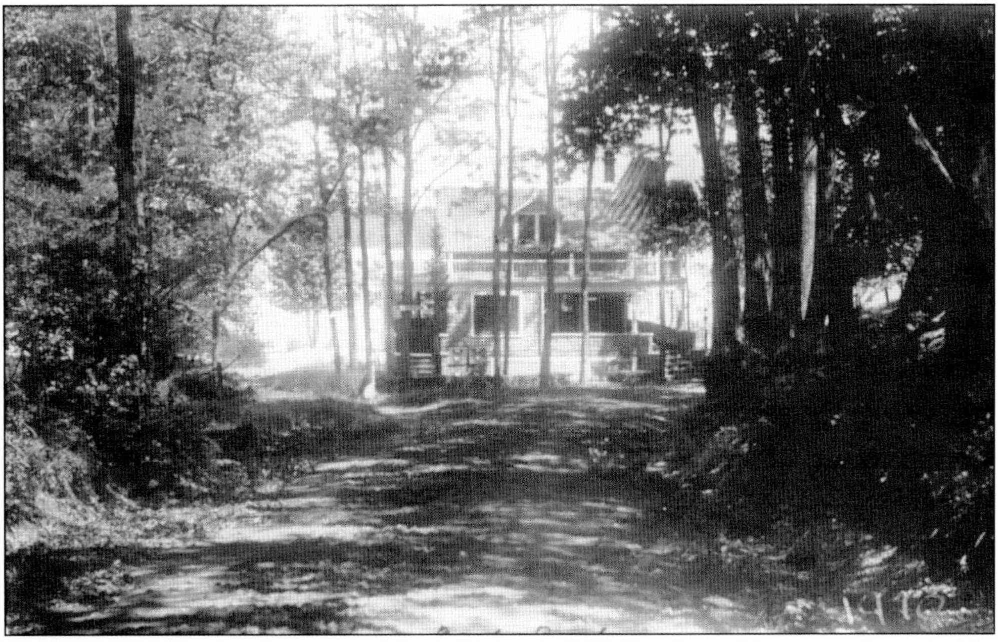

The Hoyts would name their tavern Hoyt's Casino in 1910. People would come to the casino for socializing, liquor, hot meals, and poker. The photograph shows how Pond Road looked in 1910. Note all the trees around Hoyt's and on both sides of Pond Road. In time, this tavern was sold to a Mr. Fiala and then to Herman Rugen.

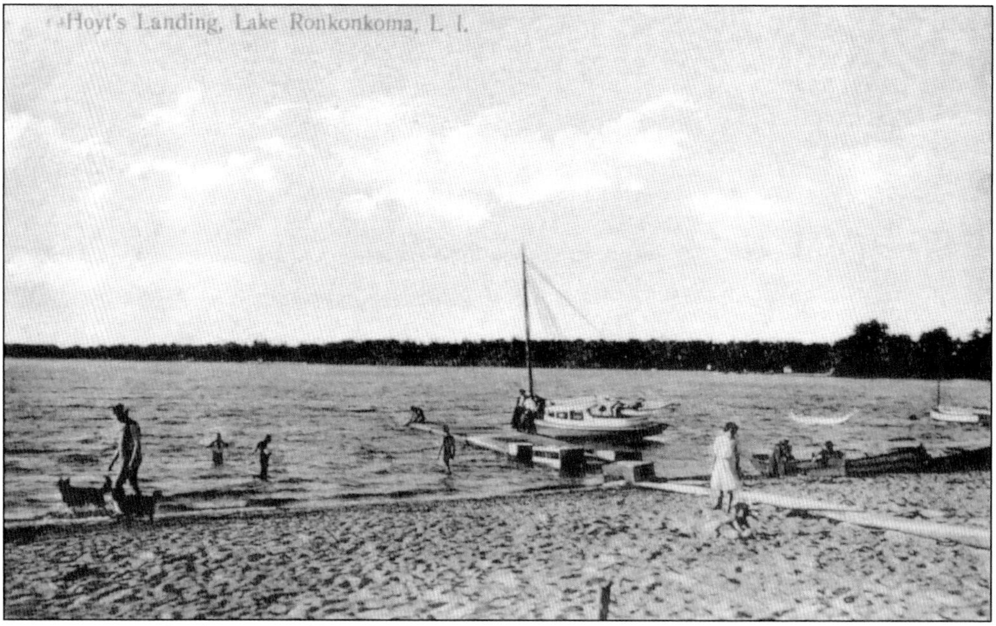

Hoyt's Casino had a strip of beach that was called Hoyt's Landing. This postcard depicts people bathing, walking their dogs, and using the landing to set off on their sailboat. Lake Ronkonkoma in the 1900s was a much more rural and easygoing place than the area would become by the 1920s.

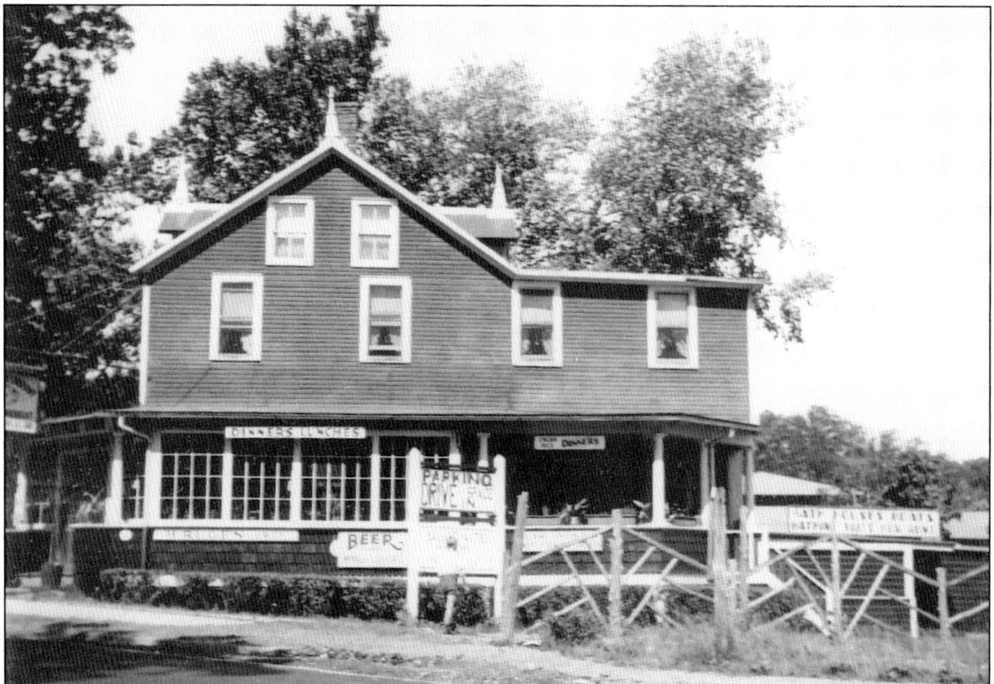

Herman Rugen was the owner of Rugen's Pavilion. James Browne Sr. took this photograph in 1937. Dinners and lunches were made at the Lake Shore Inn, and the bathhouses and beach were on the right side. Rugen's was nestled between the Green Pavilion and the Hollywood Pavilion.

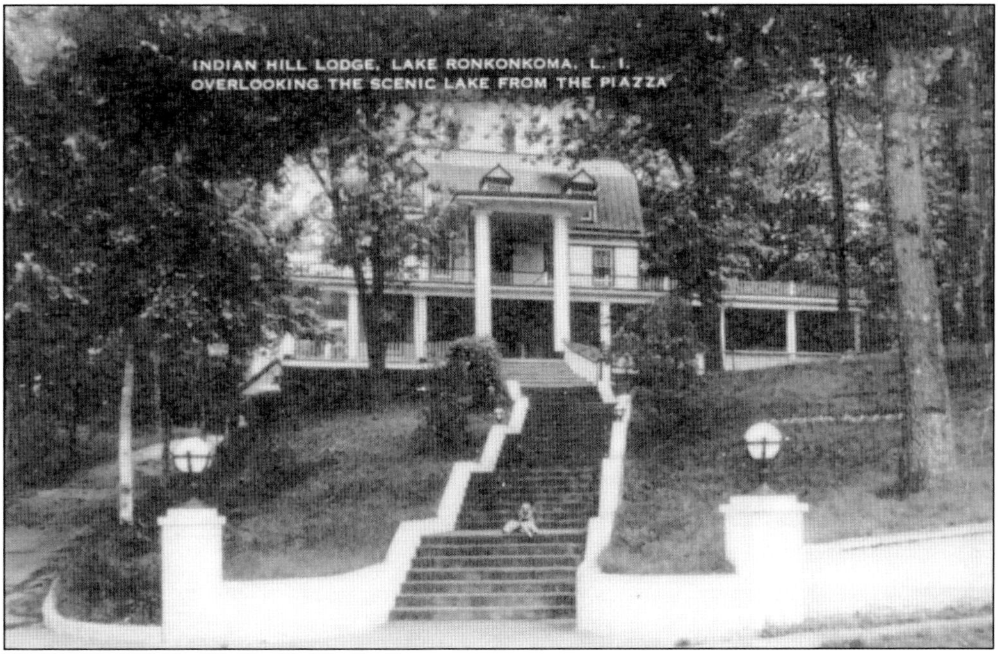

The Indian Hill Lodge was located on the bend of Pond Road, overlooking the lake. The Hoyts originally owned this property. During the 1920s, the mansion was turned into a lodge to accommodate the growing number of visitors to Lake Ronkonkoma. By 1962, the building became home to the Veterans of Foreign Wars (VFW). (Courtesy of Helen Hethy Mulvihill.)

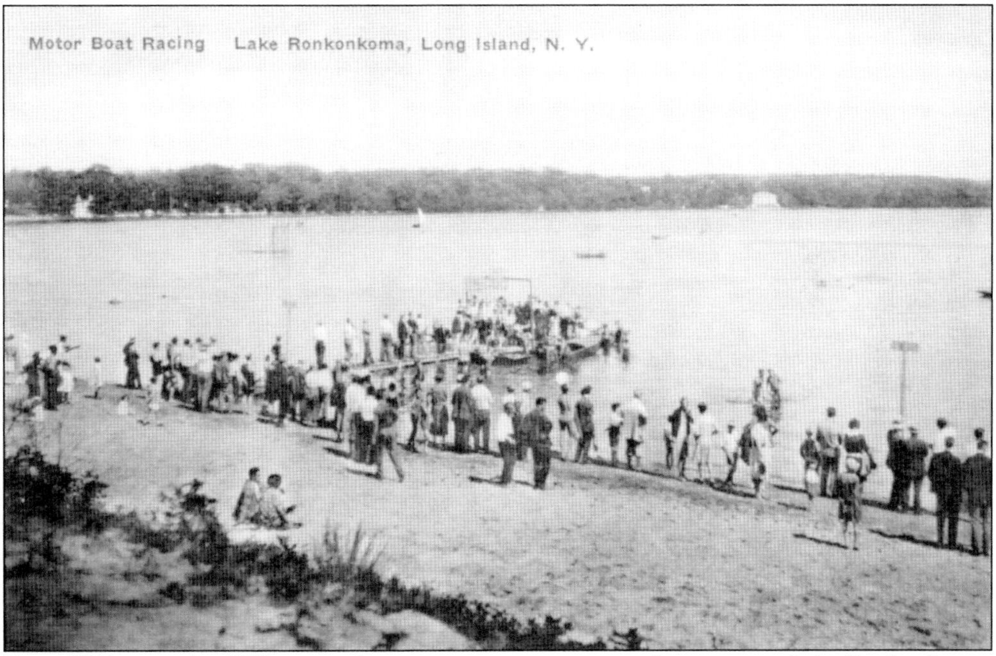

From 1920s into the 1930s, motorboat racing was a very popular event on Lake Ronkonkoma. These boats were light and very fast. Injuries did happen, but races still took place each summer. In 1934, motorboat racing and any power craft on the lake were banned out of concern for the safety of swimmers and fear of oil contamination. The law is still in place.

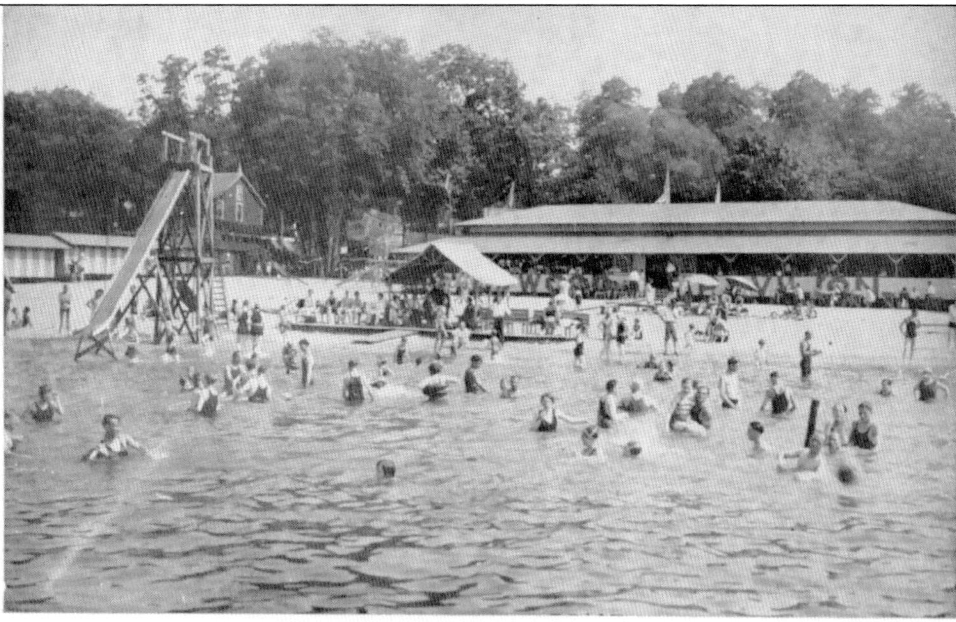

HOLLYWOOD BEACH - LAKE RONKONKOMA, L. I., N. Y.

The Hollywood Pavilion was located off Pond Road on the southeast corner of the lake near Rugen's. During the 1920s, Paula Browne built the Green Pavilion, and on the west side of Rugen's, the Hollywood Pavilion was built. The Hollywood became the favorite hangout for teenagers and young adults. Places like Duffield's and Raynor's ran a stern and meticulous operation. The Hollywood was a much more liberal and carefree place. Charlie Kruger, the proprietor of the Hollywood Pavilion, would keep the jukebox running all through the night. Everybody went dancing at the Hollywood, and if there was no room to dance in the pavilion, people would go out on the beach and dance. The picture above shows the Hollywood c. 1930. The photograph below was taken c. 1950.

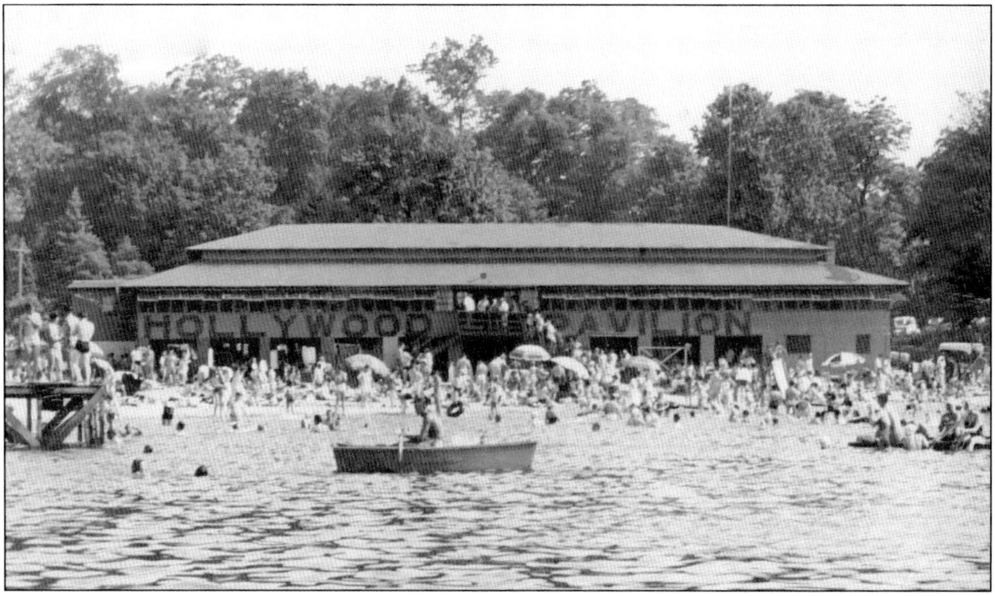

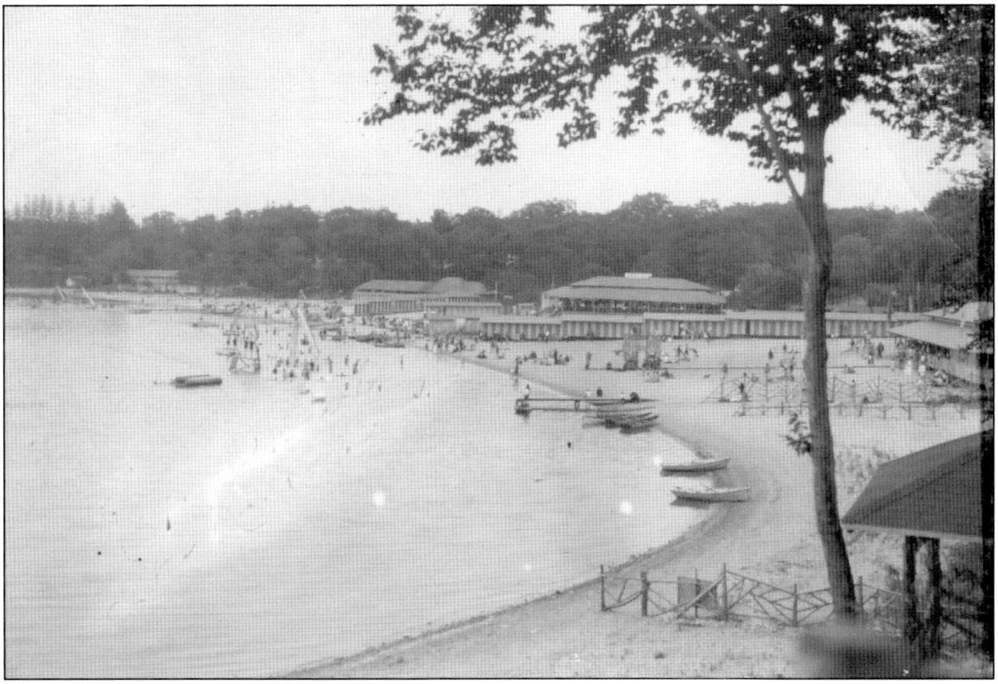

This photograph was taken at the southern tip of the lake c. 1925. Raynor's Beach (back left) is clearly visible. The pavilion in the center of the picture is the Green Pavilion. Note the row of bathhouses leading to the lake. The Hollywood Pavilion (right side) is the last pavilion on the southeast side of the lake.

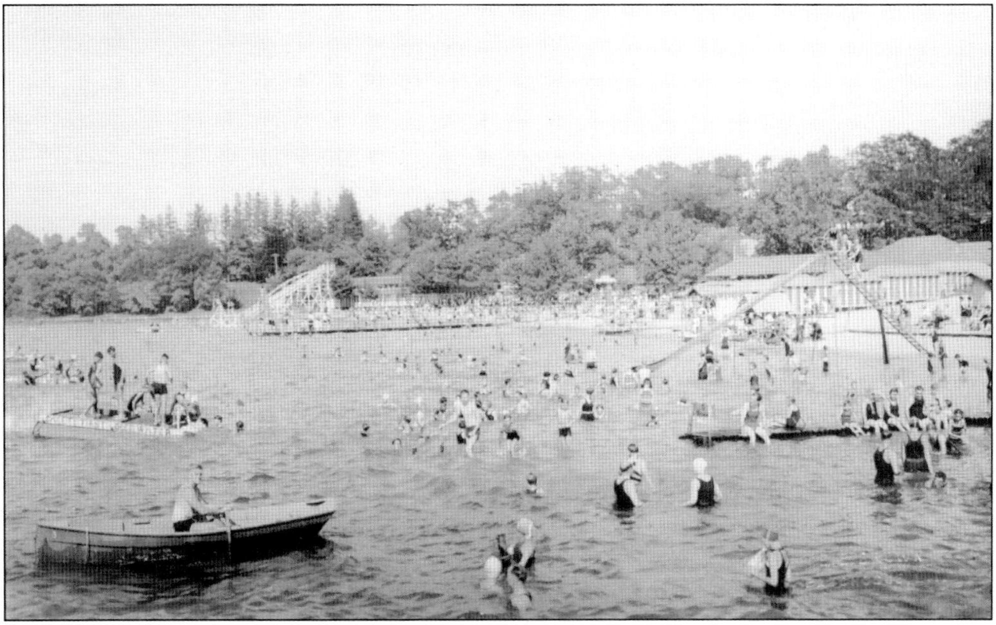

This is a magnificent photograph of Raynor's Beach c. 1930. The new toboggan slide (back center) and the waterwheel (to the left of the slide) have been assembled for visitors. Floats (front left) would be found in the deeper waters of the lake. Floating docks (front right) would be a place for adults and children to relax or take a break from all the other adventurous activities.

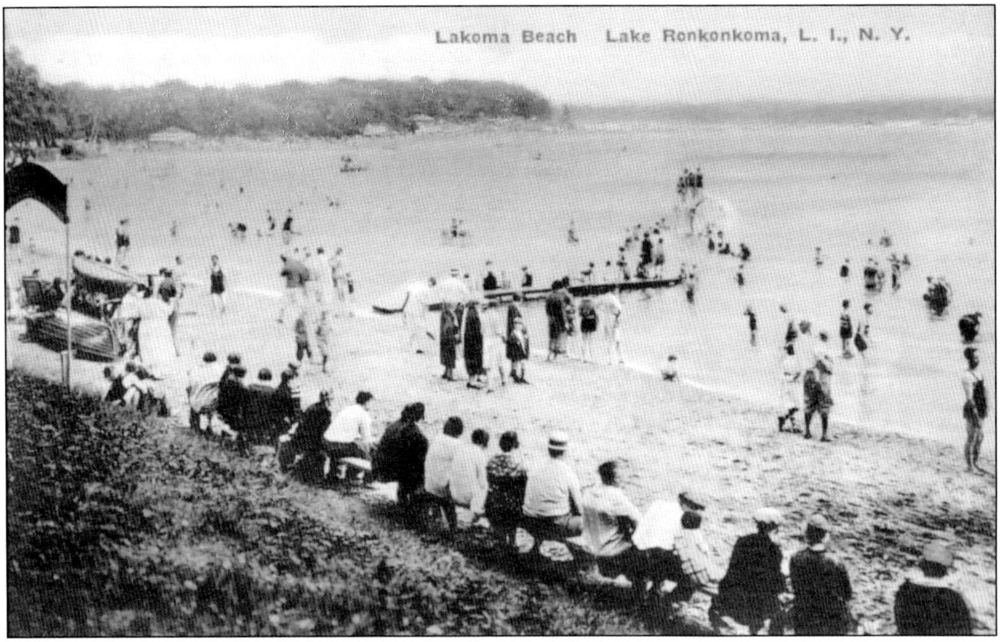

The Lakoma Beach (sometimes referred to as Heilman's Beach) was located on the west side of the lake, between Blythe's Beach and the Petit Trianon. These two postcards are from 1930 and show the activities that were available at the time. Benches lined the beach for patrons to sit, while the much more daring would attempt the waterwheel. The postcard below shows how the automobiles parked up on the embankment. Two sets of stairs were available for visitors to go from the beach to the parking lot or to the refreshment stand, where hamburgers, hot dogs, soda, and ice cream could be purchased. (Courtesy of Helen Hethy Mulvihill.)

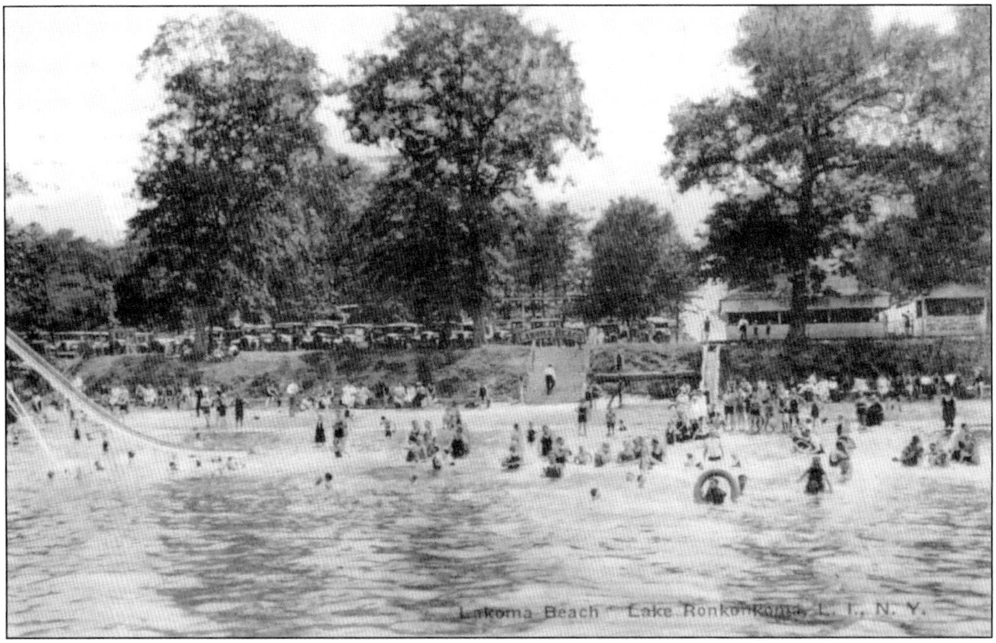

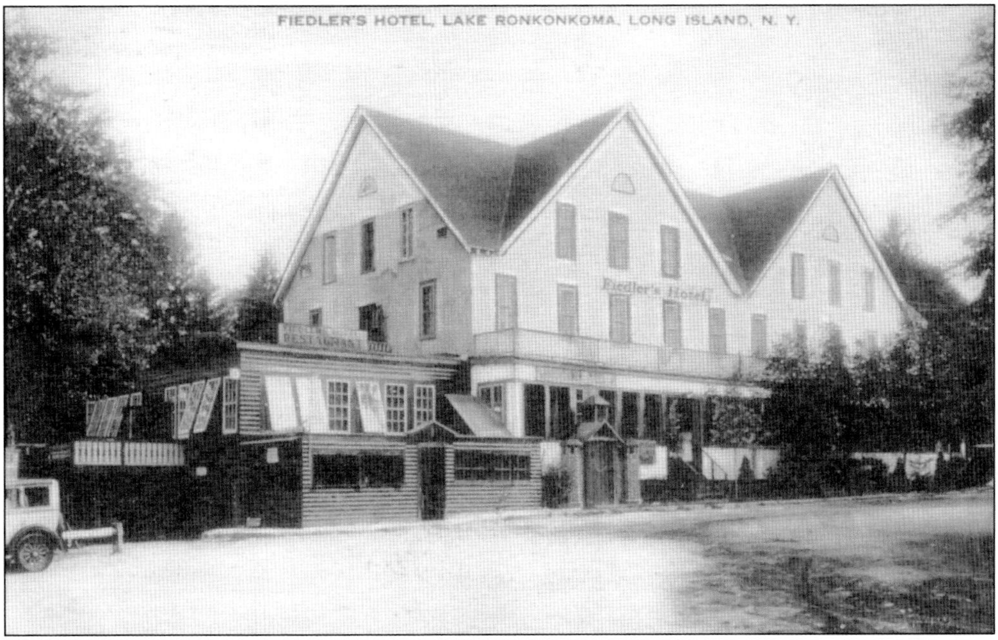

Fielder's Hotel was situated off Richmond Boulevard on the west side of the lake. Fielder's was the largest hotel on the west side of the lake. The picture of Fielder's shown above was taken around 1930. The hotel had 40 rooms and a dining room that could hold 500 guests. Banquets, weddings, conventions, and different outings were all held at Fiedler's. The postcard below shows the interior of the Munchner Brau Stube, the restaurant that was on the left side of the building. At 6:00 a.m. on May 7, 1937, an undeterred fire broke out, destroying Fielder's Hotel. (Courtesy of Helen Hethy Muvihill.)

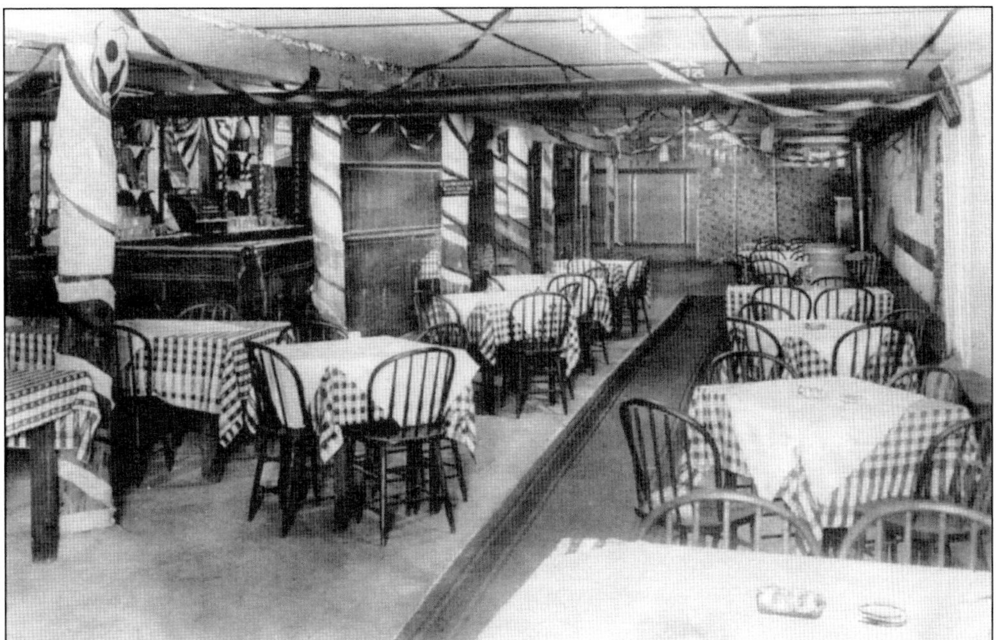

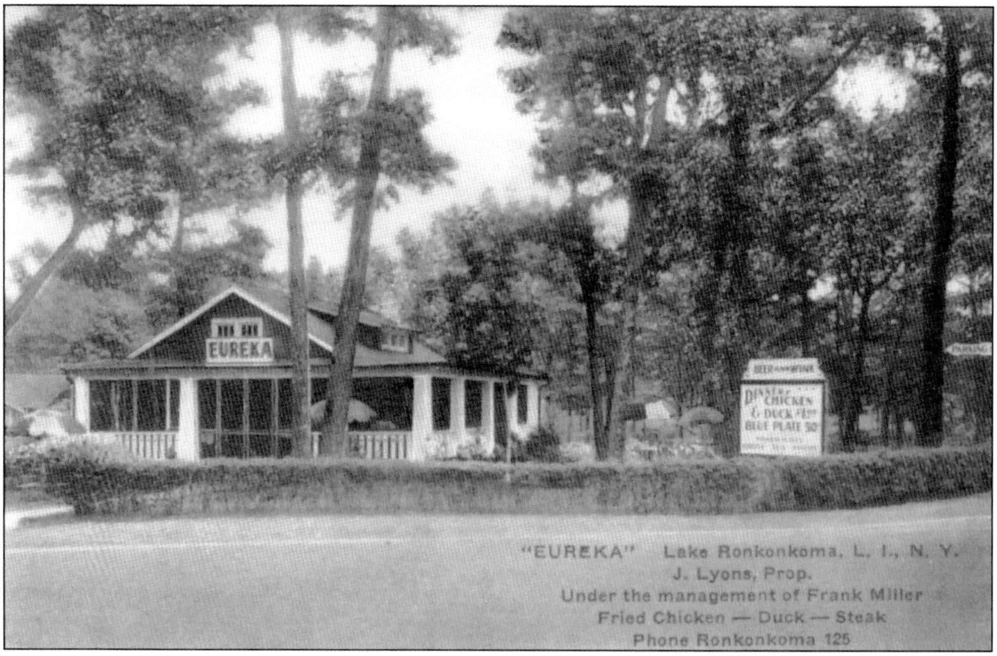

The Eureka Inn was located on the corner of Lake Shore Road and Rosevale Avenue. This postcard shows how the Eureka Inn looked c. 1930. J. Lyons was the proprietor under the management of Frank Miller. Chicken and duck dinners were only $1. (Courtesy of Helen Hethy Mulvihill.)

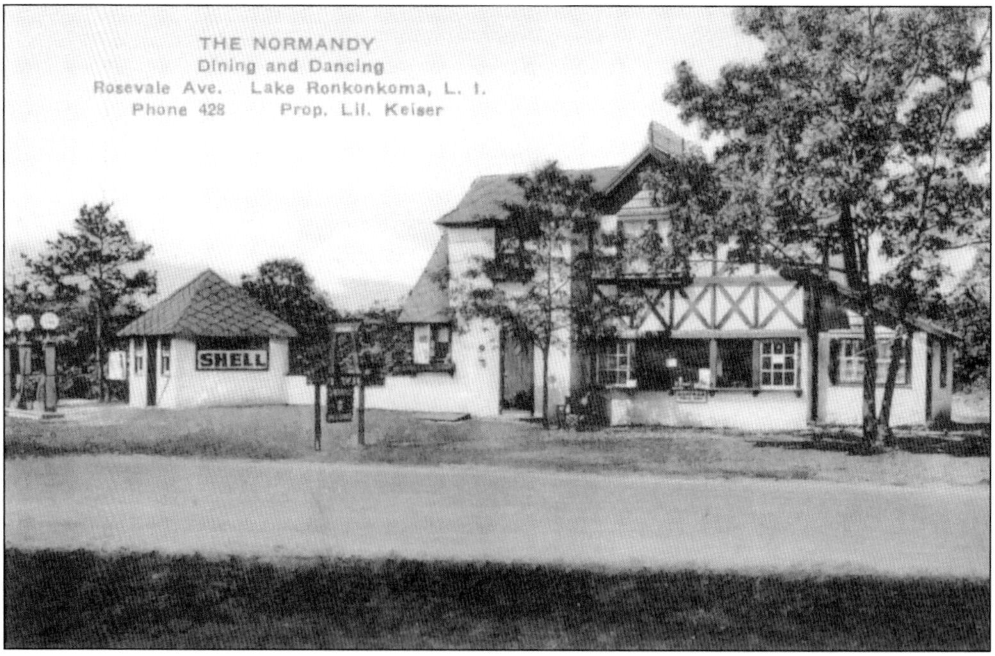

The Normandy was an inn located on Rosevale Avenue near the Clover Club (also known as the Candlelight Inn) on the west side of the lake. This c. 1930 postcard shows that there was also a Shell gas station attached to the building. (Courtesy of Helen Hethy Mulvihill.)

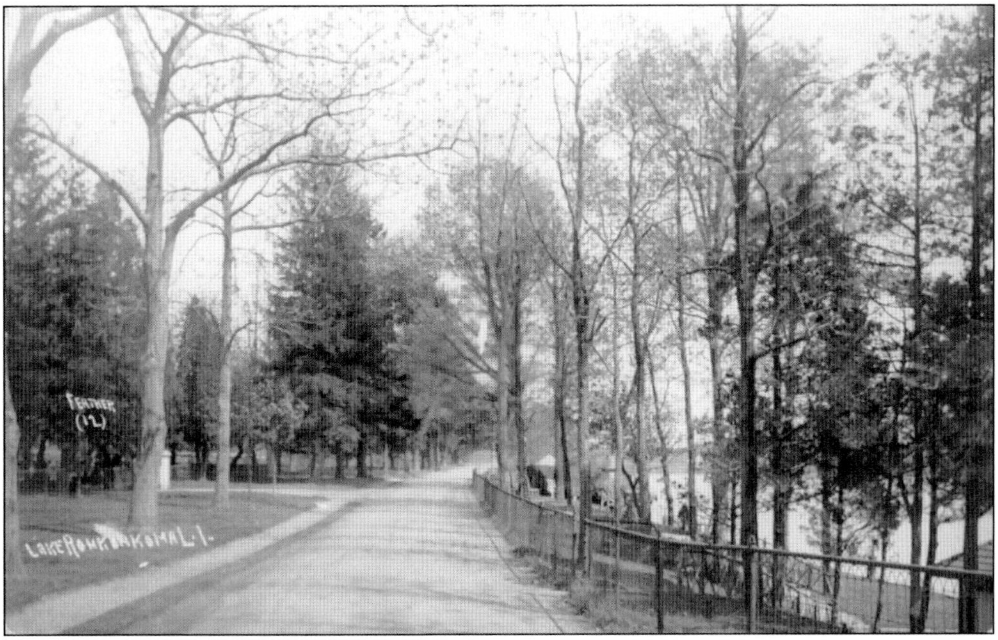

This is a scenic photograph looking east on what is now Lake Shore Road, once called Farm to Market Road. This photograph was taken c. 1915 and captures the serenity and peacefulness of the area. The Metzners' property was on both sides of the road. The entrance to the Metzners' estate can be seen in the back left of the picture.

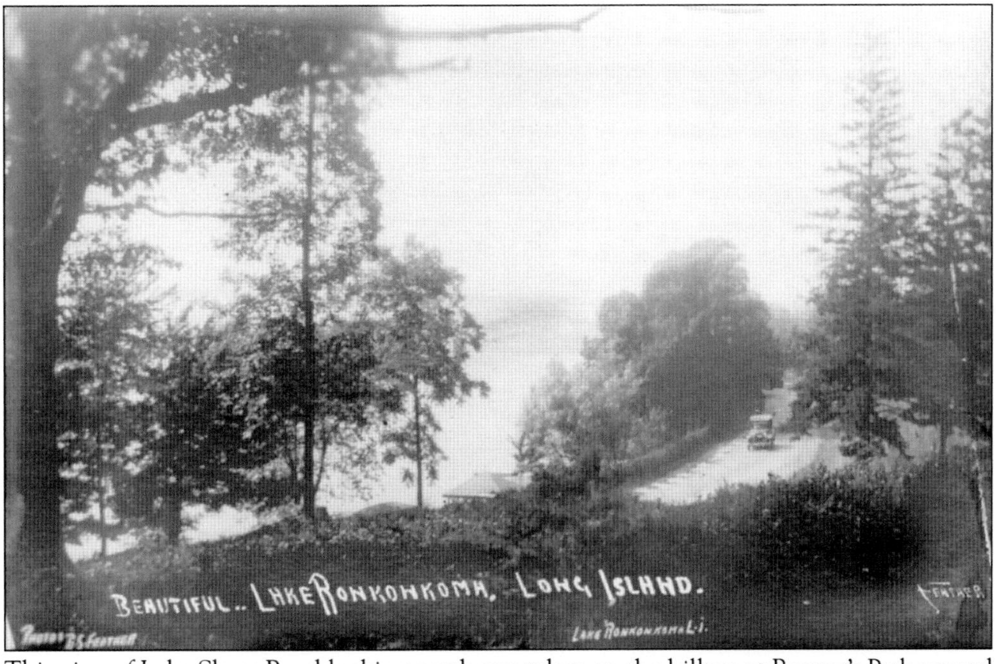

This view of Lake Shore Road looking north was taken on the hilltop at Raynor's Park around 1922. The land surrounding the lake at this time was still untouched. Within a couple of years, every ounce of land around the lake would have pavilions, refreshment stands, and thousands of visitors.

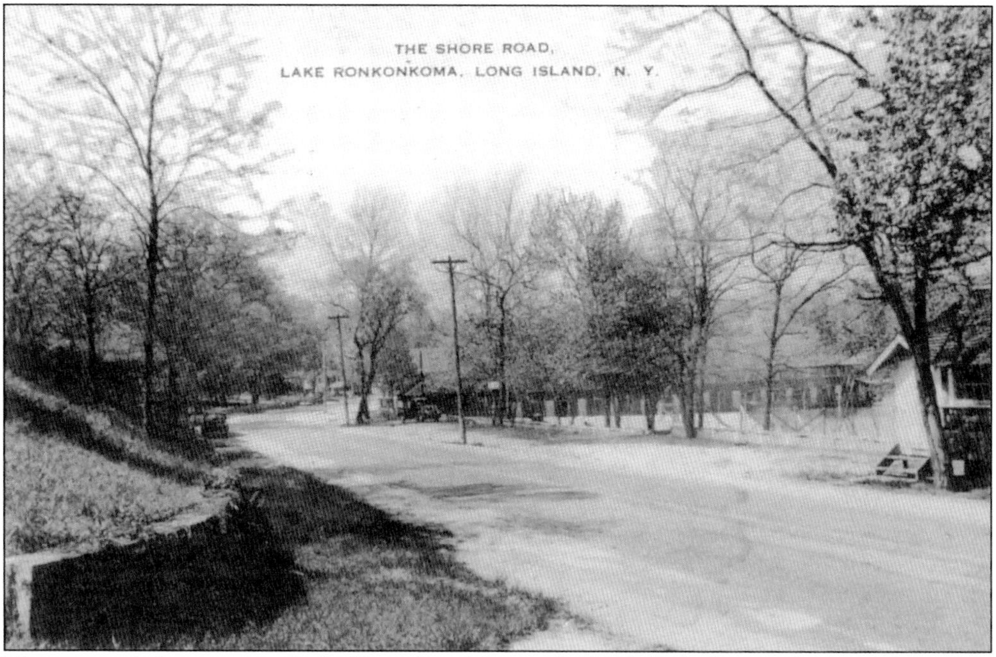

This is a south-facing view of Lake Shore Road during the 1940s. Telephone poles lined the streets, as more and more people began to reside at Lake Ronkonkoma. In the back right of the postcard is Raynor's Pavilion. Around the bend of the road would be the Green, Rugen's, and Hollywood Pavilions on the right. (Courtesy of Helen Hethy Mulvihill.)

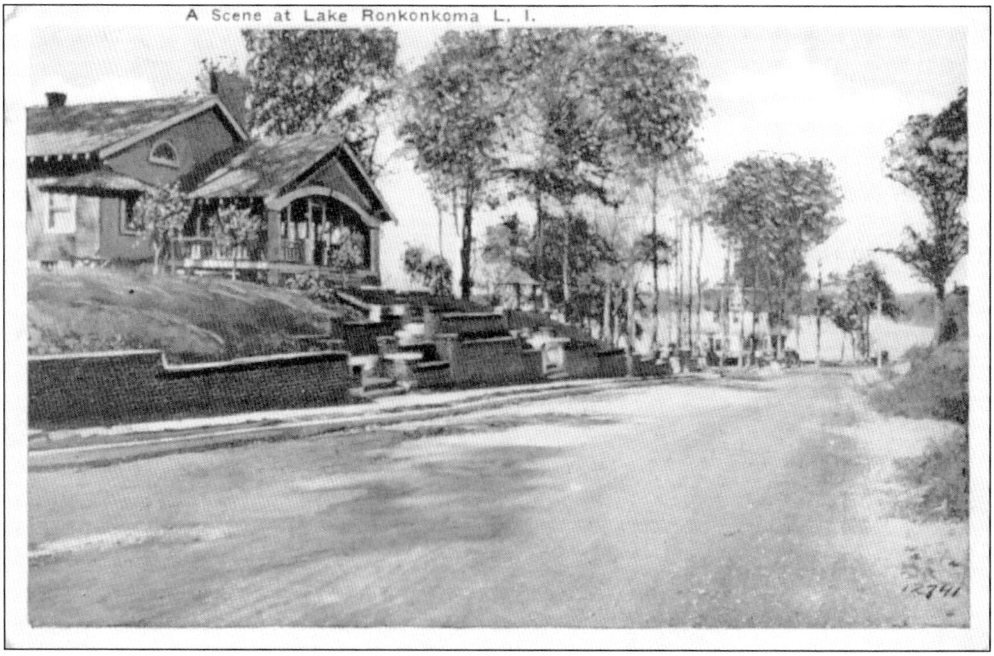

This image shows Pond Road facing north around 1920. The home on the left side is a bungalow. People would buy or rent a bungalow for the summer and return to their place of residence for winter months. The building in the background is Rugen's. (Courtesy of Helen Hethy Mulvihill.)

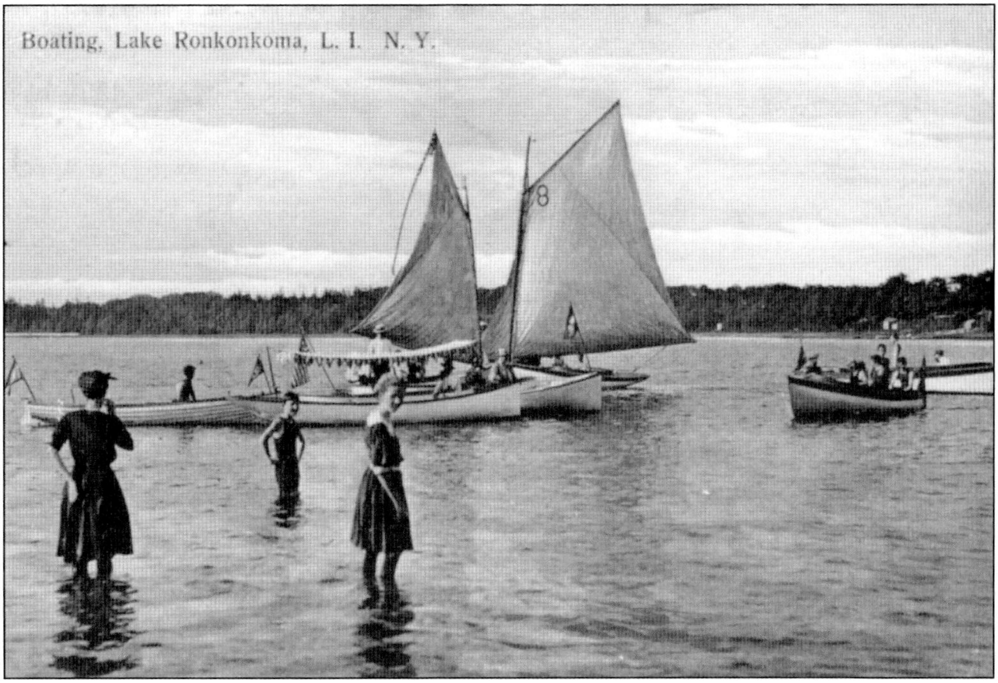

One activity everyone enjoyed while staying at Lake Ronkonkoma was boating. The lake was strictly residential in the early 20th century. Private docks ran out into the water from many of the residences. Boats were used on the lake for pleasure and for fishing. These two postcards, taken c. 1910, show the different types of boats that were out on the lake during this period of time—sailboats, rowboats, and motorboats. Boating was much more easygoing from 1900 to 1925. With the influx of visitors arriving by the thousands in the 1920s, many more obstacles became apparent.

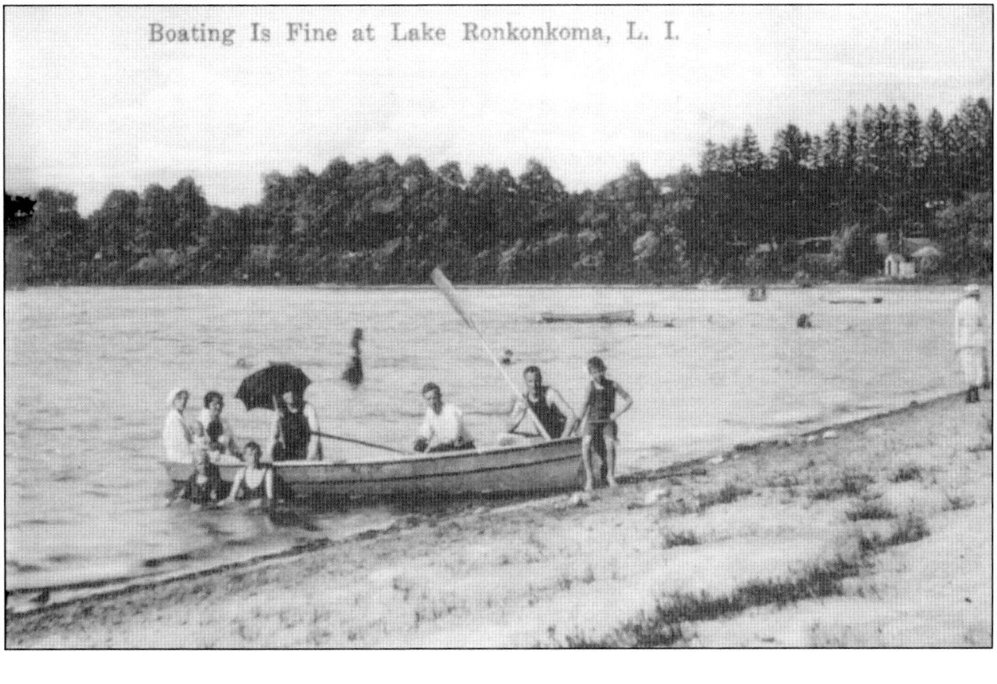

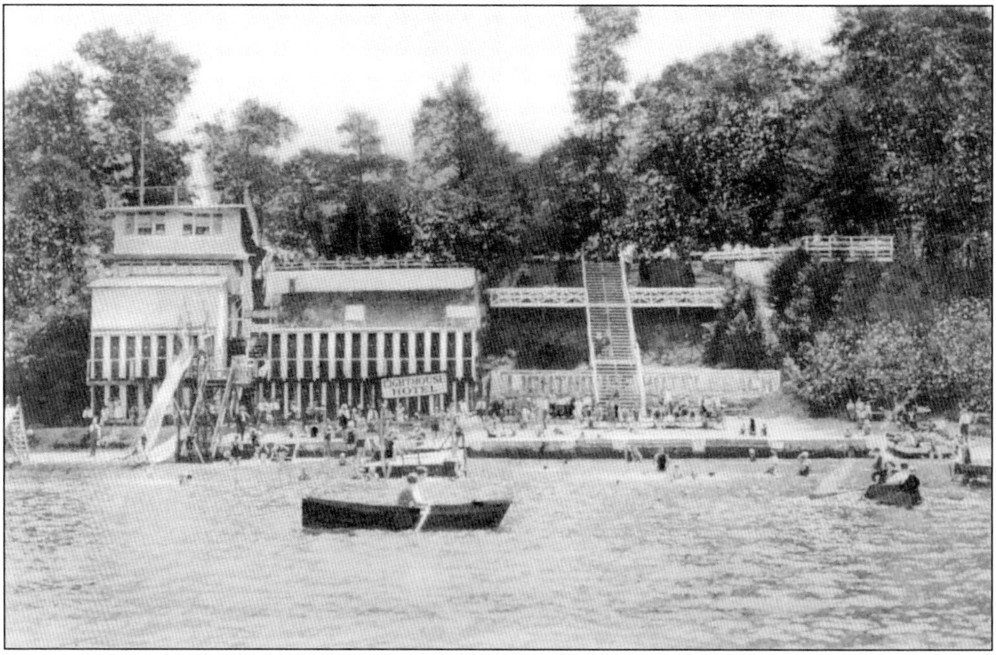

This postcard of the Lighthouse Hotel is from around 1930. This view from the lake pinpoints the different activities one could do when staying at the Lighthouse Hotel. To the left of the picture, there are two levels of bathhouses. Also take note of the steep stairs that ascend to the hotel. (Courtesy of Helen Hethy Mulvihill.)

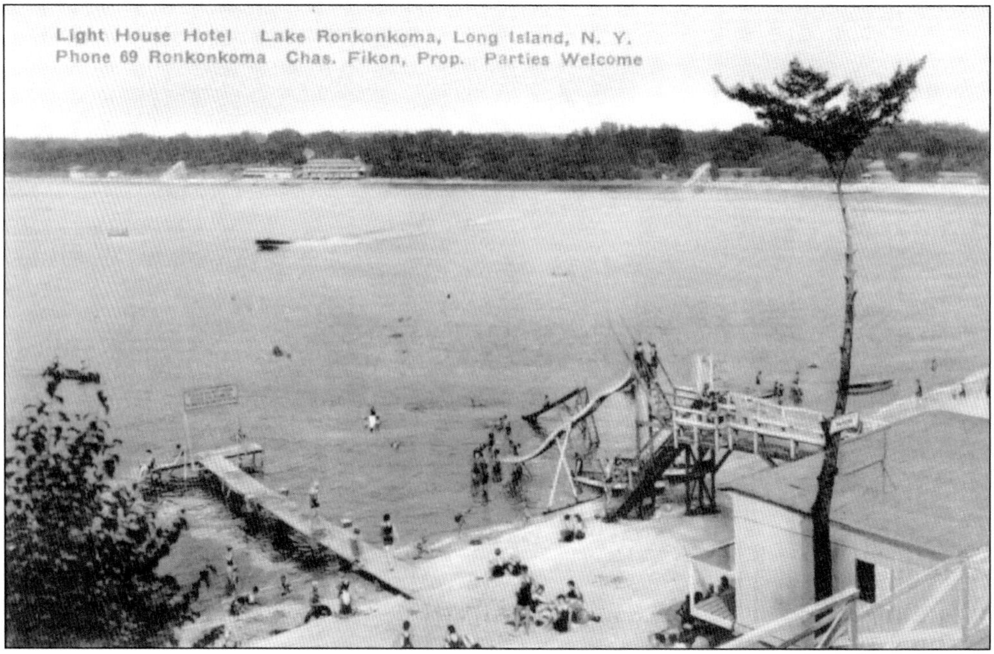

An outstanding c. 1930 view shows the floating dock and large slide at the Lighthouse Hotel. Towards the center of the postcard, there is a motorboat cruising north on the lake. In the back center of the picture is the Olympia Pavilion and to the right is Raynor's Beach. Note the toboggan slide at Raynor's. (Courtesy of Helen Hethy Muvihill.)

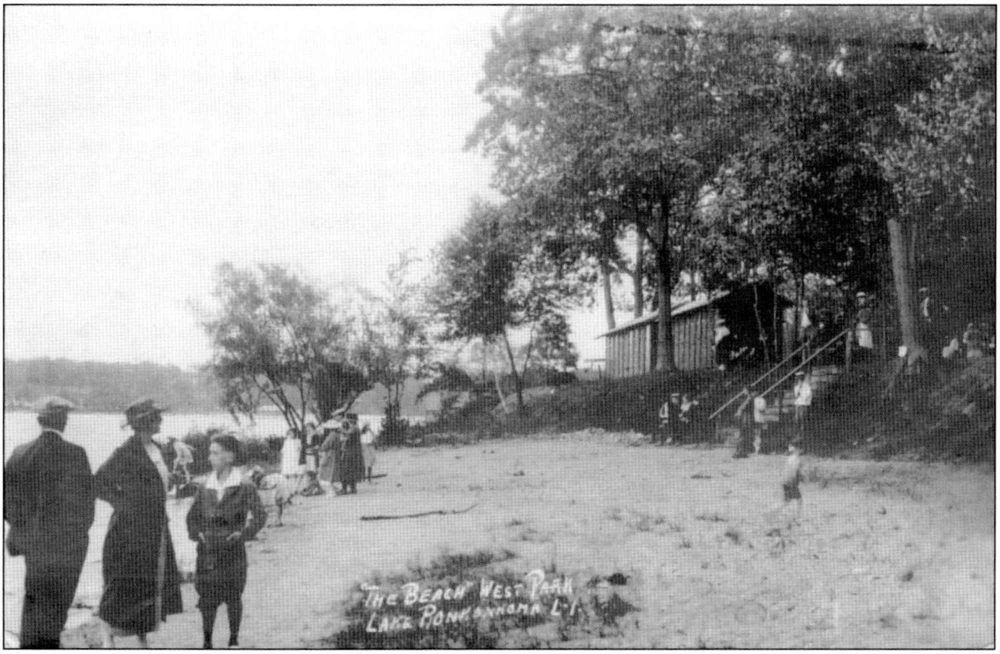

This is a very early image of Duffield's West Park Beach c. 1923. People during this time would stay fully clothed until it was time to go into the water. The crude bathhouses up on the hill would only survive a few seasons. By the end of the 1920s, Duffield's West Park Beach would become the place to go on the west side of the lake. (Courtesy of Helen Hethy Mulvihill.)

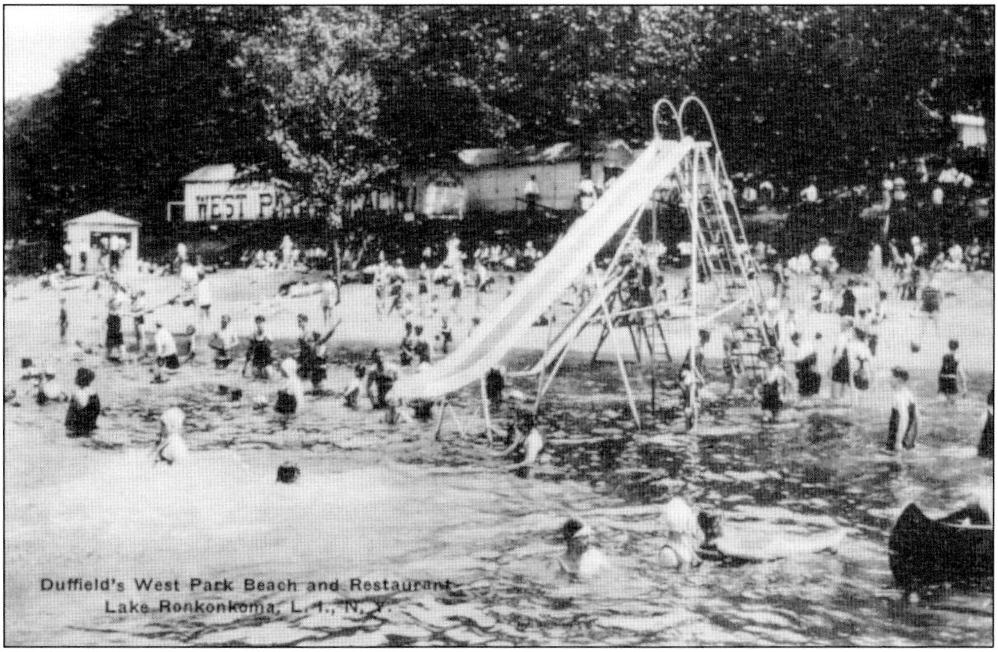

Duffield's West Park Beach is pictured c. 1928. Within a few years, Duffield's became a very successful beach and restaurant. Here is a view of the beach with a couple of slides and new and improved bathhouses. Also at this time, a tour boat named *Dark Cloud* would pick up passengers for a sightseeing cruise around the lake. (Courtesy of Helen Hethy Mulvihill.)

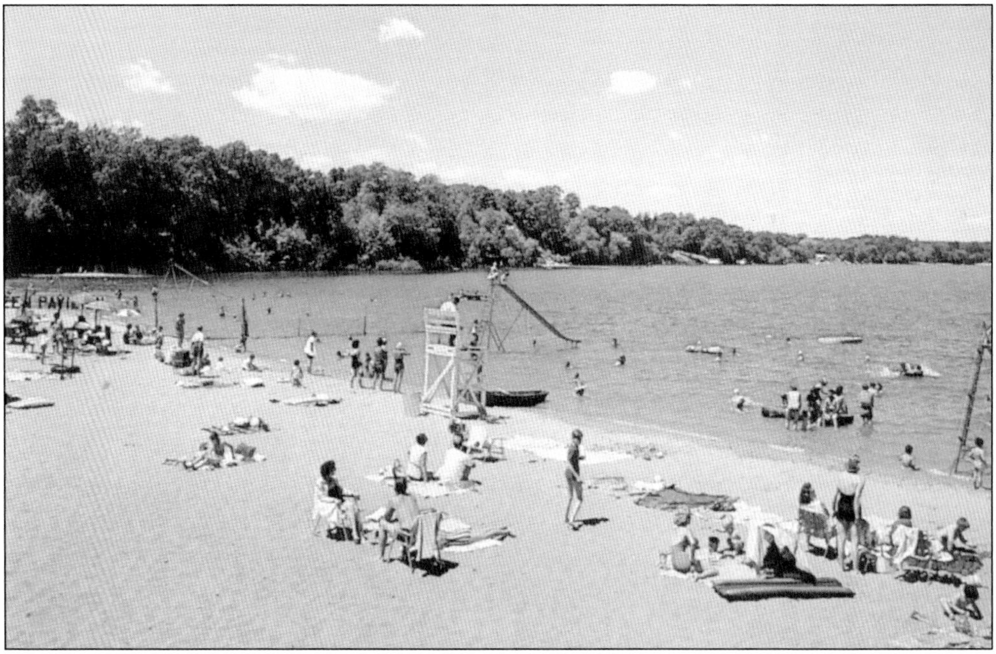

These two photographs capture the changing times of Lake Ronkonkoma during the 1960s. The photograph above is of Raynor's Beach. People still came to Lake Ronkonkoma to enjoy the lake and its beauty, but at the same time, the town that was once considered a resort was losing that title. Gone were the pavilions, hotels, and restaurants that dotted the land around the lake. Lake Ronkonkoma was now a town that had year-round residents who were going out of state for their vacations. Another large factor was the swimming pool. Most families were purchasing swimming pools during the 1960s. The photograph below shows the north side of the lake.

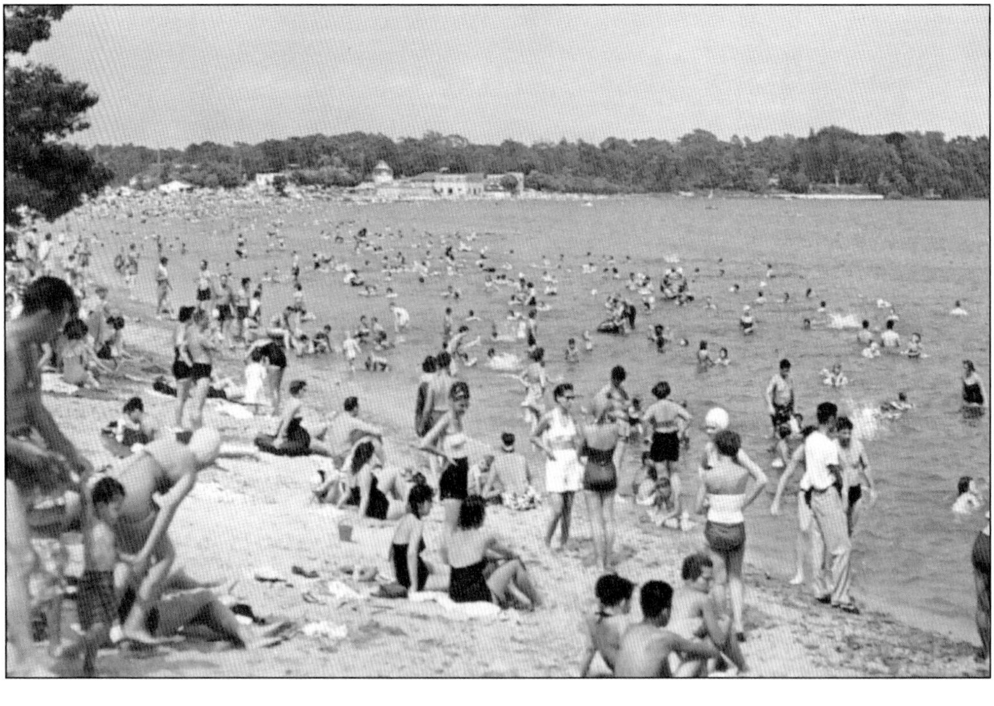

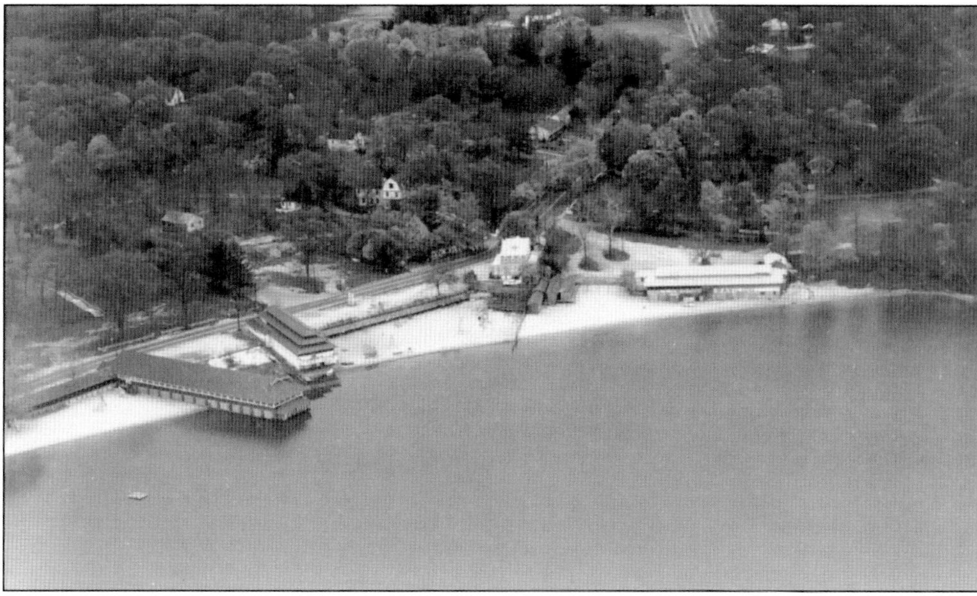

James Mooney took this photograph on November 2, 1962. This birds-eye view shows, from left to right, Raynor's Pavilion, Green Pavilion, Rugen's, and the Hollywood Pavilion. On October 4, 1962, the Town of Brookhaven purchased land where the Hollywood and Green Pavilions were standing. The Brookhaven Town Beach used the Green Pavilion until the winter of 1968, when it was destroyed by fire. (Courtesy of James Mooney.)

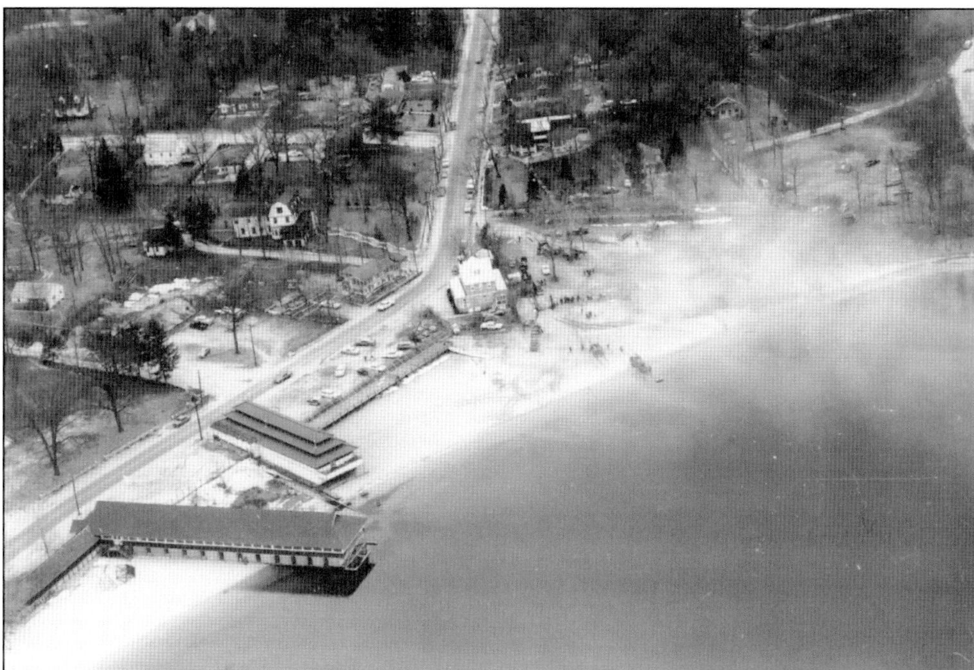

This photograph captures the end of an era at the Hollywood Pavilion. On March 8, 1964, a controlled burn by the local fire departments destroyed the Hollywood Pavilion. This was to make way for Brookhaven Town Beach. The road going up the photograph is Pond Road. (Courtesy of James Mooney.)

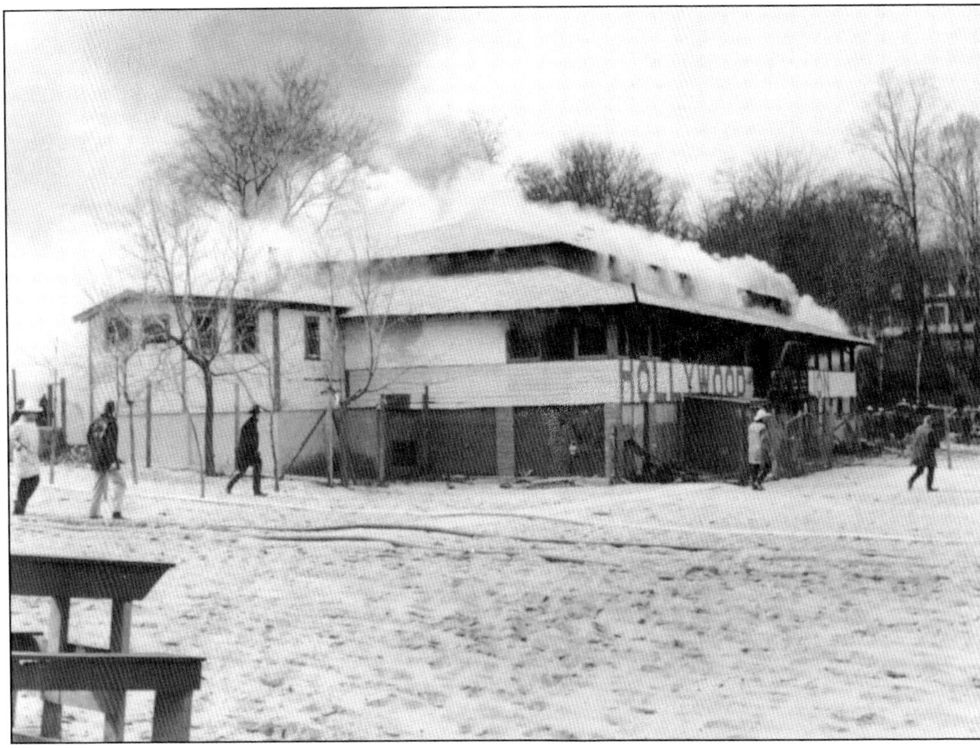

This amazing close-up shows the Hollywood Pavilion in flames. This event was big news. Firemen from the Ronkonkoma, Lakeland, Bohemia, Holbrook, St. James, and Port Jefferson fire departments all came out to assist in this event. Many people gathered around to watch this legendary place being analytically destroyed. (Courtesy of James Mooney.)

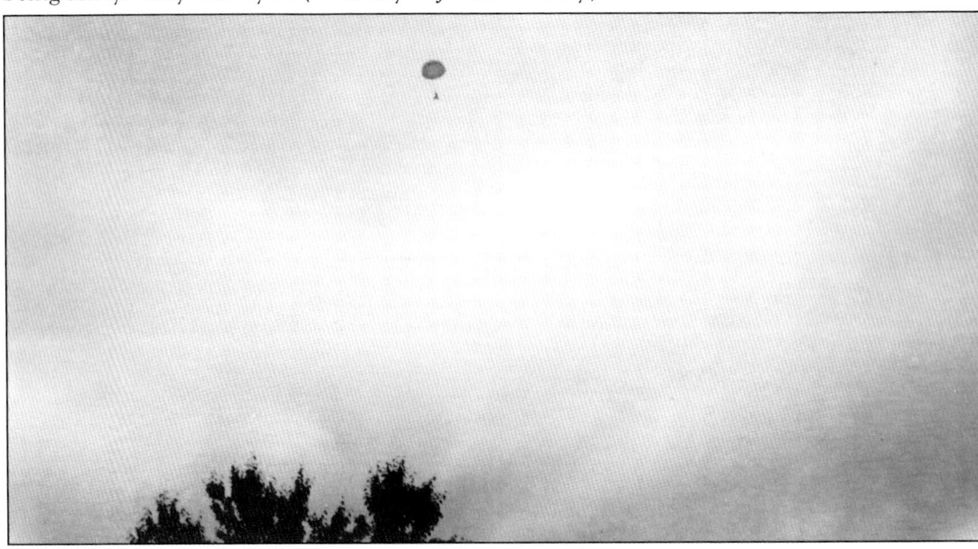

This James Browne Sr. photograph was taken in 1937. During each summer Sunday in the 1930s, Jimmy Horning would make an announcement in each of the pavilions that he was going to parachute out of a plane. On one jump over land, Horning slipped free of the harness and broke his leg so badly that it needed to be amputated. Horning continued to jump, even with an artificial leg.

Two

The Business District

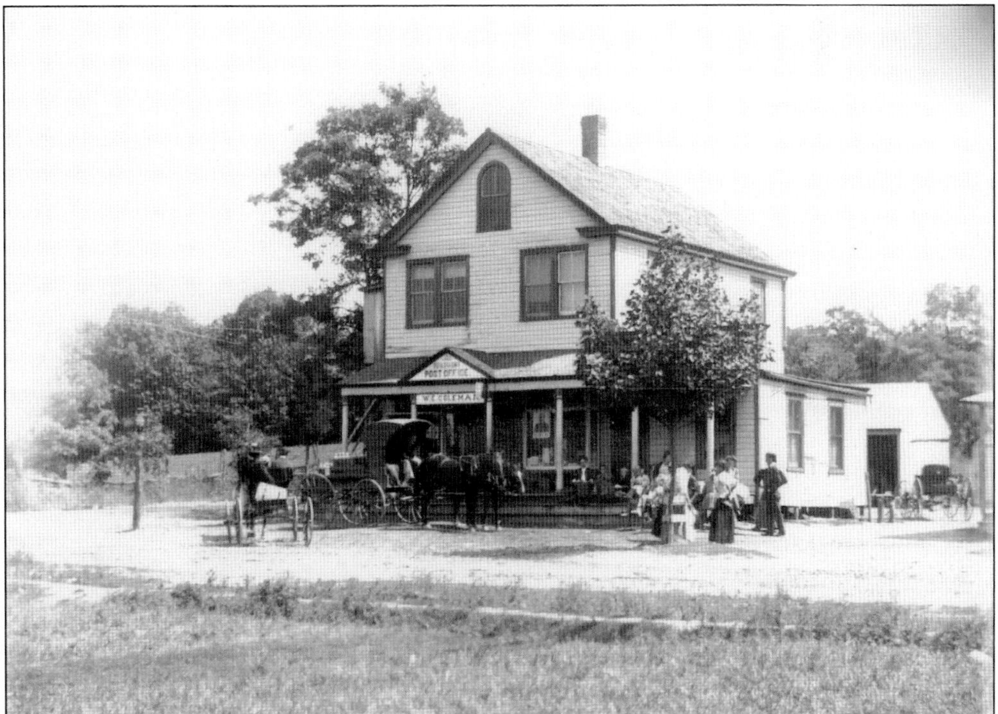

This c. 1908 photograph shows that W.E. Coleman's store was also the site of Lake Ronkonkoma Post Office. The residents of the town would meet here to socialize and receive information on what was happening in and around town. The store supplied fruits, groceries, dry goods, seasonal items, and almost all the needs of the community.

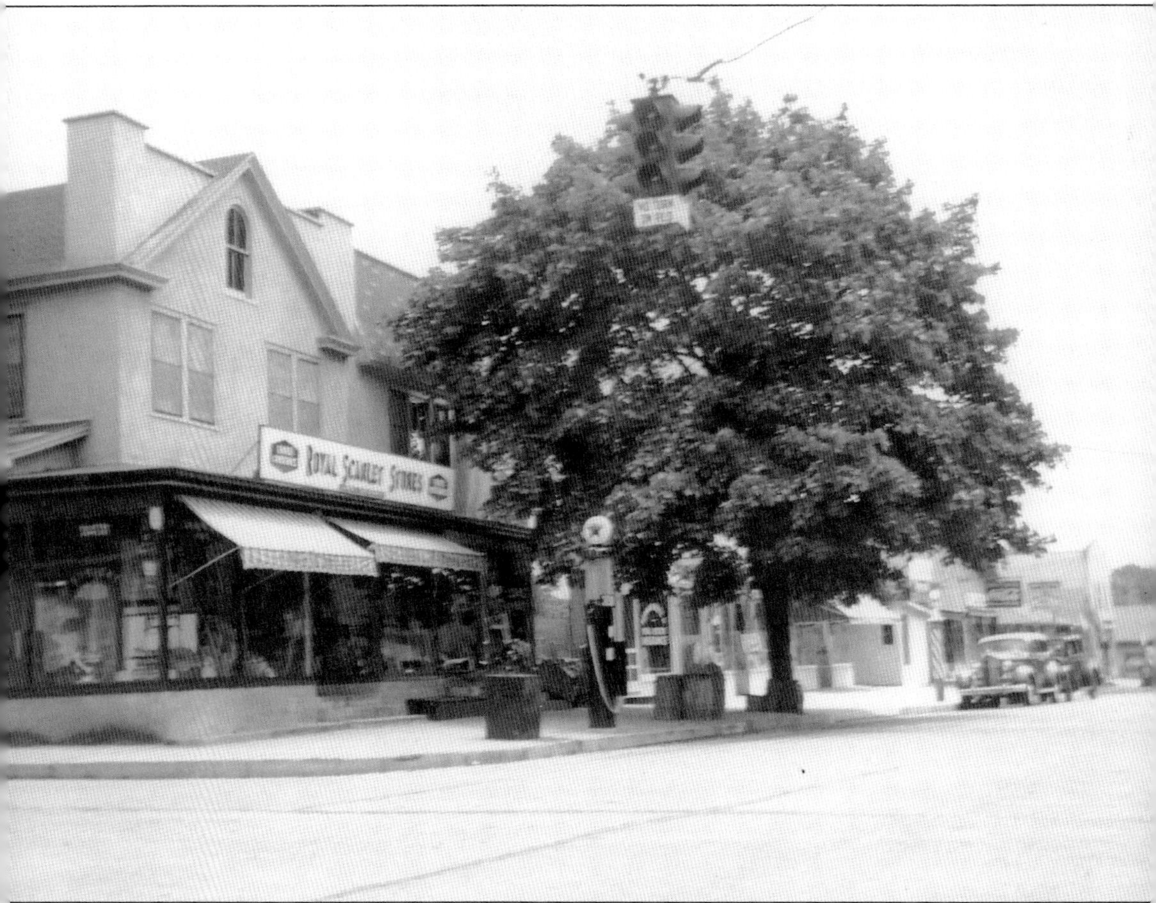

James Agnew was a Coney Island taxi driver. One of his fares wanted a ride to Lake Ronkonkoma. Seeing the town and falling in love with the area, Agnew inquired about purchasing Coleman's general store. The store was purchased for $3,000. On March 22, 1914, Agnew wrote a letter to his mother in Ireland telling her about his new and unexpected business venture. "You will be surprised to hear that I have bought a store of groceries and general merchandise, a business that has been established for about 14 years. It is located about 50 miles from New York on Long Island." He soon brought in his brother in-law Ike Taylor as a partner. In 1914, the store became Agnew and Taylor. The store supplied tools, electrical products, Radio Flyer wagons, lawn mower tune-ups, paints, plumbing supplies, and many other items. This James Browne Sr. photograph was taken in 1937.

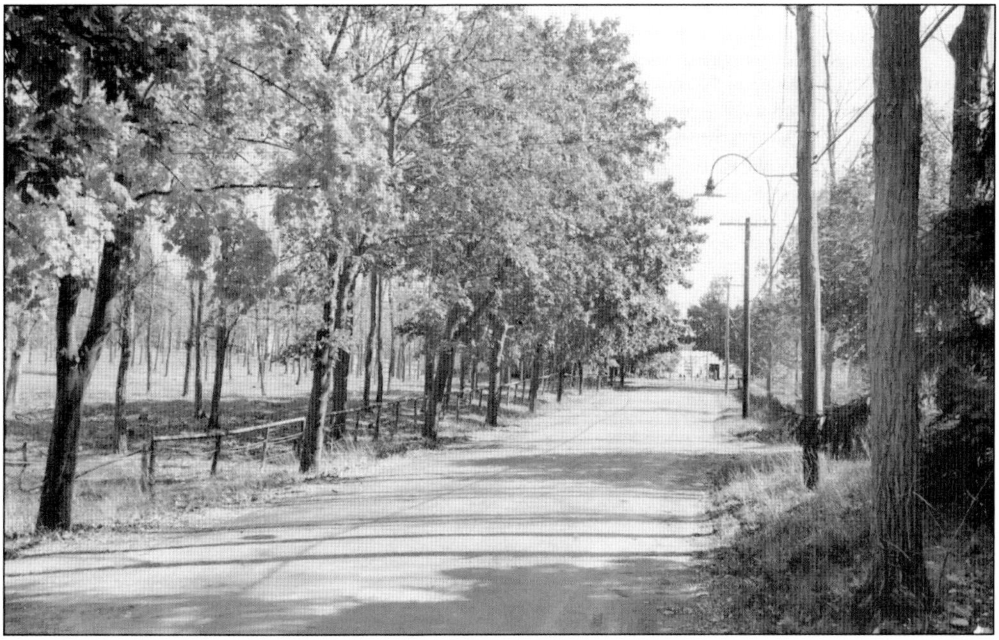

This view of Ronkonkoma Avenue is looking north towards Newton's Garage c. 1930. This wonderful photograph captures how rural the area was at the time. Towards the center of the photograph, behind the trees, is the homestead of George C. Raynor. Ronkonkoma Avenue has become one of the busiest roads in Lake Ronkonkoma.

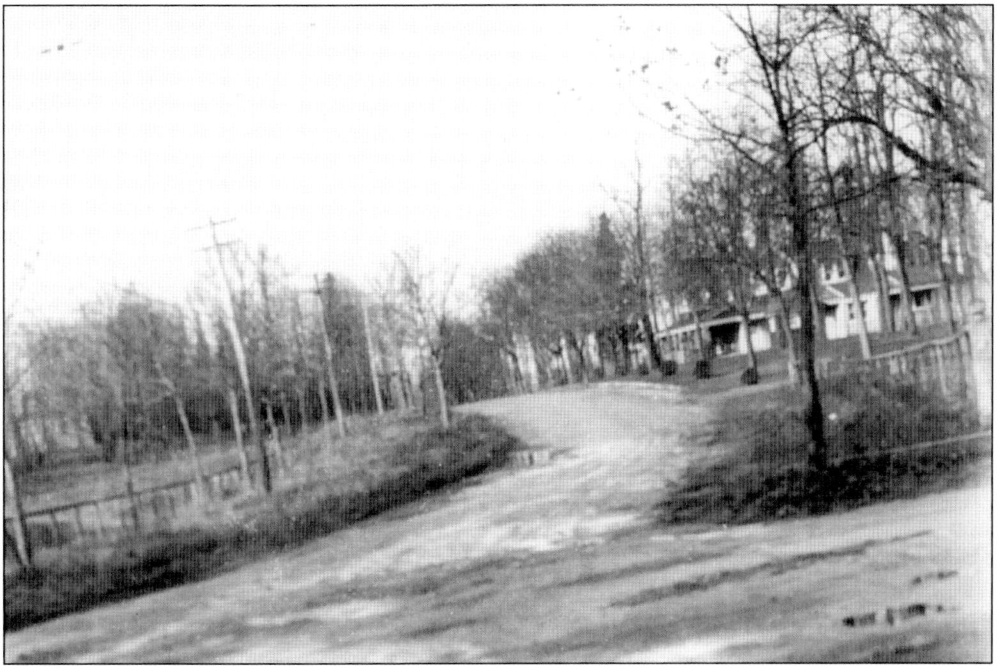

Another excellent photograph of Portion Road looks west. This is the intersection of Ronkonkoma Avenue and Portion Road taken c. 1927. The home on the right side of the photograph is the Raynor's homestead. Note that both roads have not yet been paved. Also take note that telephone poles and trees dominated the landscape during this time.

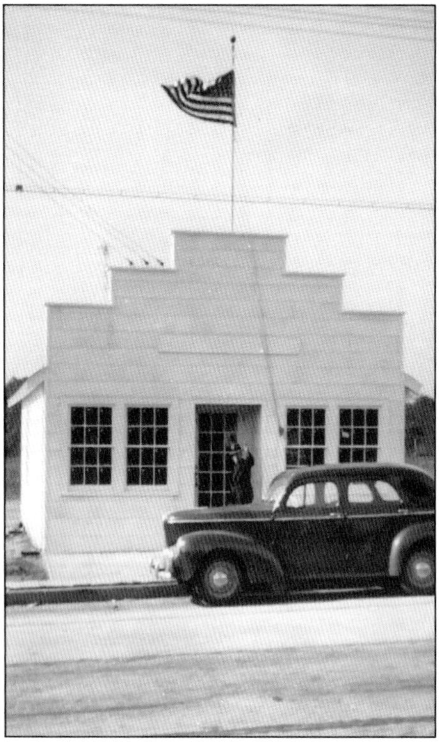

Lake Ronkonkoma Post Office was originally located in Hallock's general store in 1899. Willis Hallock was the postmaster, until Walter Emmett Coleman bought the general store c. 1907. Coleman would become postmaster until 1913, when he sold the store to James Agnew. Agnew was the postmaster from 1913 to 1933. When Franklin D. Roosevelt was elected president, the post office was moved out of Agnew and Taylor and given to Gus Gehweiler, a Democrat, who had a novelty store just down the road. Gehweiler was postmaster from 1933 to 1941. In 1941, Lake Ronkonkoma Post Office would move across the street to a brand-new building. These two photographs show what the building looked like in 1941. Alexander Matson was postmaster from 1941 to 1943, and Joseph L. McKernon was postmaster from 1943 to 1959.

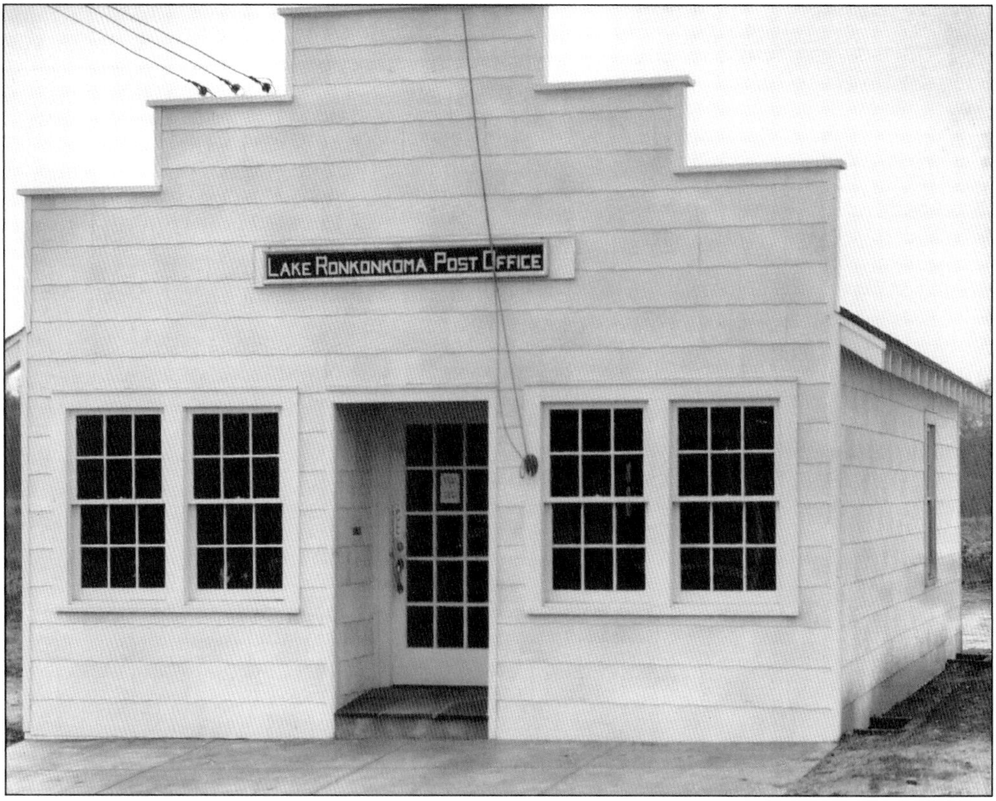

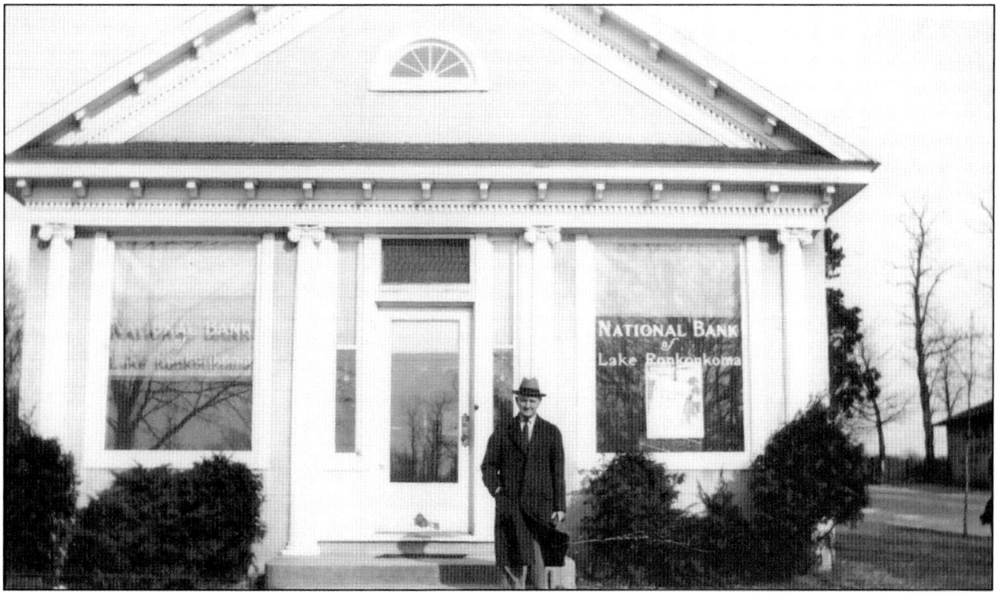

The National Bank of Lake Ronkonkoma was located on the northeast corner of Hawkins Avenue and Portion Road. The bank was organized in September 1927 with George C. Raynor as president. On its first day, April 9, 1928, $43,000 was deposited. This 1937 photograph shows Ralph B. Wheeler in front of the bank.

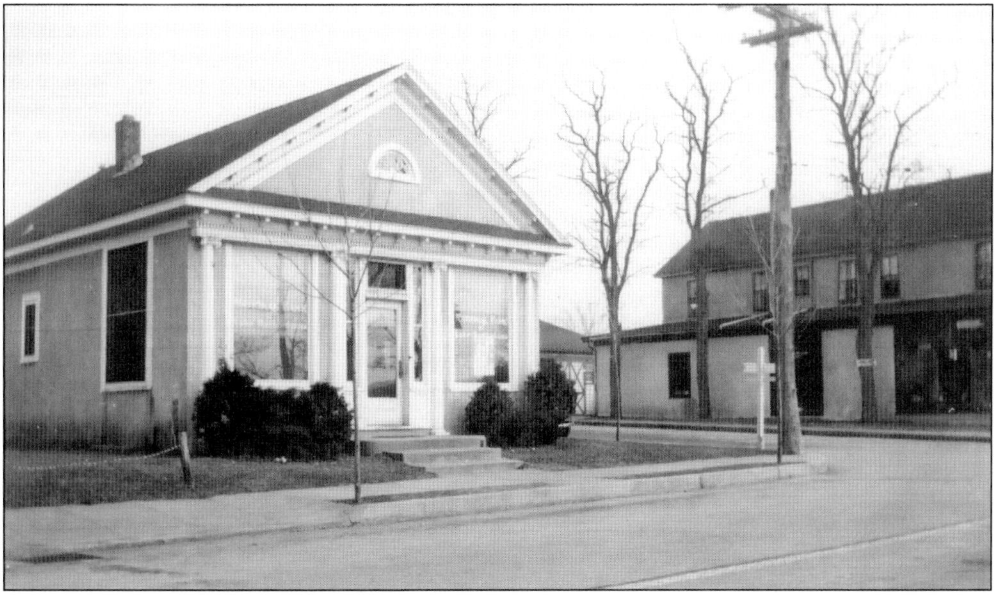

This angled view of the bank was taken from Hawkins Avenue in 1937. When the bank first opened, the directors were George C. Raynor, Louis Heilman, James Agnew, Joseph A. Kirk, Clarence R. Dare, and Giles C. DeGroot. The building on the right side of the photograph is Agnew and Taylor.

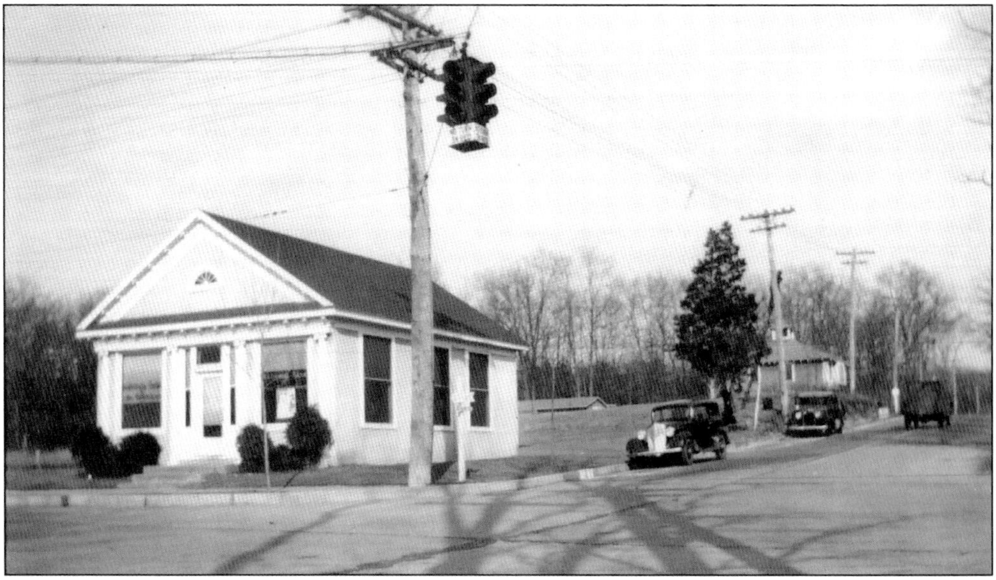

Another angled view of the bank was taken from Portion Road in 1937. The traffic light seen at the top of the photograph was installed in 1929 to control traffic at the busiest intersection in the community. The firehouse can be seen in the background. The First National Bank of Lake Ronkonkoma served its community until 1995, when the building was taken over by the Lake Ronkonkoma Fire Department.

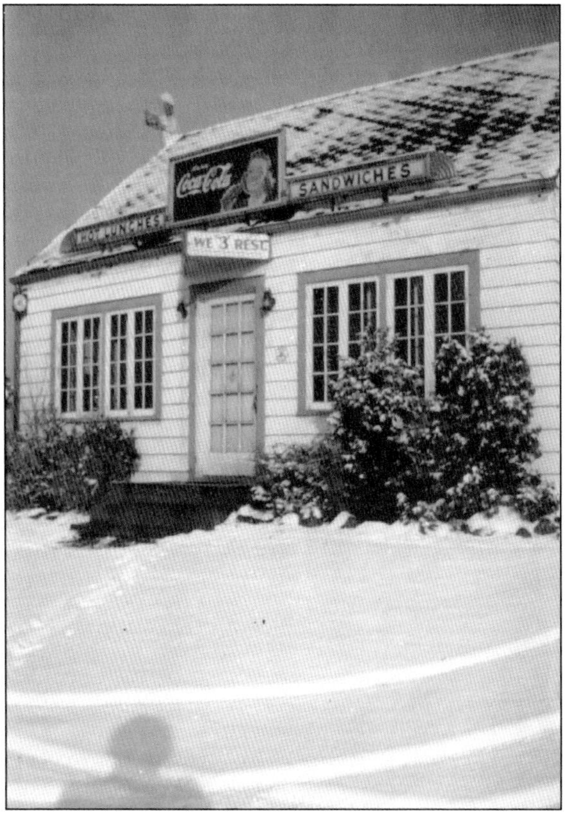

This photograph shows Margaret's Restaurant, located on Portion Road just east of the First National Bank of Lake Ronkonkoma, in 1942. Margaret's, owned by Margaret Curtis, sold hot lunches and sandwiches. Her sister-in-law was Ann Farnum Curtis, the first president of the Lake Ronkonkoma Historical Society. By the 1970s, the site of Margaret's Restaurant had become the parking lot of Barclay's Bank.

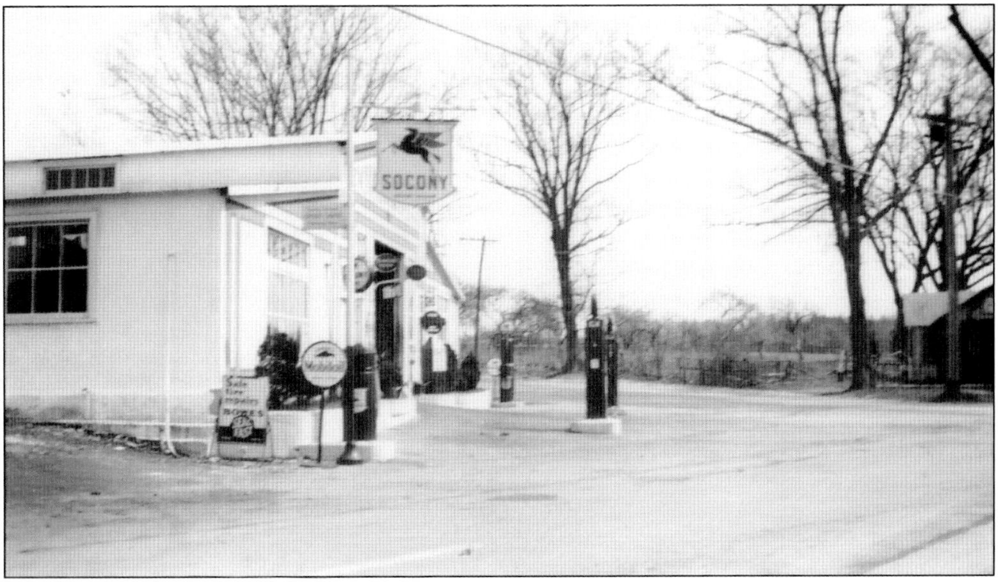

Newton's Garage is located on the northeast corner of Portion Road and Ronkonkoma Avenue. In April 1923, Sumner Newton decided to build a garage to repair automobiles. The Newton family was one of the earliest to settle in the Lake Ronkonkoma area and contributed to the growth and development of the town. Newton's Garage was the first automobile service station in town. When visitors would drive their automobiles out to Lake Ronkonkoma during the summer months, Newton's Garage was the place that everyone used for repairs and maintenance. The photograph above is a view of Newton's Garage taken from Ronkonkoma Avenue in 1929. James Browne Sr. took the photograph below in 1937. Newton's Garage is now a Town of Brookhaven historic landmark.

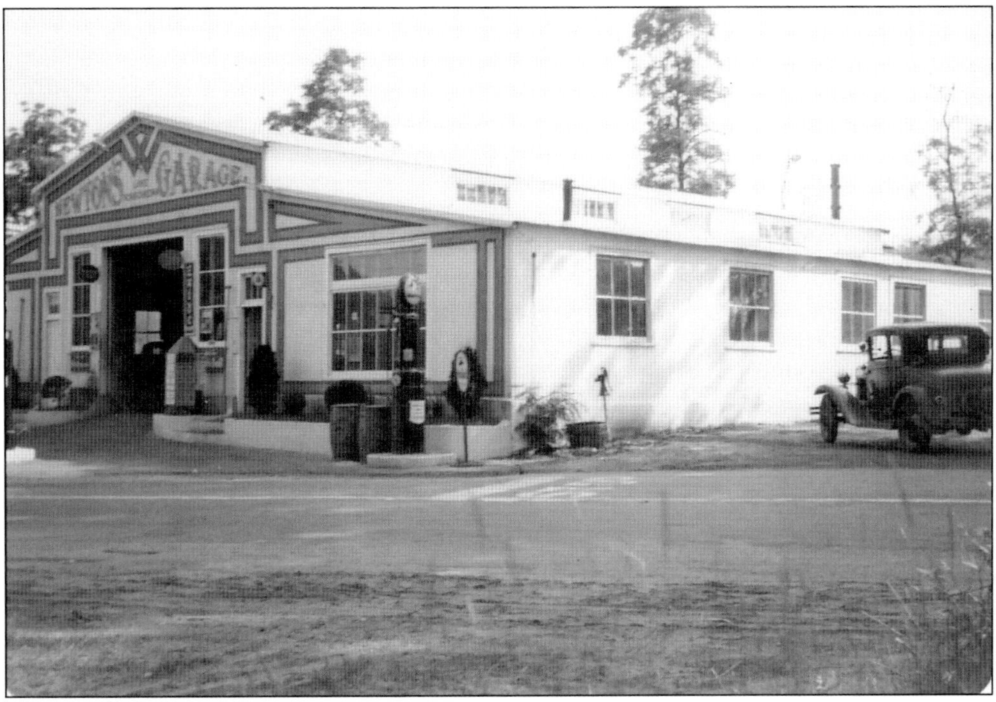

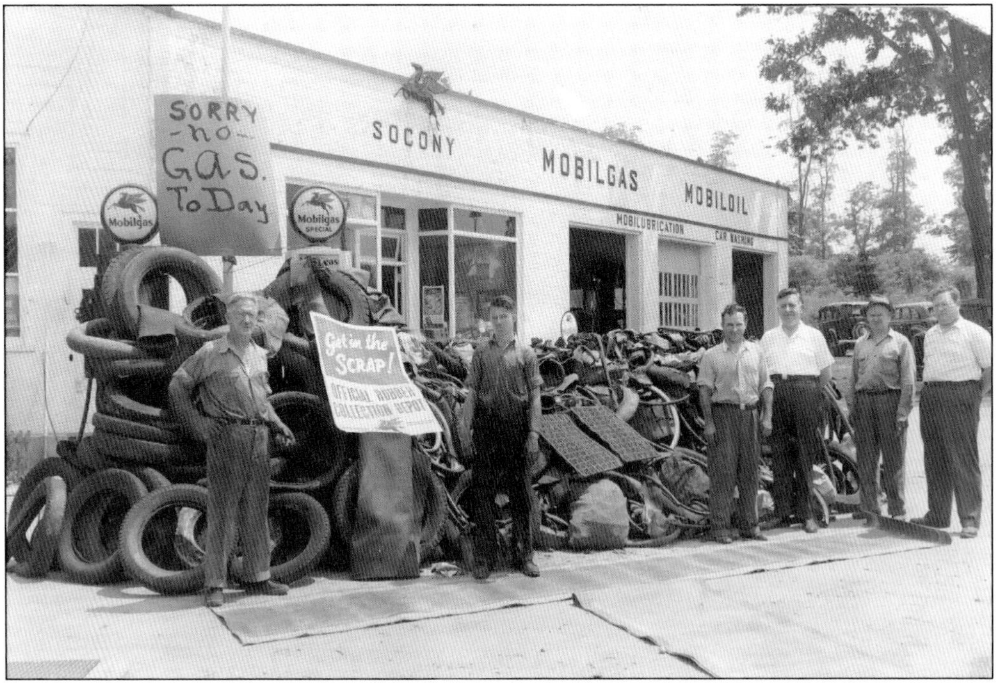

During World War II, Newton's Garage organized a scrap drive. Towns throughout the United States would gather iron, rubber, and gasoline to assist with the war efforts overseas. Note the two large signs in the photograph. Pictured are, from left to right, Sumner Newton, Herman Lax, Henry Lax, Joe Kirk, Dick Newton, and Dr. Walter Roettinger.

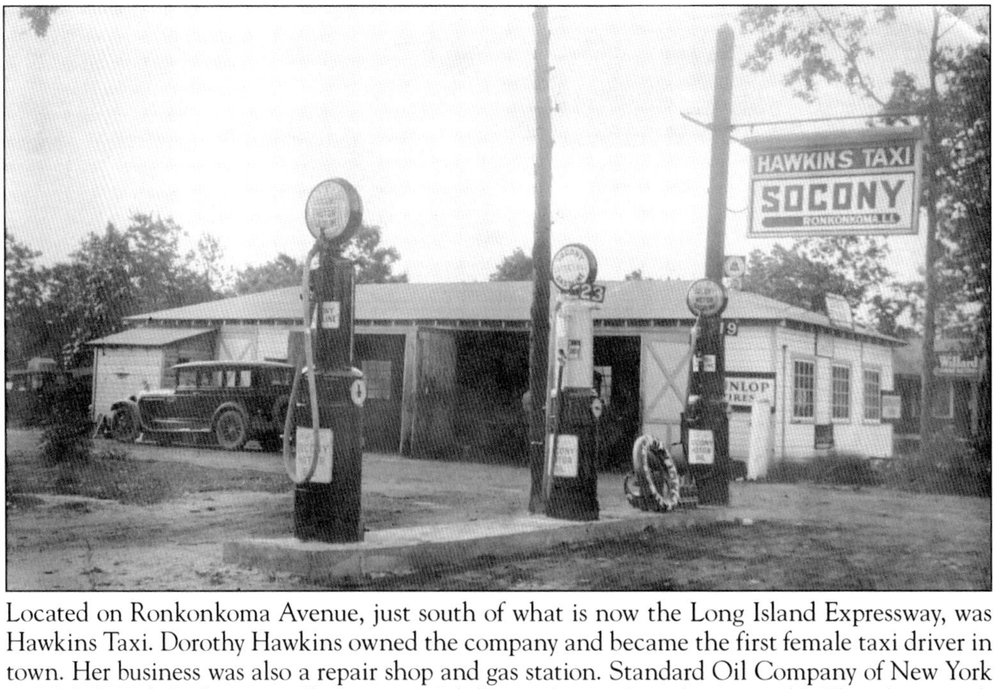

Located on Ronkonkoma Avenue, just south of what is now the Long Island Expressway, was Hawkins Taxi. Dorothy Hawkins owned the company and became the first female taxi driver in town. Her business was also a repair shop and gas station. Standard Oil Company of New York or SOCONY (which eventually became Mobil) was the gasoline that was sold. This photograph was taken in 1928.

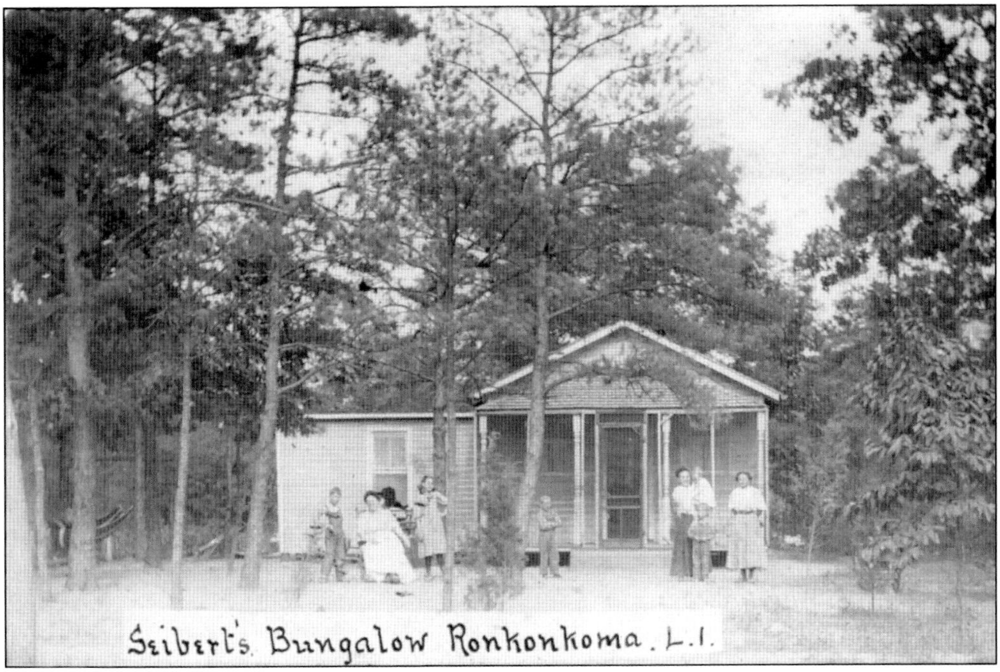

The photograph pictured above is dated 1911 and shows the Seibert's summer bungalow located on the east side of Hawkins Avenue. During this time, W.E Coleman's general store was the only place around to purchase food and goods. The Seibert's would change their summer bungalow into Lake Ronkonkoma's first bakery. The photograph pictured below was taken c. 1930 and shows Hawkins Avenue facing north. The building to the far left of the picture was the location of Seibert's summer bungalow, now the Ronkonkoma Bakery. The smaller building in the center was a real estate office for the Overton's. The house to the right of the picture was John Overton's home. Today, all of these buildings are still in existence.

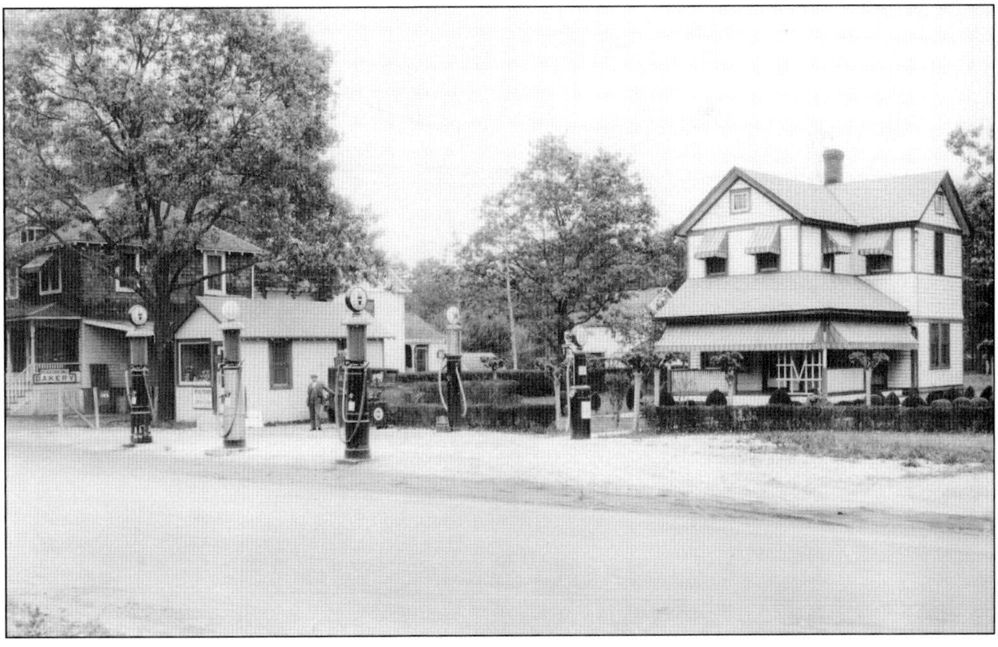

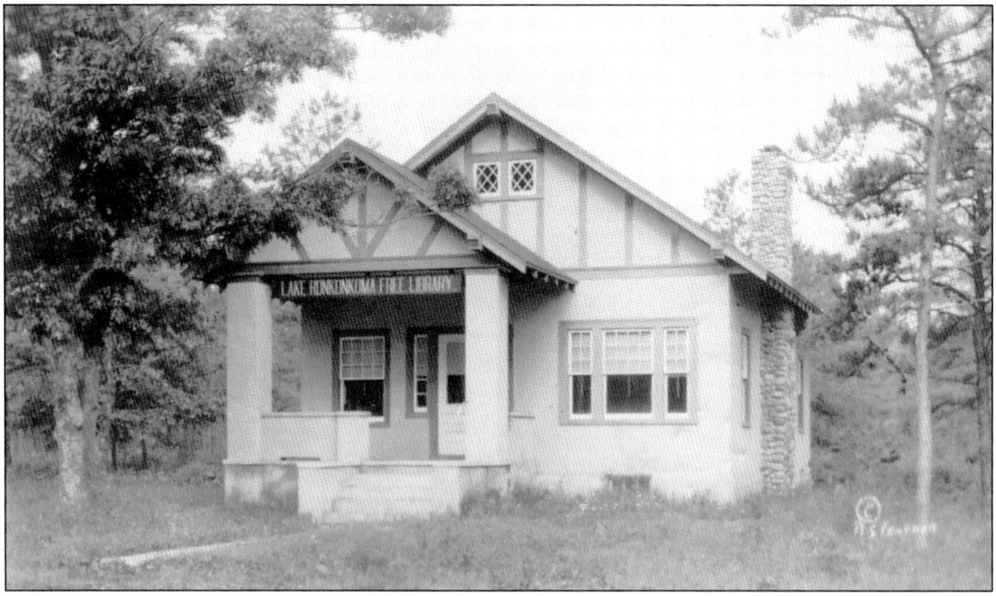

Helen DeVere, a militant suffragette, managed to get a collection of 18 books from the Equal Franchise Society. In 1914, she set the foundation on what would become the Lake Ronkonkoma Public Library. In order for her to keep these books, she needed five men to sign a letter stating that they were going to form a community library. Frank Newton, Morris Hawkins, W.E. Coleman, David Seibert, and Timothy Morrisey were the signers. George Raynor and W.N. Hallock donated property for the library. In 1961, voters approved plans for a new, larger building because of the increase in population. Land was acquired on Holbrook Road in Holbrook, and in 1966, the new library opened. In 1976, Lake Ronkonkoma Historical Society leased the building. The photograph below is the grand opening of the historical society c. 1978.

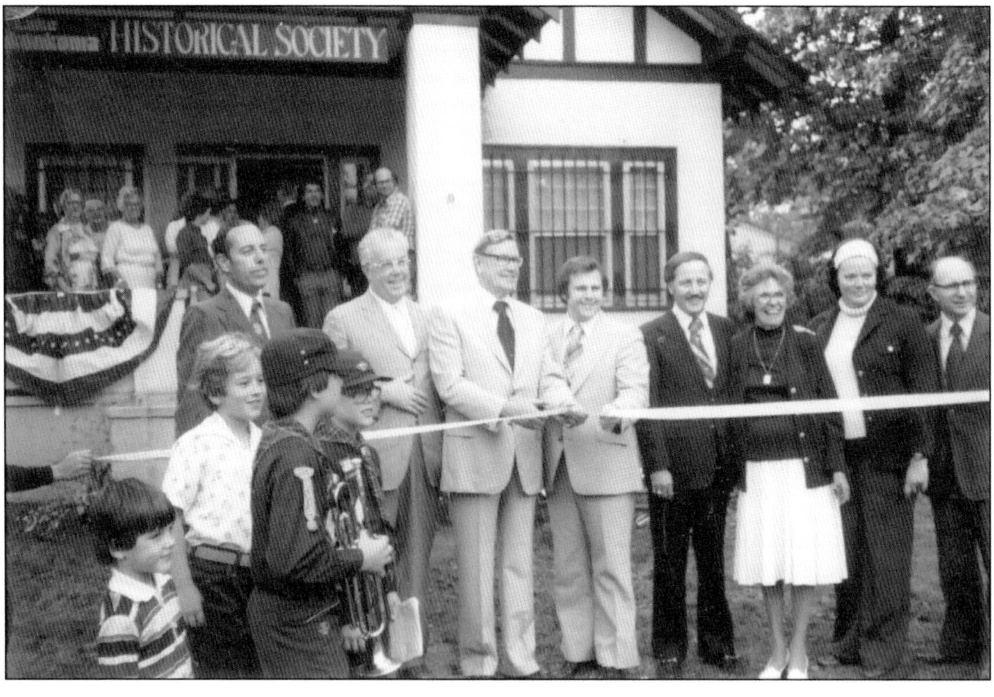

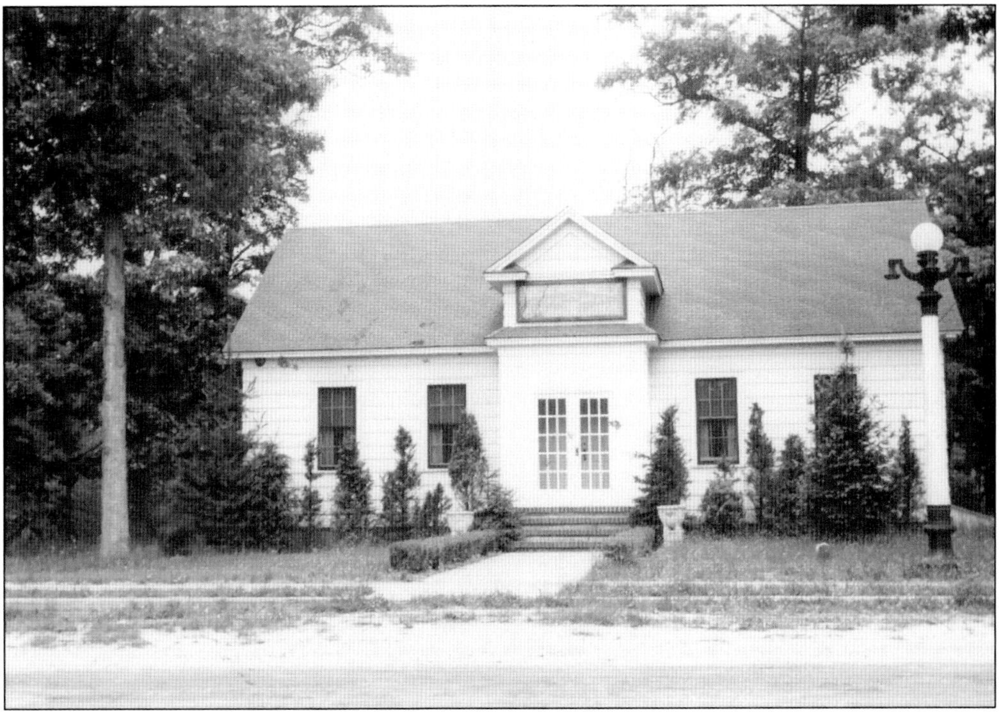

During World War I, Fitzgreen Hallock's only son, William Merritt, died in battle at Belleau Wood in France. In 1926, a group of veterans in Lake Ronkonkoma started their own legion post. They named the post in honor of William Merritt Hallock. This photograph, taken in 1937 by James Browne Sr., shows the American Legion Hall on Church Street.

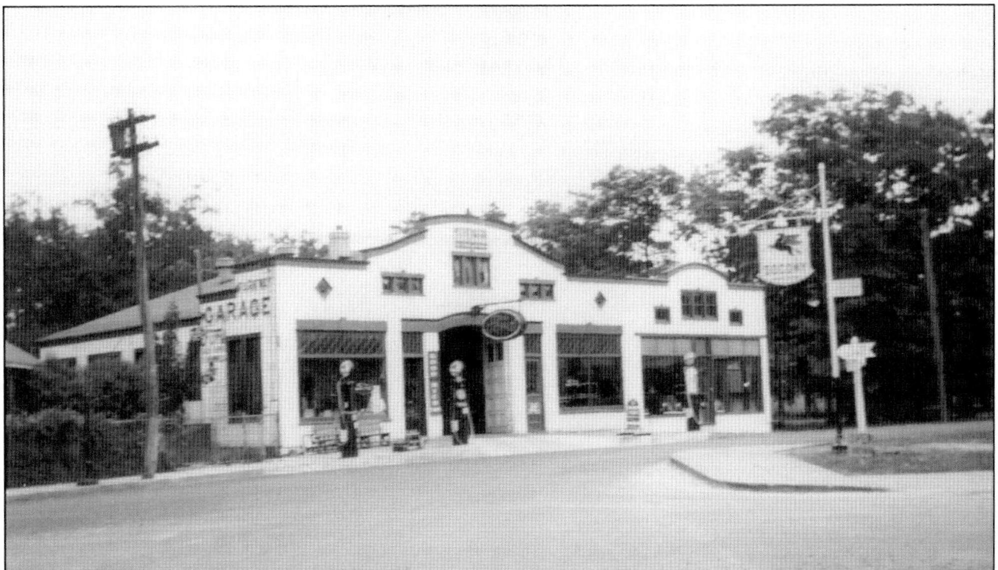

This James Browne Sr. photograph of Rummel's Garage was taken in 1937. Frank Rummel opened a Ford Agency and garage on the corner of Church Street and Pond Road c. 1926. To the right of the picture, there is an open lot where Rummel would sell new Fords. The original Rummel's building was destroyed by fire in 2002.

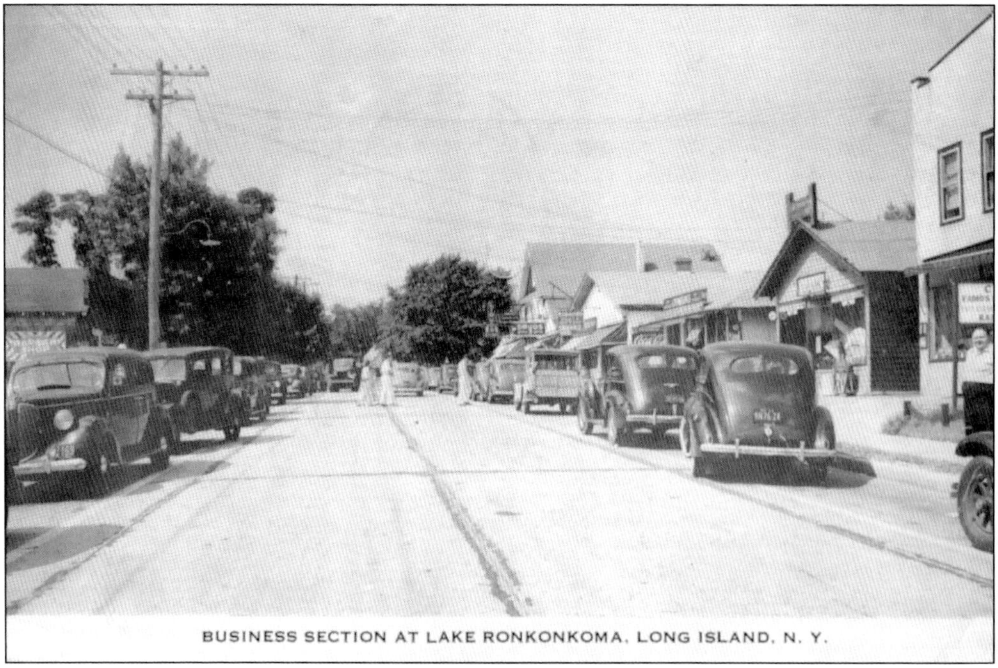

This is a postcard of Hawkins Avenue looking north c. 1943. At this time, the road was made with concrete. Some of the businesses are noticeable on the right side of the postcard. There is a liquor store, Fayne's drugstore, Straub's Meat Market, Conklin's, and the building on the left was a barbershop.

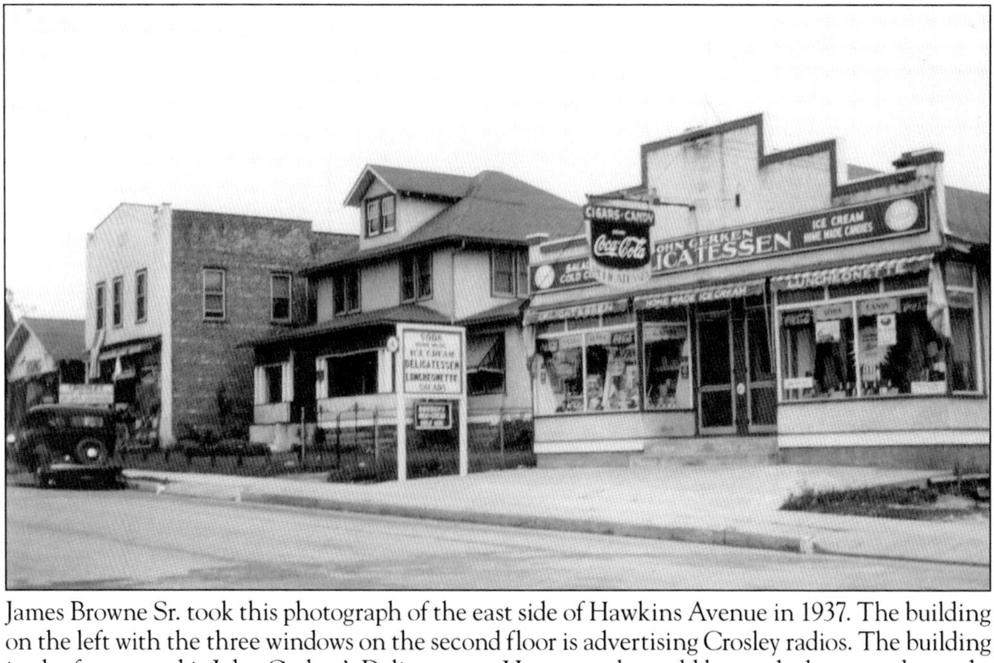

James Browne Sr. took this photograph of the east side of Hawkins Avenue in 1937. The building on the left with the three windows on the second floor is advertising Crosley radios. The building in the foreground is John Gerken's Delicatessen. Here, people could buy soda, homemade candy, homemade ice cream, salads, cigars, and dairy products.

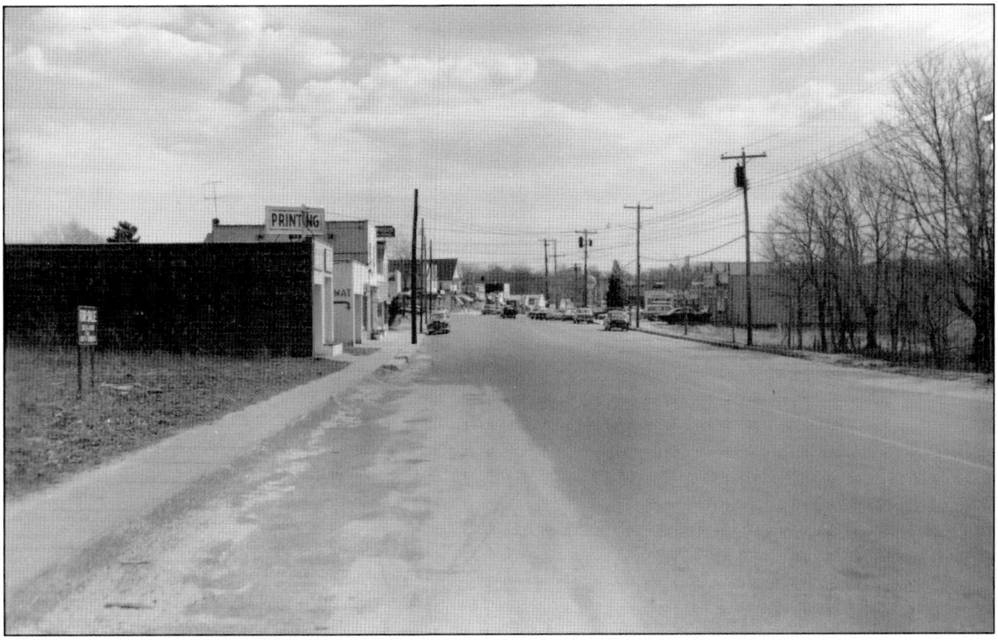

This James Mooney photograph was taken on April 4, 1961. The picture is of Hawkins Avenue looking south towards the intersection of Portion Road. The first building on the left was a printing company, next door was a laundry mat, then an office supply company. Agnew and Taylor is visible on the left side, and across the street is the Shell gas station. (Courtesy of James Mooney.)

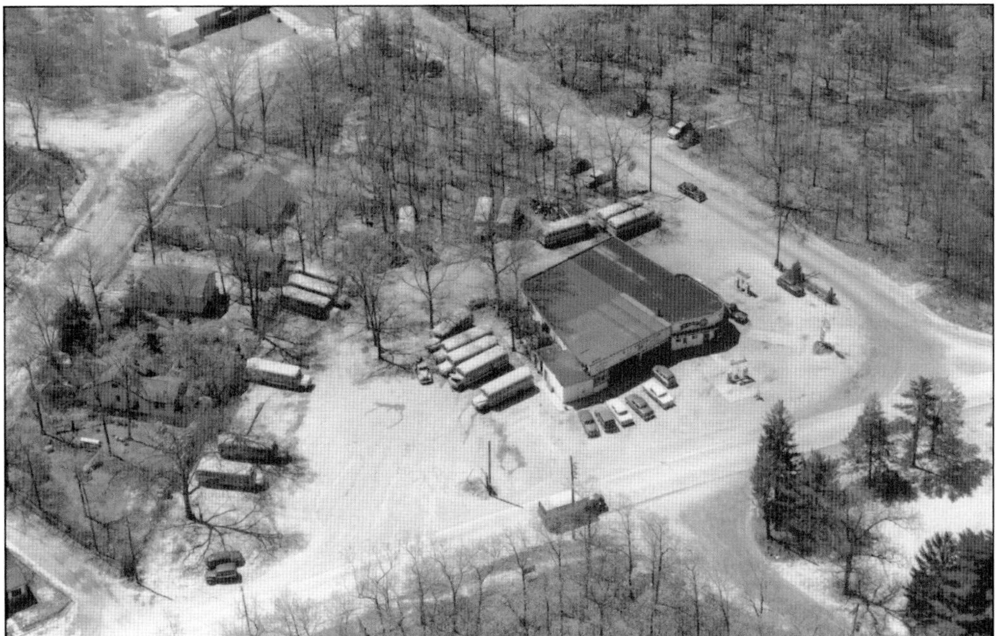

Seen here is Rosevale Avenue and Smithtown Boulevard looking south. James Mooney took the photograph on May 14, 1959. D and E distributors occupy the building in the foreground. Lake Ronkonkoma Beverages occupies this building today. The road at the bottom right of the picture is Gibbs Pond Road. (Courtesy of James Mooney.)

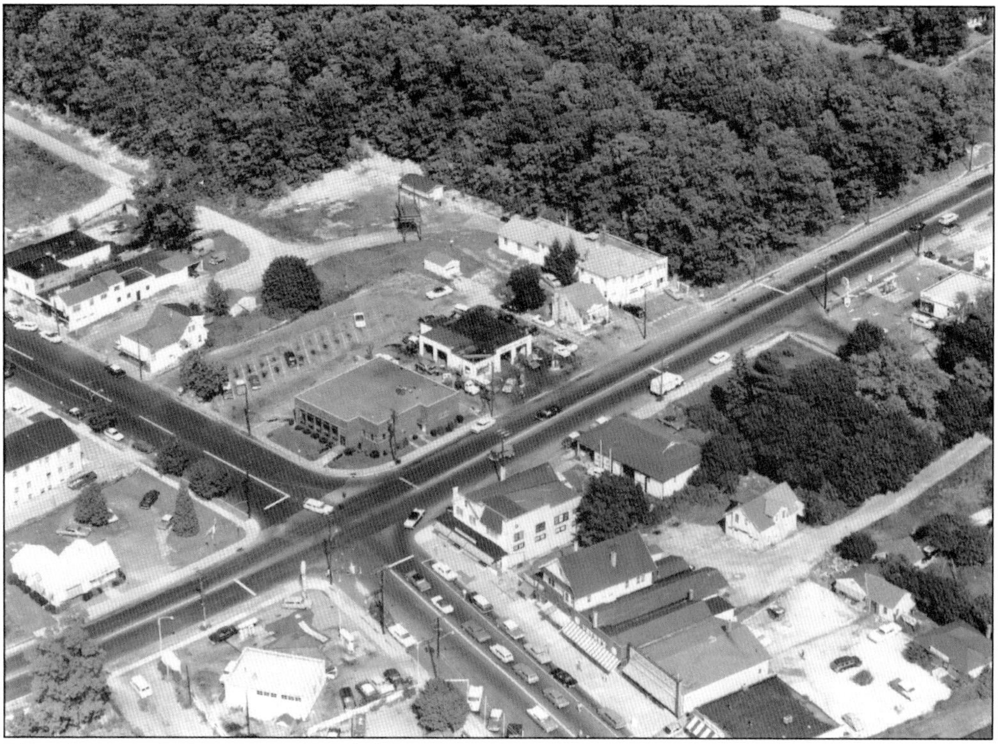

The photograph above is a view of the intersection at Portion Road and Hawkins Avenue taken on September 28, 1963. On the northeast corner of Portion Road and Hawkins Road is the First National bank, Agnew and Taylor is on the southeast corner, and the Shell gas station is on the southwest corner. The photograph below was taken on April 25, 1964, and is a view of Lake Ronkonkoma looking northeast. Hawkins Avenue runs from the bottom right to the top left. Portion Road crosses at the top. At the very top right of the photograph was the brand-new Lake Shore Commons shopping center. The vacant lot on the east side of Hawkins Avenue towards the bottom of the photograph is where Slater Drugs would be built in 1966. (Both, courtesy of James Mooney.)

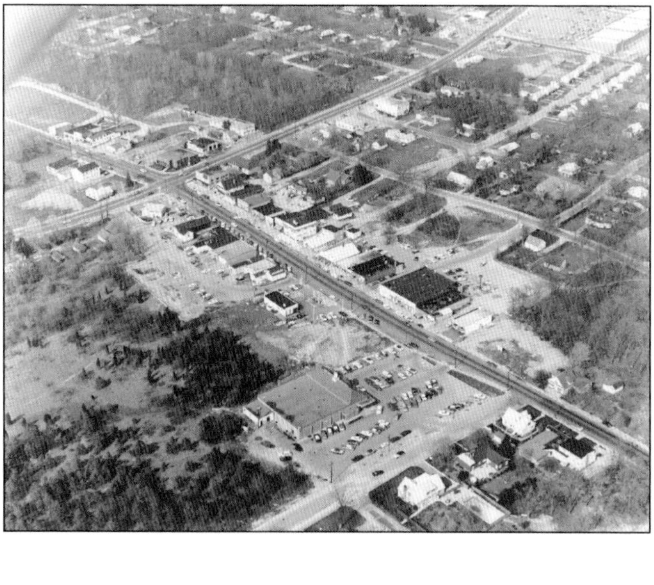

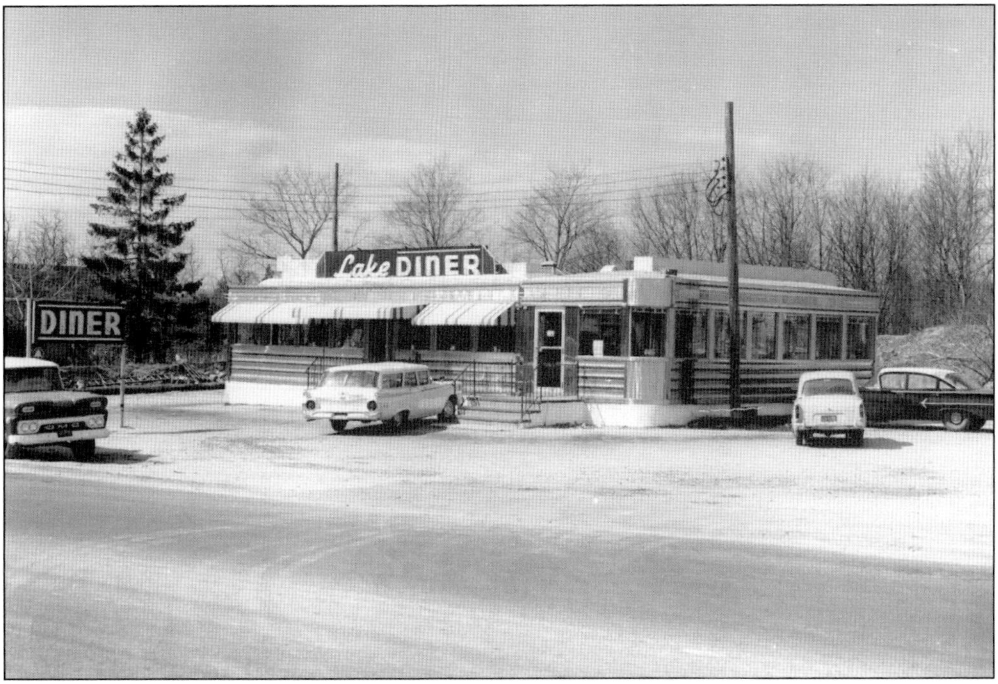

Located on the north side of Portion Road between Ronkonkoma Avenue and Hawkins Avenue was the Lake Diner. This James Mooney photograph was taken on April 5, 1961, and was the first diner in town. During the early 1980s, the Golden Wok was built on this site. In the 2000s, Dunkin Donuts and Baskin Robbins took the place of the Golden Wok. (Courtesy of James Mooney.)

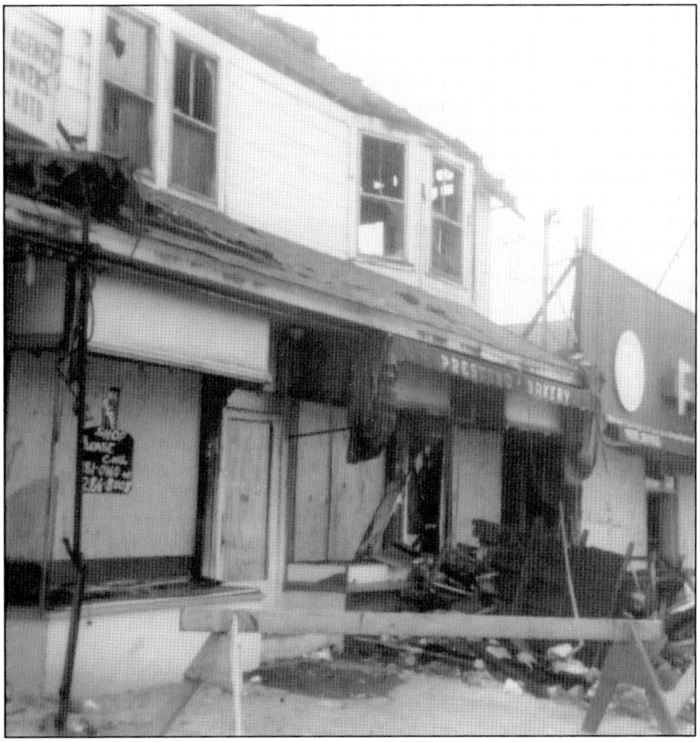

On May 16, 1980, a fire broke out in Prestano's Bakery, destroying Dolson Insurance Agency, the Stove Shop, Fayne's Drug Store, and Straubs Market. In 1981, wreckers began tearing down the fire-gutted buildings. This photograph, taken in 1980, shows Prestano's Bakery. To the left of this building is Agnew and Taylor.

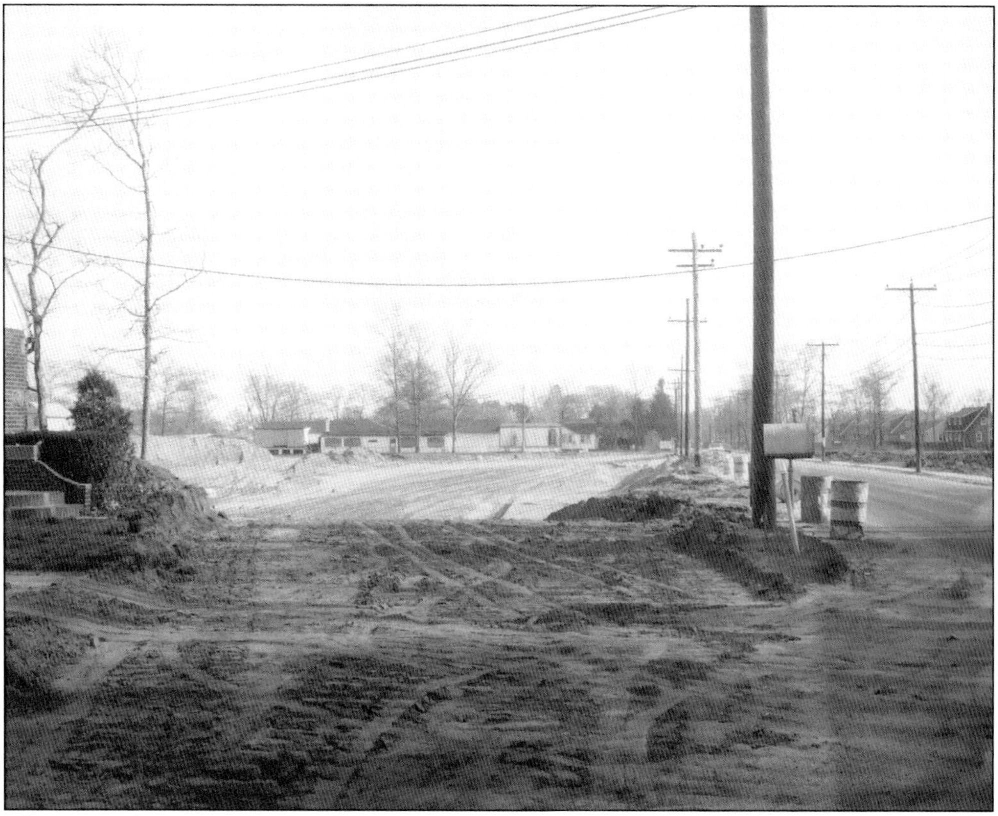

These two photographs were taken on May 6, 1965. The Long Island Expressway was already completed in Queens and Nassau Counties. By 1963, the Long Island Expressway reached Veterans Memorial Highway near Islandia. Exits 58 and 59 would be completed in 1964. In 1965, Hawkins Avenue would become exit 60. By the spring of 1965, people began losing their properties and homes to the Long Island Expressway. The photograph above is Hawkins Avenue facing south. This would become an intersection for the service road of the Long Island Expressway. The photograph below is Hawkins Avenue facing north. Louis and Emma Bruno's house is on the right.

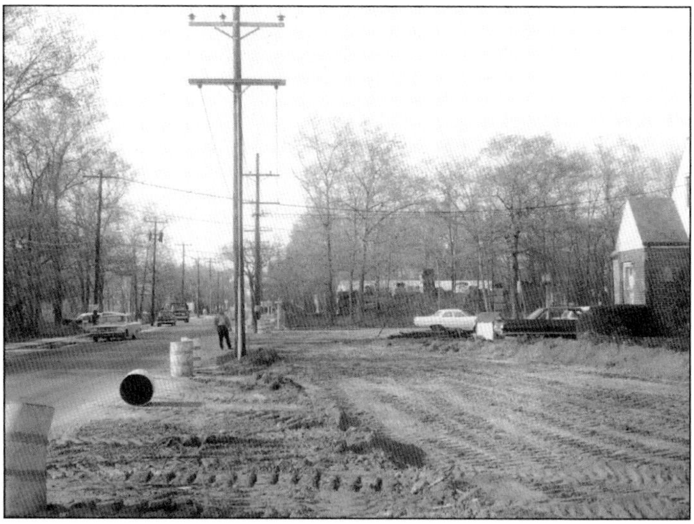

Three

The Homes of Lake Ronkonkoma

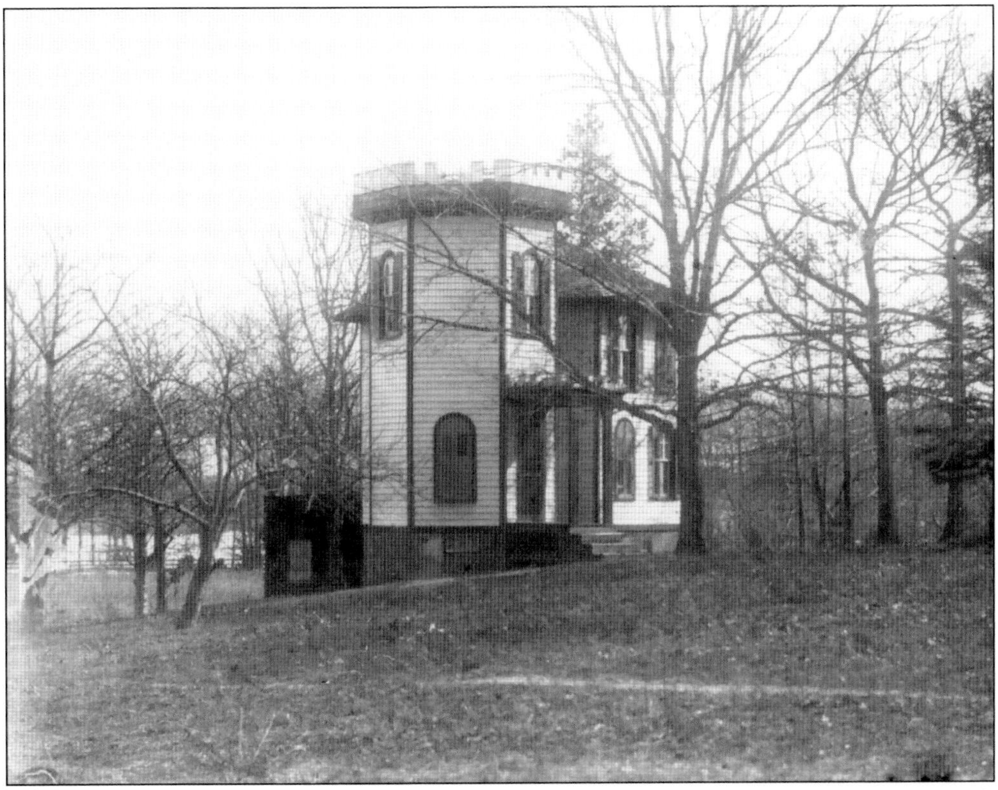

The Kirk family was originally from Ireland and moved to Manhattan. In the 1840s, John Kirk bought land around the lake. He bought a house known as the Castle, located on land that is now the Ronkonkoma Town Beach. The home had a tower similar to an Irish round tower. The Castle was described at the time as a secluded, mysterious place. The Castle burned to the ground c. 1882.

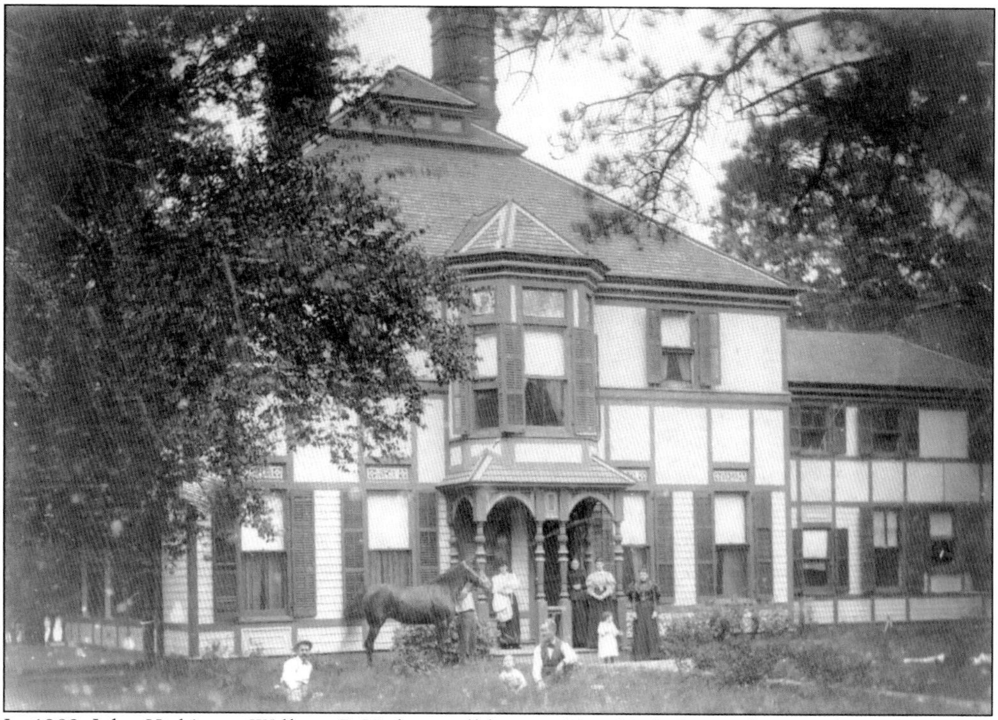

In 1882, John Kirk's son William P. Kirk, a well-known New York City politician, built this estate off Rosevale Avenue. The estate had a huge porch that wrapped around two sides of the home and overlooked the lake. Once in the home, there was a spiral staircase carved out of mahogany. Also, many windows of the house were decorated with stained glass. The above photograph was taken around 1900. The photograph below is of the Kirk Estate during the 1950s. After Joseph Kirk (the grandson of John Kirk) died, his wife, Flossie Kirk, remained in the house until 1979, when she died at age 87. In 1987, a Dix Hills developer named Thomas Naoum bought the Kirk Estate. On May 5, 1988, a suspicious fire destroyed the estate. Within five years, residential homes would be constructed.

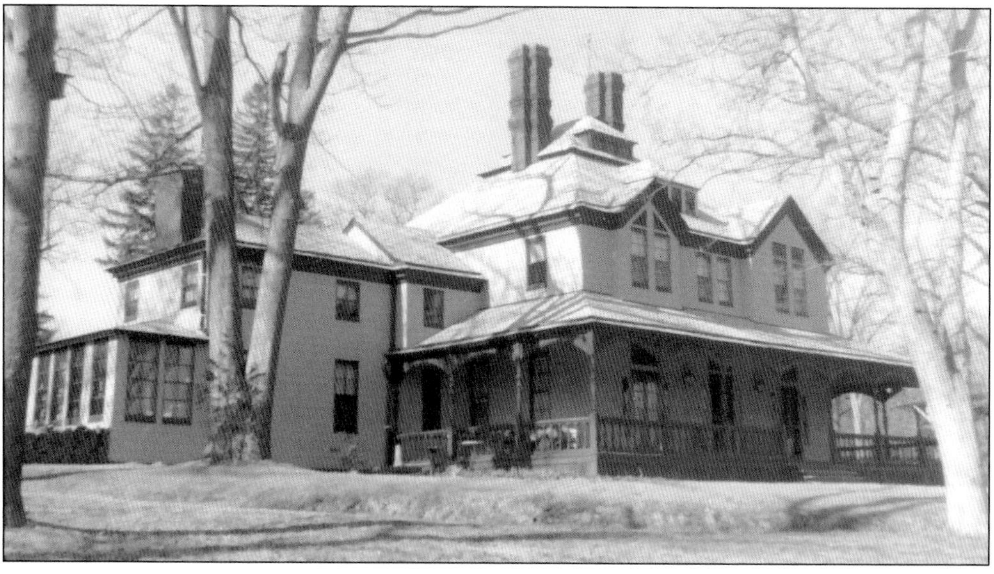

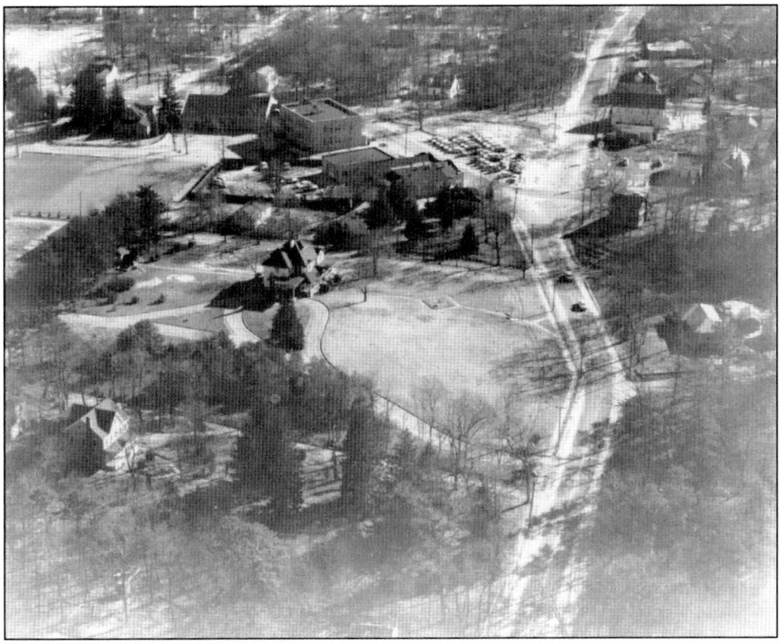

James Mooney took this photograph on February 22, 1959. Pond Road is seen here going north to south in this picture. The Fitzgreen Hallock house (bottom left) was built in 1888. The Kirk house (center) was built in 1913. St. Josephs Church (top left) can be seen facing south. (Courtesy of James Mooney.)

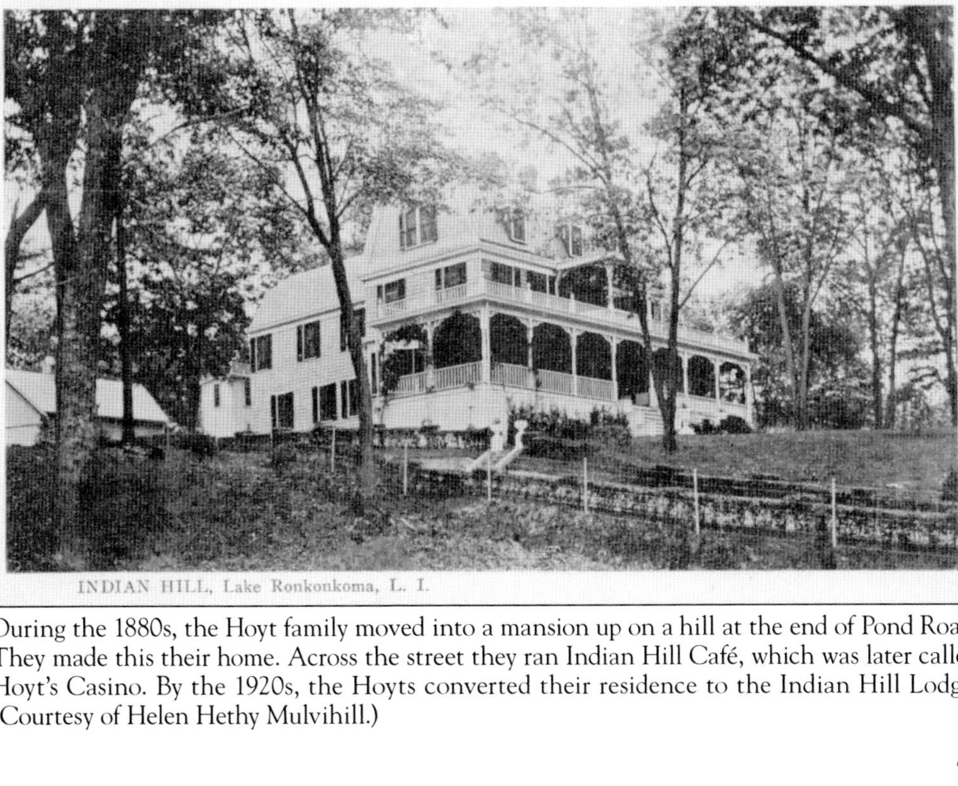

INDIAN HILL, Lake Ronkonkoma, L. I.

During the 1880s, the Hoyt family moved into a mansion up on a hill at the end of Pond Road. They made this their home. Across the street they ran Indian Hill Café, which was later called Hoyt's Casino. By the 1920s, the Hoyts converted their residence to the Indian Hill Lodge. (Courtesy of Helen Hethy Mulvihill.)

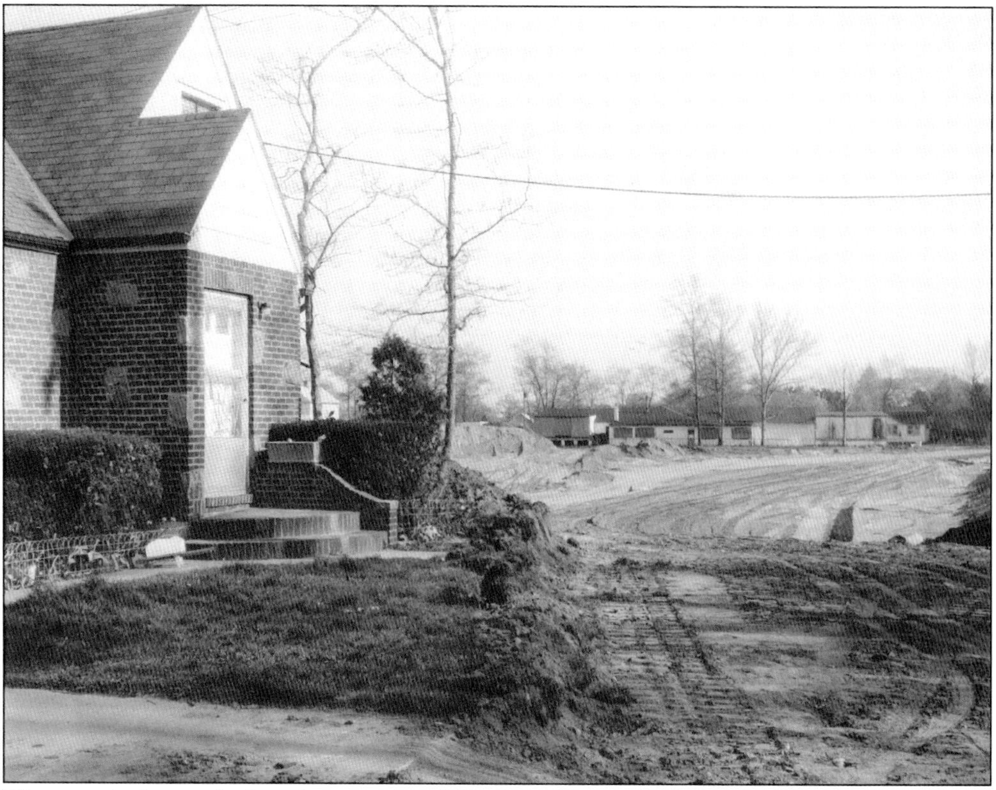

These are before and after photographs of Hawkins Avenue looking south in 1965. Louis and Emma Bruno's home is on the left. During the 1940s, Louis Bruno sold coal and ice by truck. After World War II, homes were being built with oil heating, so coal was not in demand. Bruno needed an idea to make money. In the late 1940s, he began selling soda, ice, and beer. The original Bruno's beer distributor was on the corner of Hawkins Avenue and Thorne Street. In 1954, Louis Bruno has a heart attack and in 1955 sold the beer distributor to Oliver "Duke" Mulvihill. The building was demolished when ground was broken for the Long Island Expressway in 1965.

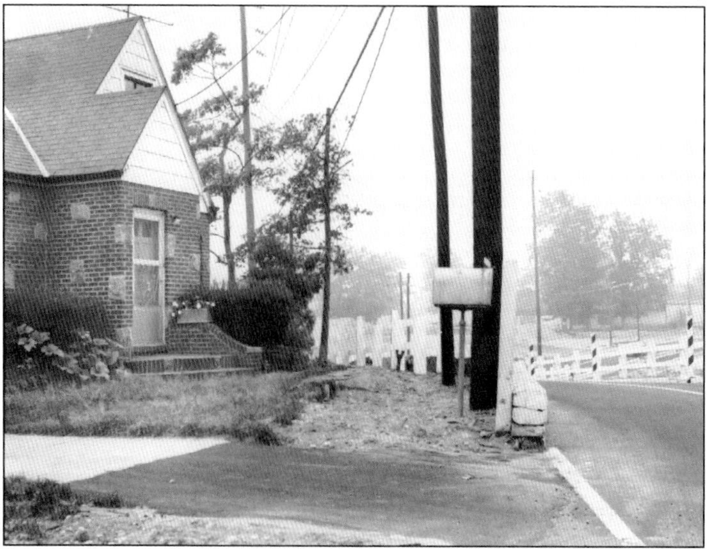

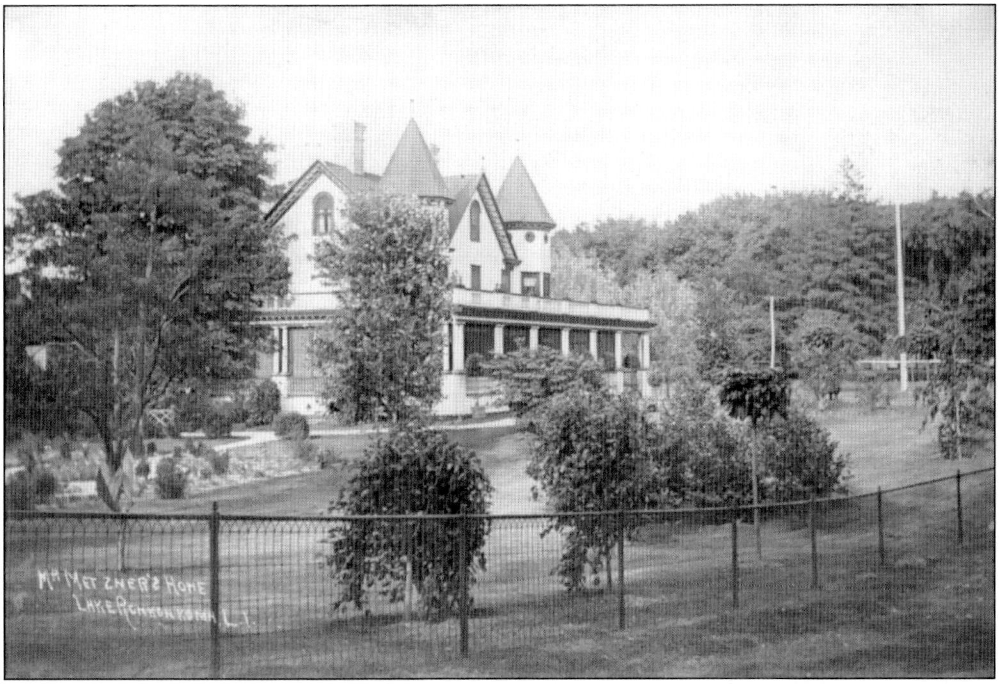

Marin Metzner (1859–1925) formed a partnership with Nicholas P. Young (1864-1941) and established the Young and Metzner bagging company. Metzner made his fortune in manufacturing sacks for sugar. In 1899, the Metzners' home was built in Lake Grove. During the 1900s, Martin and Johanna E. Metzner built their summer home, known as Lake Towers, on the north side of the lake. The household moved twice a year between the two homes. Lavish parties were common at Lake Towers, where as many as 65 guests would arrive by train for a long weekend. A large guesthouse on the shore of the lake provided extra sleeping room. These two photographs of Lake Towers were taken c. 1910.

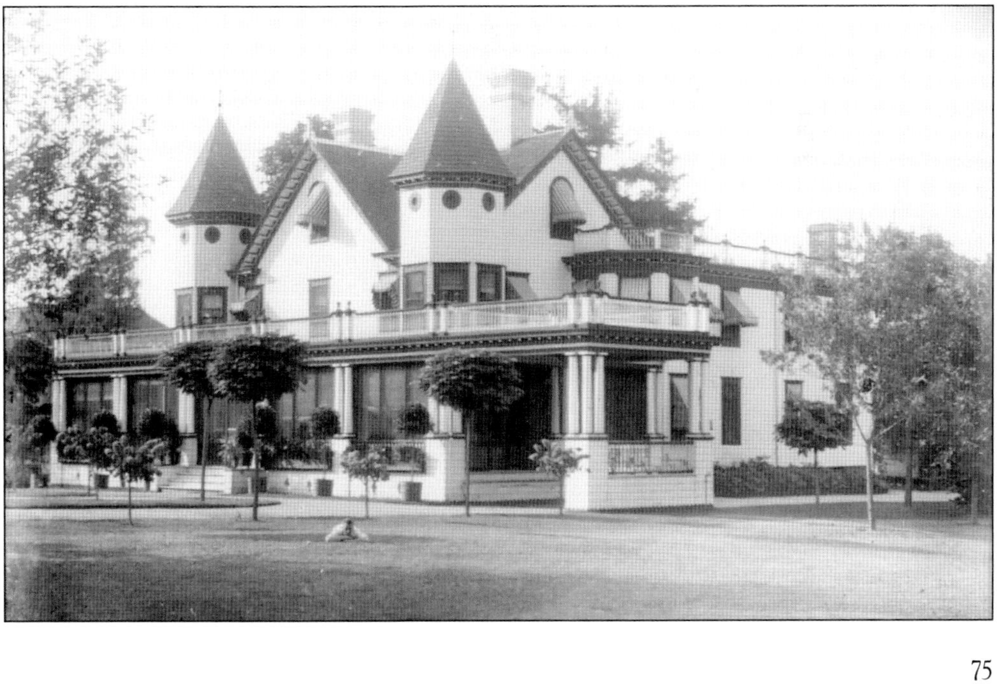

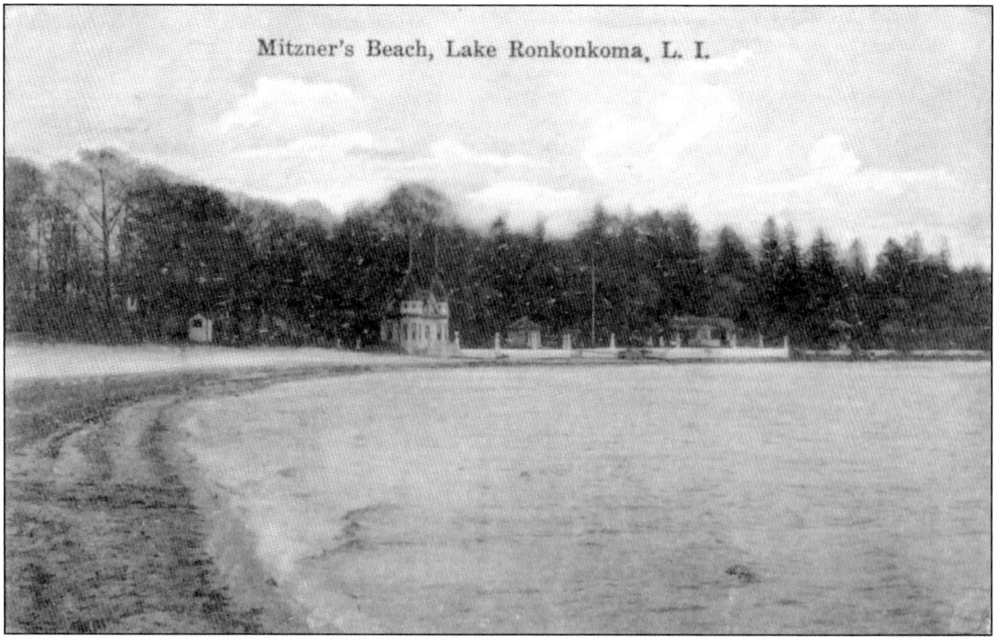

In the postcard above, Lake Towers is seen on the shoreline of the lake. The Metzners had a pump house that pumped water directly to the barnyard. It also helped water the peach, pear, and apple trees and the lawns. Horses were kept in the stables during the winter. The entire estate was illuminated at night with gas lamps. Each year, the Metzners would invite all the local children to the house for a Christmas party. The Metzners had four children, Alma, Nicholas "Les," Rose Foley, and Magie Robinson. At the age of 18, Les died in an automobile accident in Florida. On July 22, 1936, Alma Metzner sold Lake Towers and all its furnishings. The estate became a rest home for rejuvenating people with illness for a number of years. Both postcards were taken around 1915.

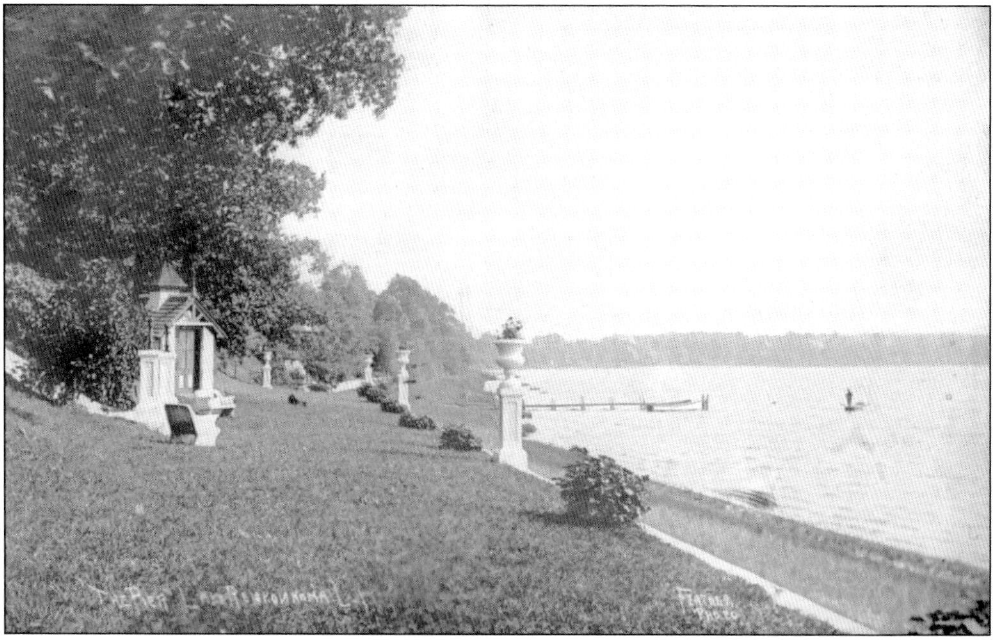

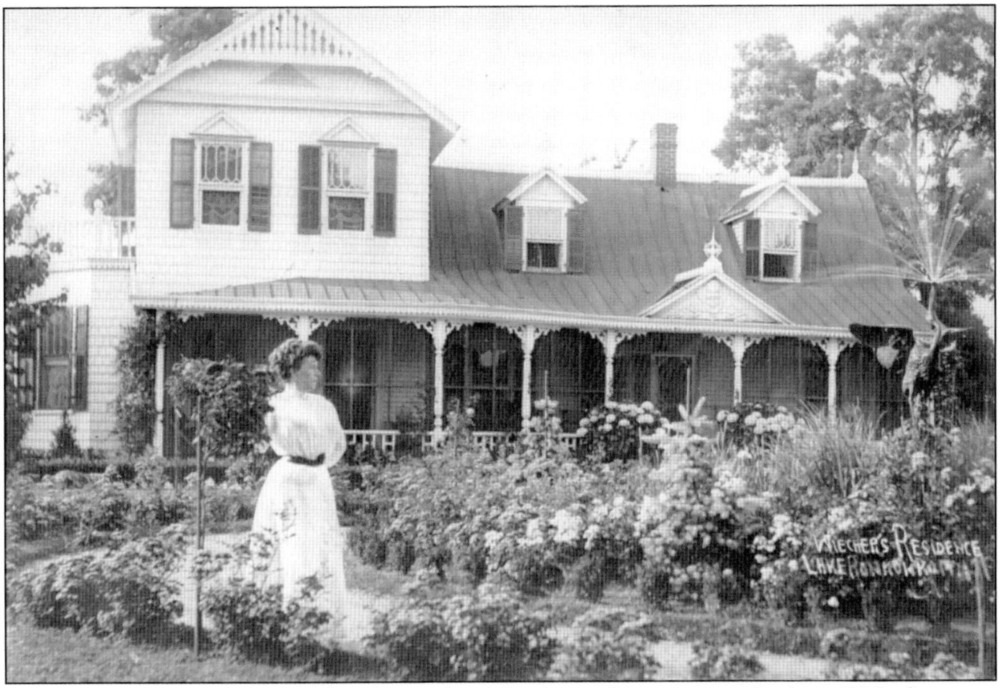

When Adolph Wiechers sold his shipyard in Hamburg, Germany, in the late 1800s, he came to the United States and invested heavily in land. Wiechers first went to Queens and Nassau Counties and, at one time, owned the land around LaGuardia Airport, Shea Stadium, and the world's fair. He also owned land where Levittown is today. From Nassau County, he came to Lake Ronkonkoma and became one of the largest landholders of property. These two photographs show the Wiechers estate (also known as Wiechers' Italian Garden) c. 1900. It was located off Smithtown Boulevard and went down to Turner's Beach and back to Gibbs Pond Road. Steuben Boulevard, named by Wiechers, went through the property and was the road to his estate.

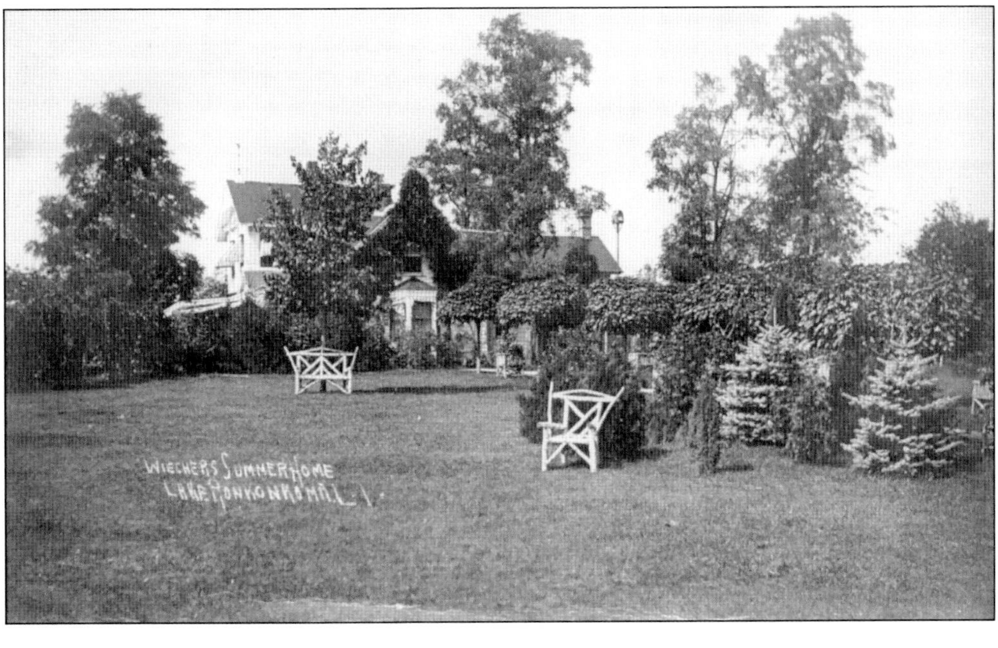

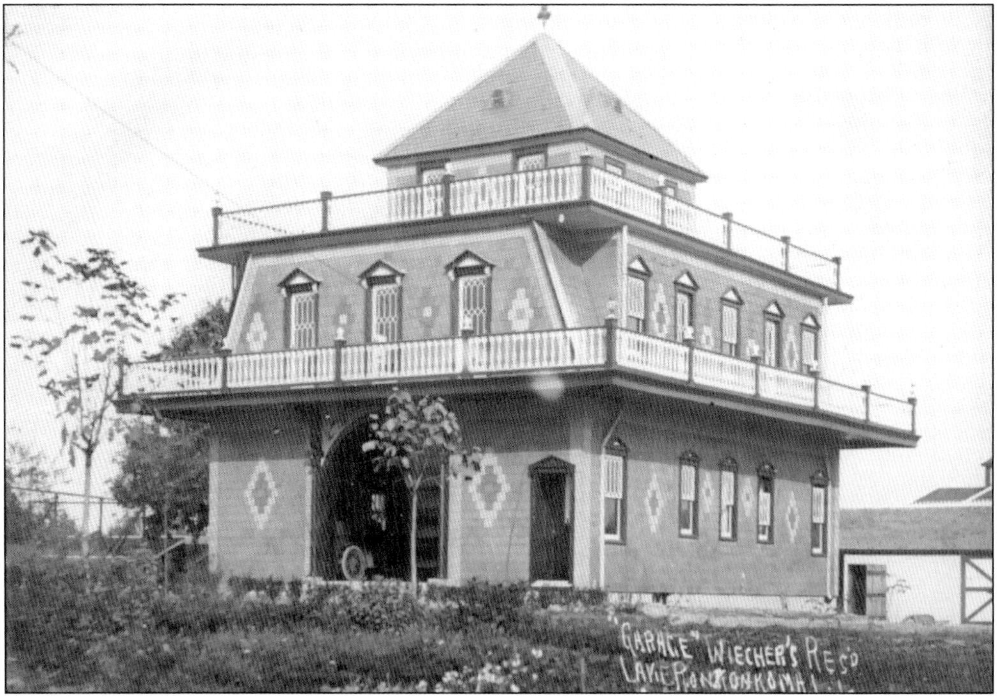

This was the Wiechers' garage c. 1910. Adolph Wiechers owned and operated a realty company and was president of the Clifton Game and Forest Society. They were known for breeding and handling quail, ducks, and other birds. Wiechers second estate was on Lake Terrace Road and Lake Shore Drive. This home would later become the Ondawa Hotel. Wiechers also owned property from Lake Terrace Road to the railroad station.

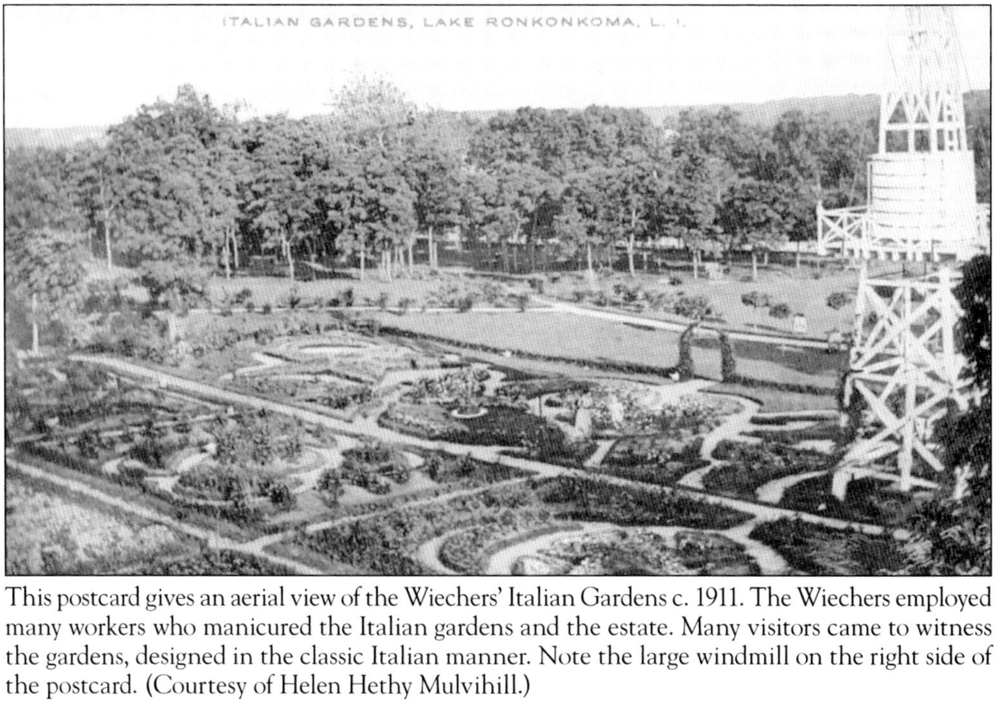

This postcard gives an aerial view of the Wiechers' Italian Gardens c. 1911. The Wiechers employed many workers who manicured the Italian gardens and the estate. Many visitors came to witness the gardens, designed in the classic Italian manner. Note the large windmill on the right side of the postcard. (Courtesy of Helen Hethy Mulvihill.)

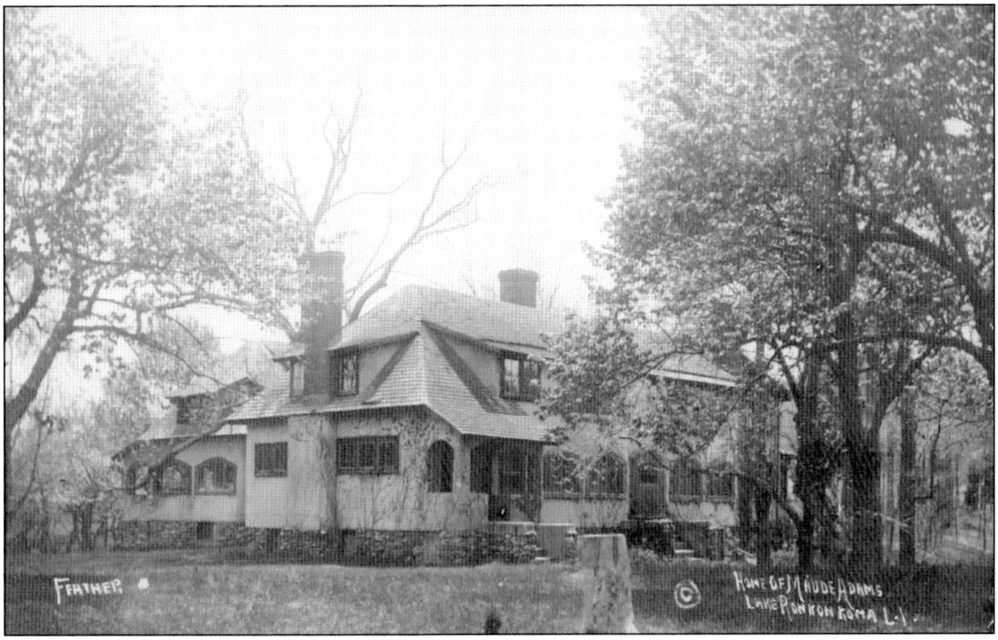

Dating back to 1720, this home is one of the oldest houses in the Lake Ronkonkoma area. It is the original Mooney Smith Homestead. The house and farm served the Smith family until the late 1800s. The actress Maude Adams bought the house, also called Sandy Garth, and property in 1898. Adams added two north wings to the original farmhouse and began enhancing the property. She purchased other land in the area, totaling 700 acres. In 1922, she turned her estate over to the Sisters of the Cenacle, who built a Catholic retreat house on part of her property. She continued to live at Sandy Garth until her death in 1953. Sachem High School now resides on some of Adams's land. These photographs were taken during the 1910s.

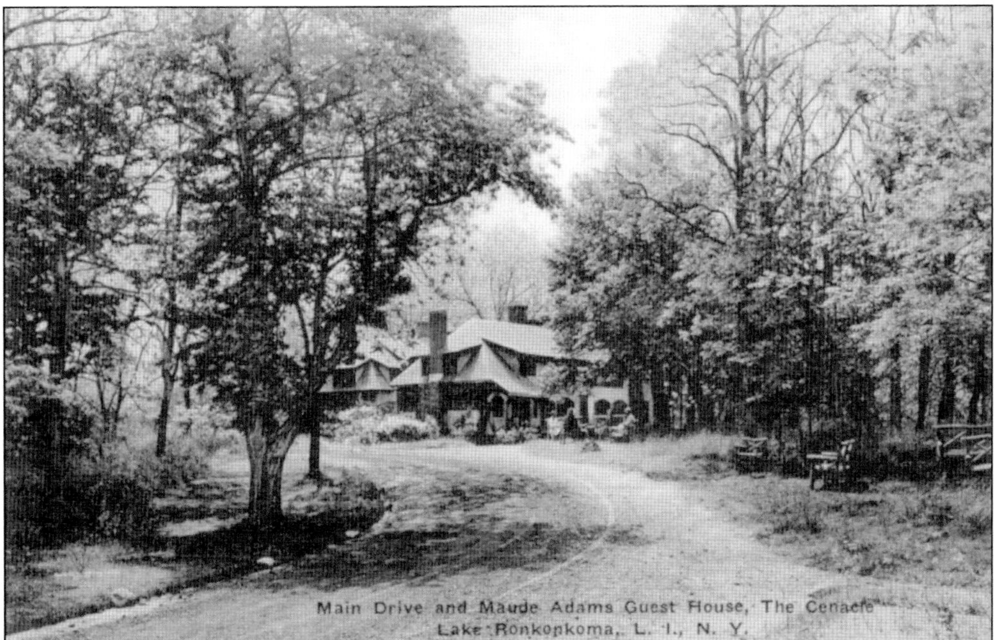

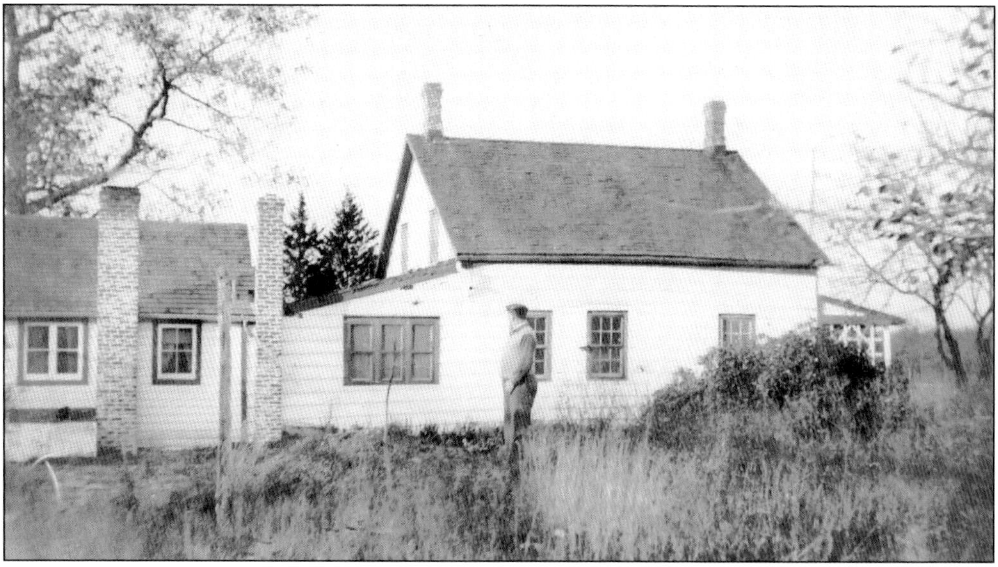

In 1853, Adam Peterman built a home on the west side of Holbrook Road. The property contained a pigsty, a horse barn, an outhouse, a cistern (an underground tank storing rainwater), and three barns. In 1906, Theodore and Dora Vollgraff bought the home from Peterman. The Vollgraffs lived there until 1934, when Walter Hethy bought this home for his mother, Ilona Korcz Hethy. She fell in love with the place after seeing a semicircle of lilacs on the property. The photograph pictured above shows the extension Hethy built to the original home c. 1935. Before 1934, there was no electricity, fireplaces, or bathrooms in the house. The two photographs were taken in 1937. (Courtesy of Helen Hethy Mulvihill.)

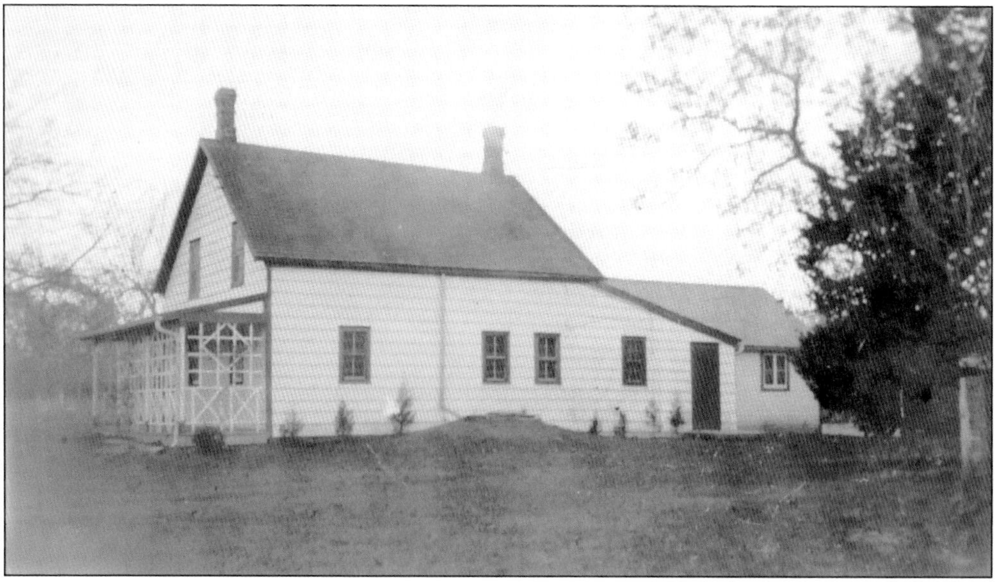

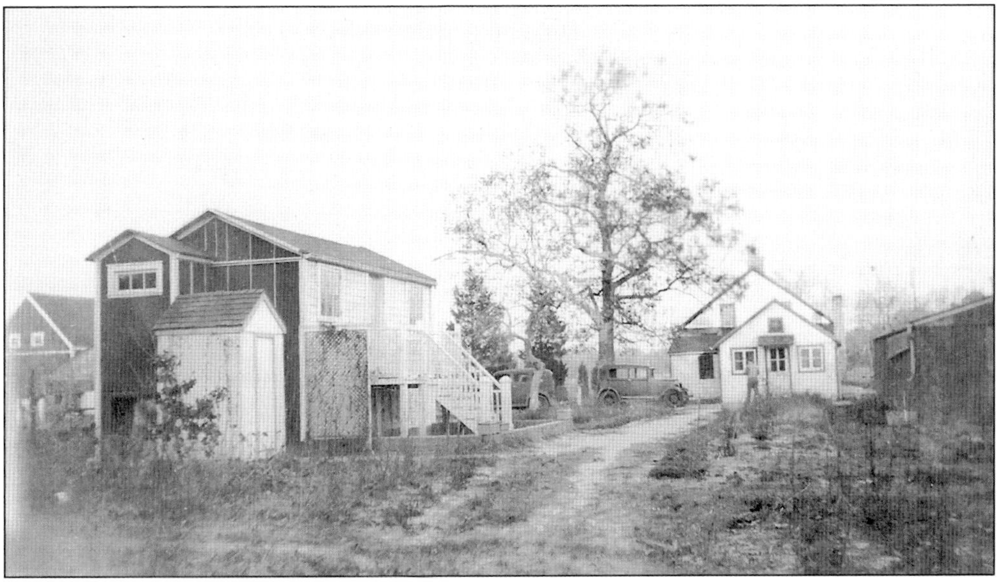

Here is a view of Walter Hethy's house looking east in 1937. The pigsty is seen in the foreground with the outhouse by its side. Behind the pigsty on the left is the horse barn, built in the 1850s. Hethy's daughter Helen Hethy Mulvihill currently resides here. (Courtesy of Helen Hethy Mulvihill.)

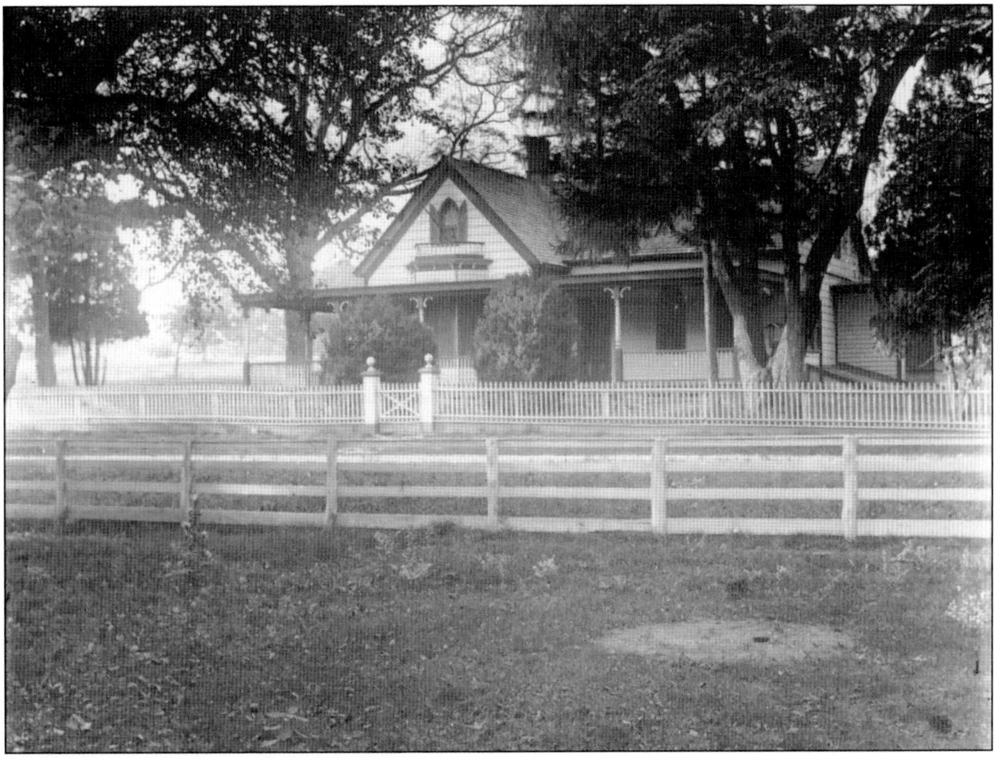

This home was photographed c. 1905. Located on Smith Street just west of the Methodist Church, John Newton originally owned this homestead back in 1873. The Puleston and Henkel families later resided here. Today, many homes from the early 1900s have disappeared. The few that remain are important assets to the town and community.

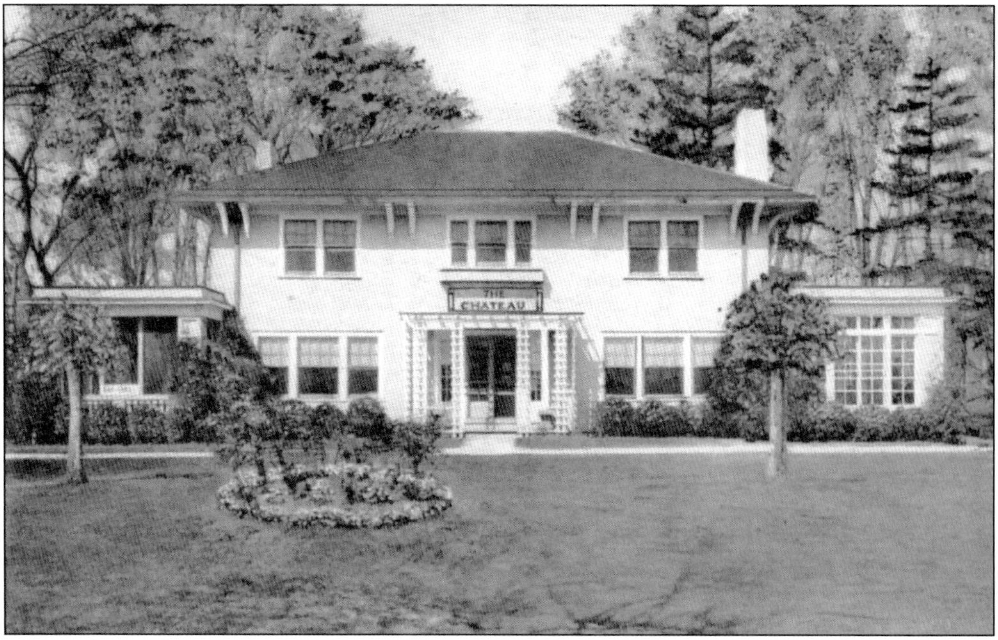

The Heilmans first settled in the Lake Ronkonkoma area in the 1880s. In 1905, Charles Heilman and two of his sons constructed this home. The Heilmans owned a butcher shop in New York City and made the commute each day back to their home on Lake Shore Road. The home is still in existence today. The postcard is dated 1910. (Courtesy of Helen Hethy Mulvihill.)

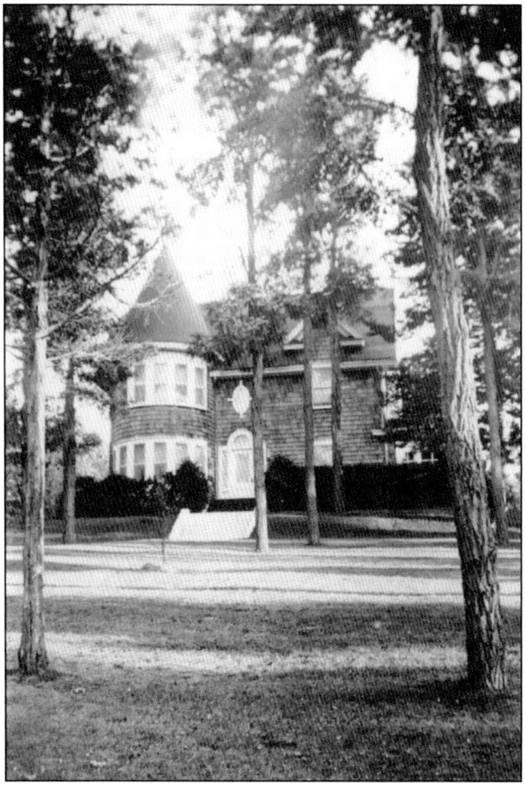

Located on the south side of Portion Road, Ed Parsons built this home c. 1905. Parsons, who had previously lived in Lake Grove, raised and trained fighting cocks as a hobby. In the 1920s, George McKay purchased the home for his family to use during the summer months. This picture is dated 1951. The home still exists today.

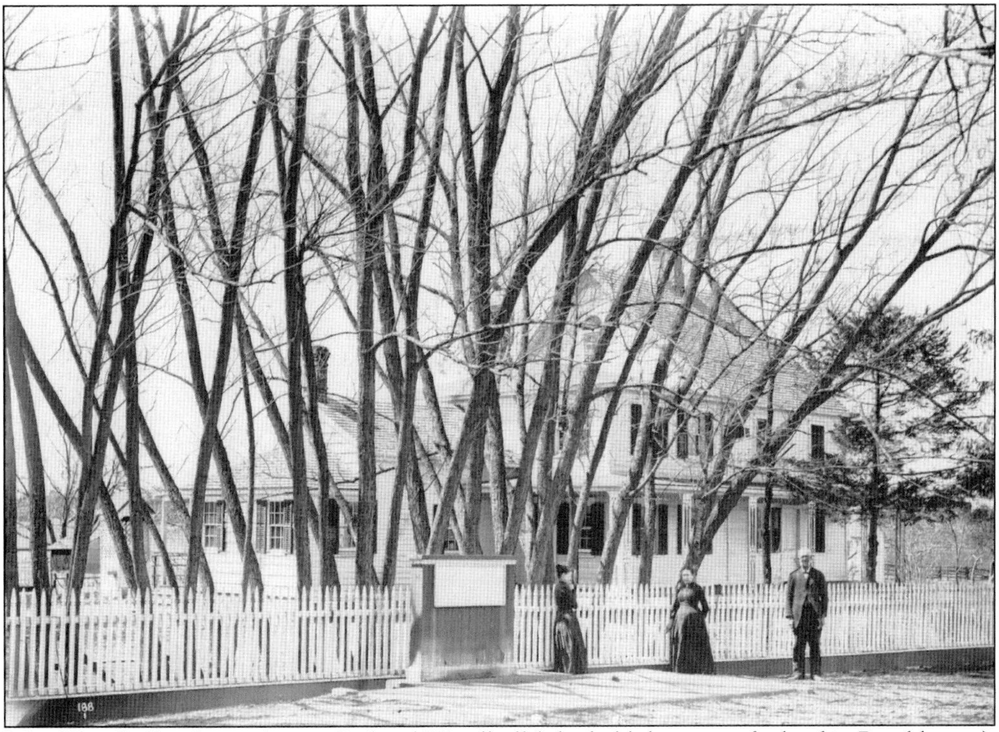

John Woodhull, a descendant to Richard Woodhull (who held the patent for land in Brookhaven), built a house on Portion Road in 1796 about a half-mile east of the lake. Woodhull's son Richard Woodhull Newton became the first in the Newton family to live in the homestead. The Newtons had a few barns, a corncrib, an icehouse, and a windmill on the property. The above photograph, dated 1905, shows the willow trees in front of the homestead. In 1964, the town felt the homestead was in danger of being lost in the town's expansion. The Newton family decided to have the home moved to a safer spot on Division Street (pictured below). The Newton Homestead is the oldest home in Lake Ronkonkoma.

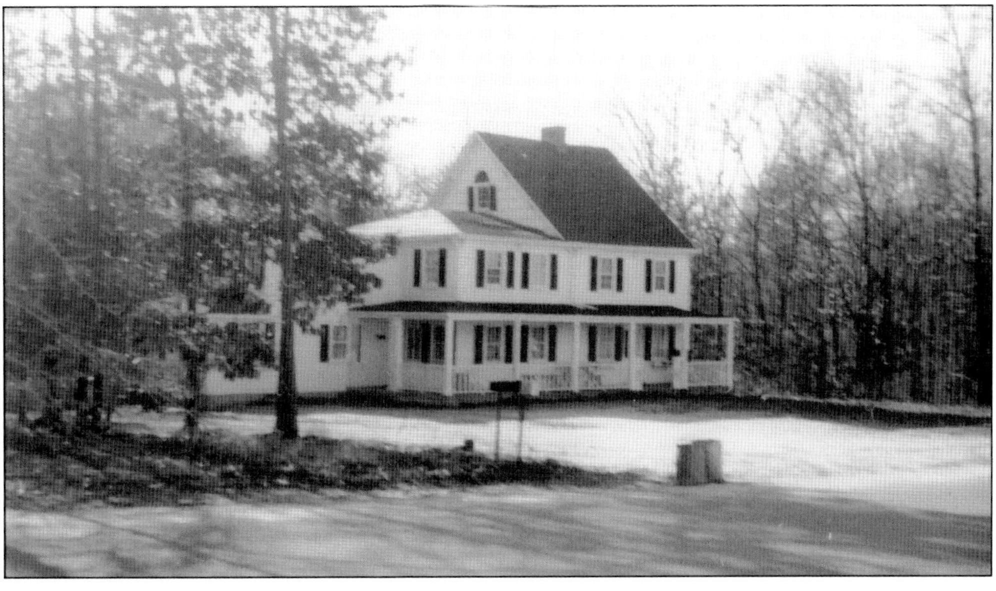

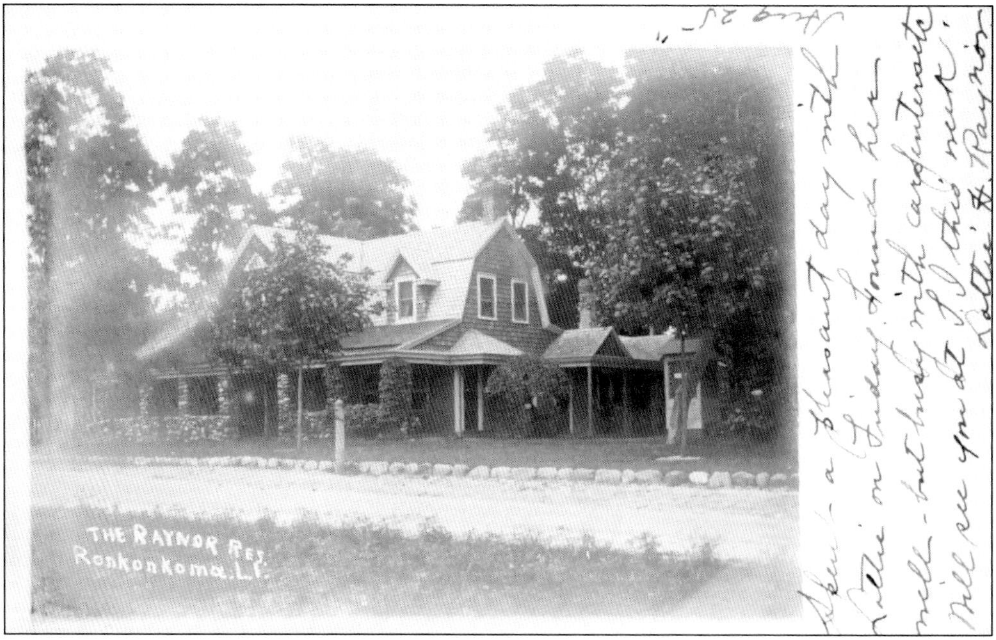

George C. Raynor was born in this home located on the north side of Portion Road in 1868. The home consisted of a one-and-a-half-story gabled roof, a wide porch, and a cobblestone fireplace. Prior to 1909, the front facade was redesigned with a second-floor pavilion, cobblestone porch, and two gabled dormers. This photograph, taken in 1907, shows how the home looked with these changes. (Courtesy of Helen Hethy Mulvihill.)

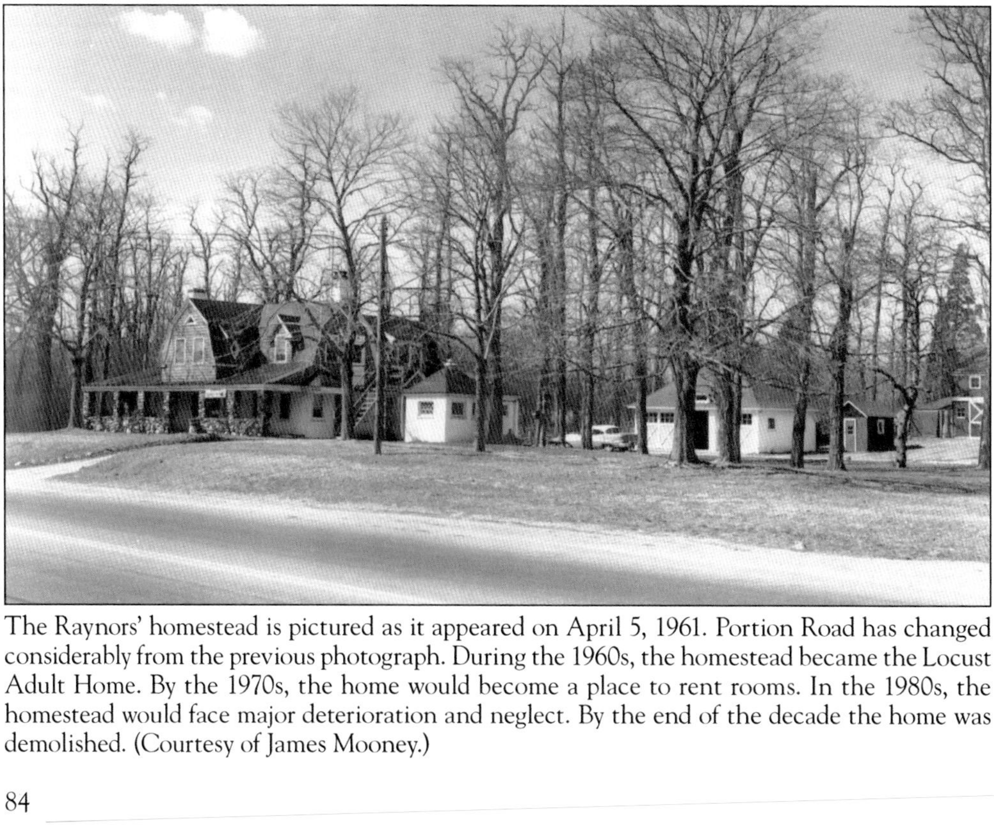

The Raynors' homestead is pictured as it appeared on April 5, 1961. Portion Road has changed considerably from the previous photograph. During the 1960s, the homestead became the Locust Adult Home. By the 1970s, the home would become a place to rent rooms. In the 1980s, the homestead would face major deterioration and neglect. By the end of the decade the home was demolished. (Courtesy of James Mooney.)

Four

The People of Lake Ronkonkoma

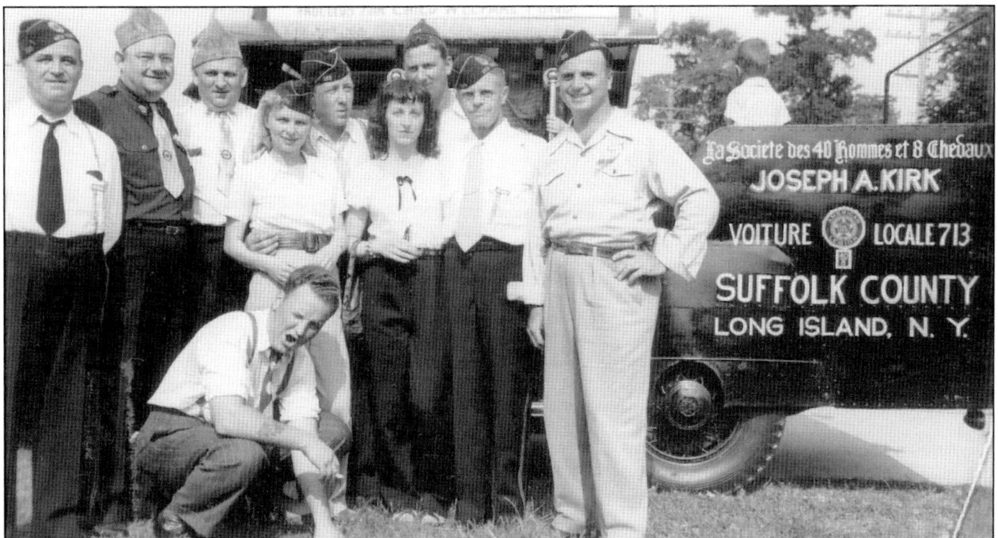

This photograph was taken in front of the William Merritt Hallock American Legion Post on June 28, 1947. Pictured are, from left to right, (kneeling) Chad Benjamin; (standing) Carl Haas, Joe Barnickel, Bill Berger, Lil Sevenliss, John Sevenliss, Bibs Davis, unidentified, Jim Browne Sr., and Carl Gregory.

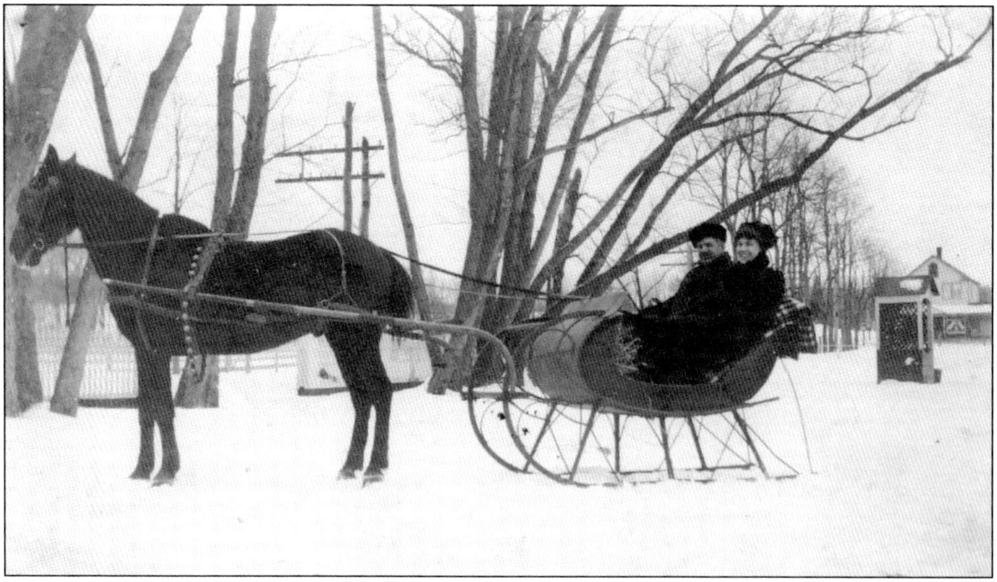

Frank Newton (1869–1940) is seen here with his second wife, Henrietta D. Baker (1885–1950). The photograph was taken in 1915 and shows the Newtons sitting on a horse-drawn sleigh in the front yard of their home, the Willows. Agnew and Taylor can be seen in the back right of the picture.

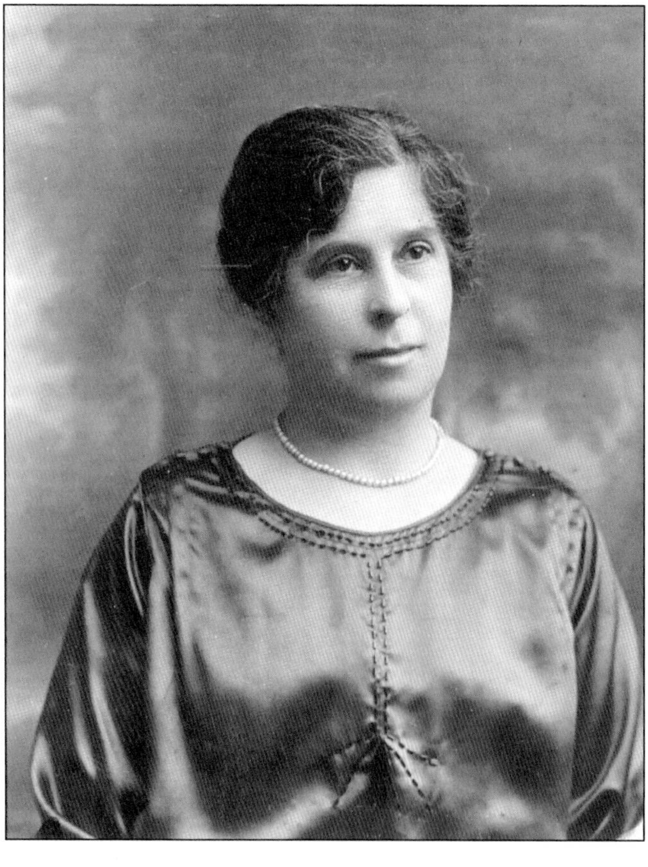

Ada "Purdy" Overton (1872–1962) was married to John B. Overton and lived in the Overton house on Hawkins Avenue. In 1917, Lake Ronkonkoma had their first library, and Helen DeVere was in search of a librarian. The Overtons lived right across the street from the new library, and Purdy Overton inquired about the position. In 1917, she became Lake Ronkonkoma's first librarian. She would step down a year later.

Joseph A. Kirk (1890–1944) was a veteran of World War I. He was the founder of the William Merritt Hallock American Legion Post and was treasurer of the Duffield Construction Company, a well drilling firm. Kirk was the president and a founder of the National Bank of Ronkonkoma (as seen in this picture c. 1930). He was also a former fire chief of the Lake Ronkonkoma Fire Department.

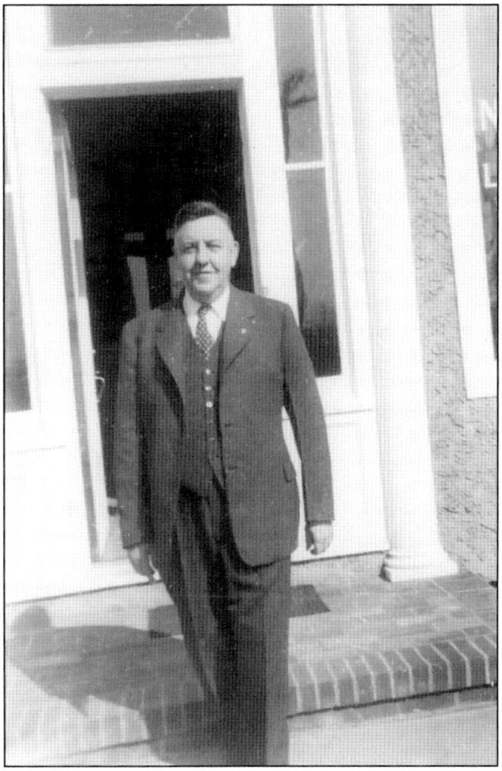

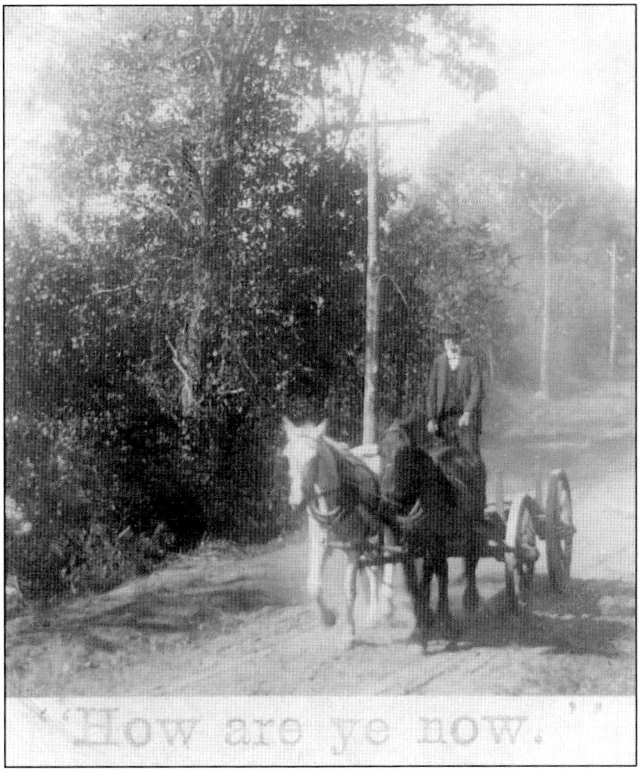

Richard Woodhull Newton (1834–1901) was born and raised in Lake Ronkonkoma. He was one of the 13 children of Samuel Newton (1802–1877) and Caroline Jane Rhodes (1808–1866). Around town, people would call him "Uncle Richard," and his favorite saying was "How are you now?" Newton arranged to have the Lakeland railroad station moved to Lake Ronkonkoma in 1883. This photograph was taken c. 1900.

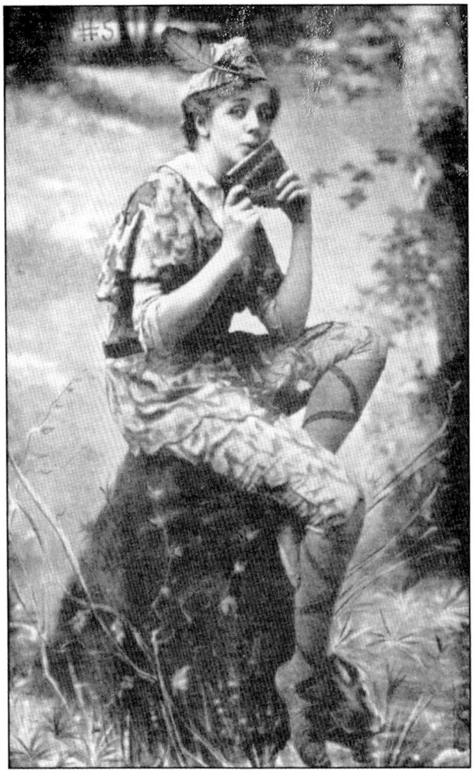

Maude Adams (1872–1953) was born Maude Ewing Kiskadden in Salt Lake City, Utah. She was an American stage actress who achieved great success as Peter Pan. In 1898, Adams bought a farm called Sandy Garth and 700 acres in Lake Ronkonkoma. In 1922, she donated her estate to the Sisters of St. Regis and had Cenacle Retreat House built for them. Adams is buried at the Cenacle.

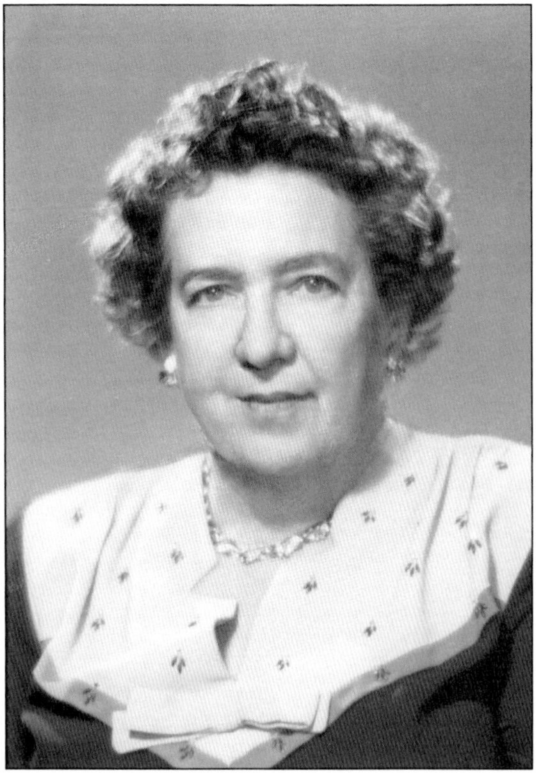

Rosemary Cleary, c. 1960, was the founder of the Cleary School for Deaf Children. In 1925, she opened Camp Peter Pan, the first summer camp for deaf children in the United States. In 1930, she opened the Cleary School, located on Smithtown Boulevard in Lake Ronkonkoma. In 1960, Catholic Charities supplemented county and state funds and provided for capital improvements to the school.

Morris Hawkins (1867–1958) and Lizzie H. Hawkins (1870–1947) were married on November 26, 1891. They had five children—E. Bassford Hawkins, Alice Coleman, Jessamine Sanford, Leona Meyer, and Erma Bednar. The Hawkins had a farm on Smith Road east of the Five Corners. There were peach and apple trees, strawberries, blueberries, and other fruit, and Hawkins also grew turnips and squash. They would travel to Lakeland and Sayville to sell their produce. Morris Hawkins was one of six brothers playing with the Hawkins Nine, a Lake Ronkonkoma baseball team during the late 1800s and early 1900s. These two photographs were taken at Ruescher's in Brooklyn in 1896.

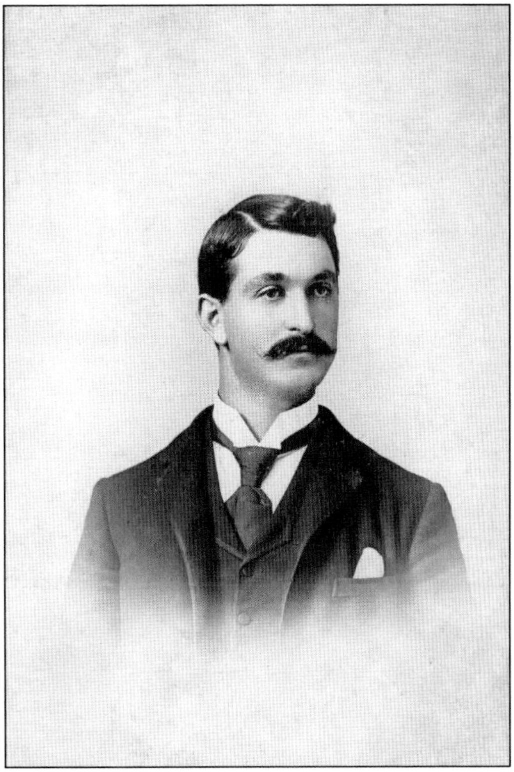

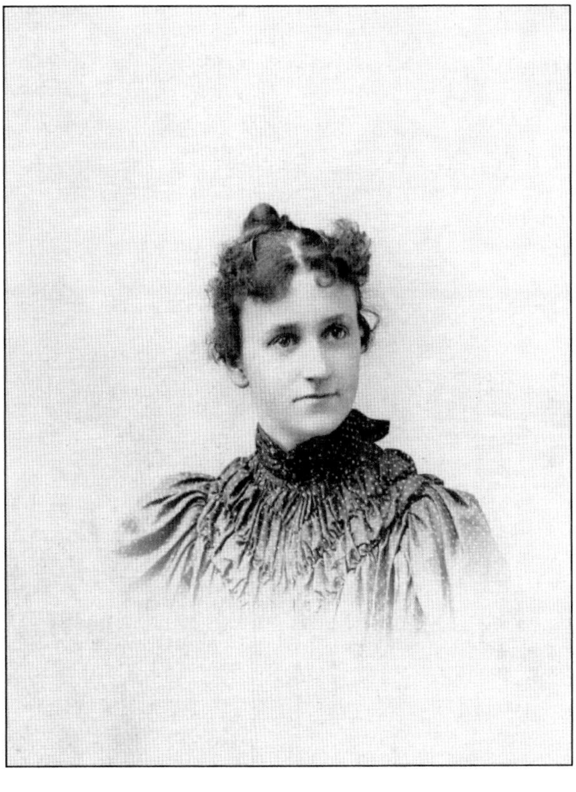

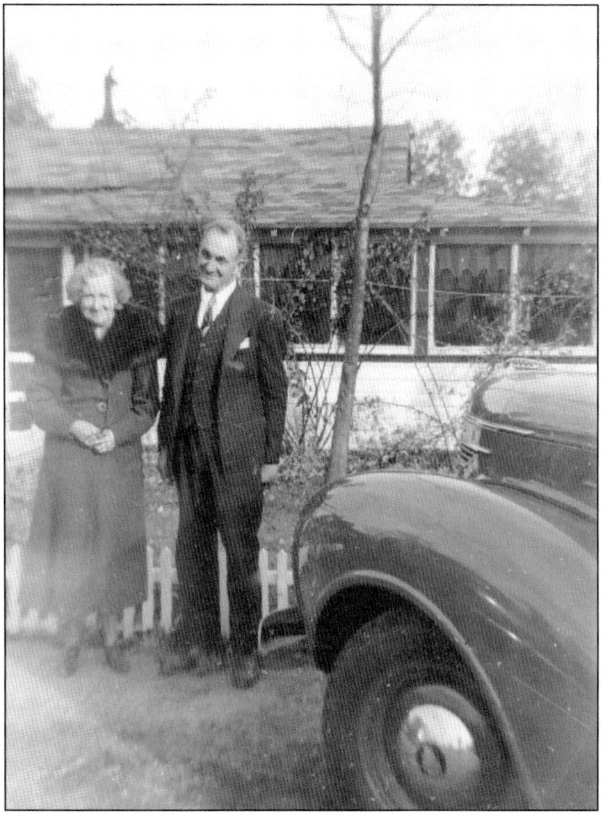

This is a picture of Lizzie and Morris Hawkins taken in 1939. Besides farming, Morris Hawkins was the town justice of the peace from 1896 to 1914 and was a school trustee for 15 years. He would also clear land, take down trees, dig out stumps at cemeteries, dig graves, and even act as a pallbearer at many funerals.

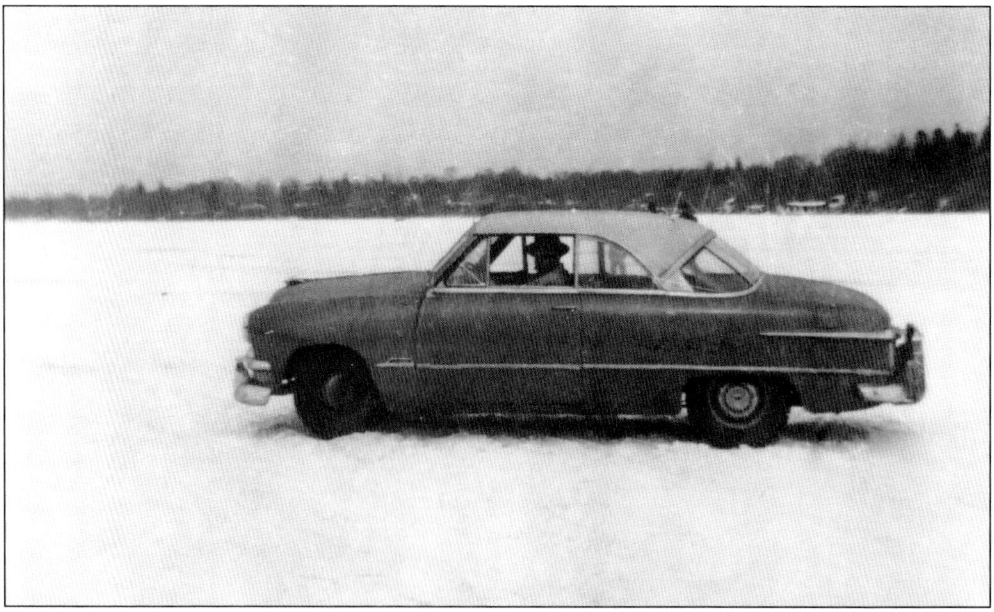

Jim Muldoon, in the winter of 1952, drove his car across the lake from the Green Pavilion (Brookhaven Town Beach) to Ronkonkoma Shores (Bavarian Inn). His two children were ice-skating near Ronkonkoma Shores. Muldoon's wife, Kate, took this photograph. Over the years, there have been many unsuccessful attempts to drive across the lake.

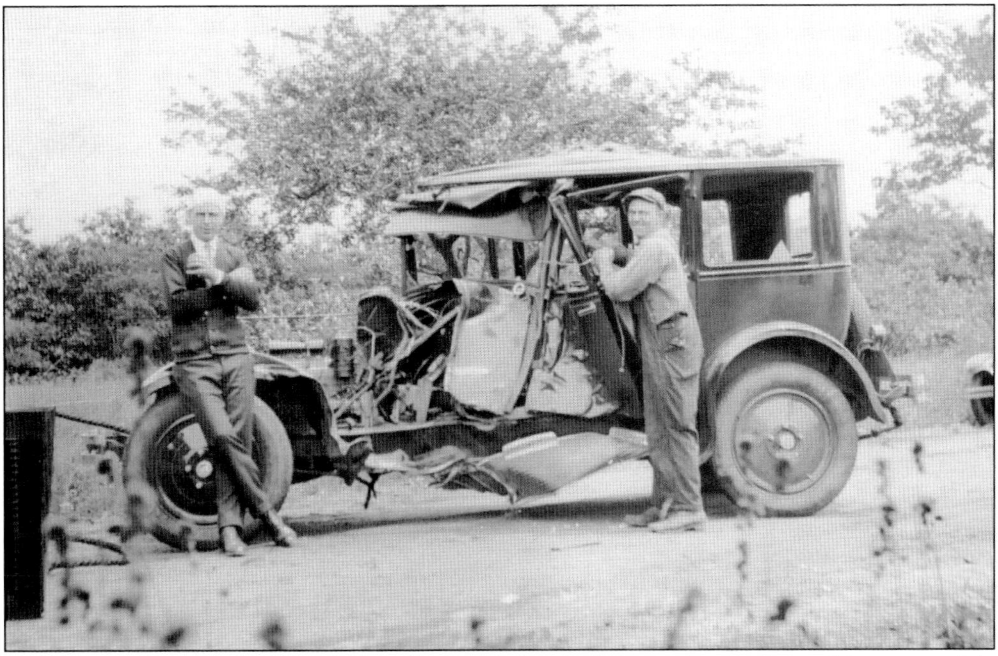

This photograph shows Dick Newton (1889–1945) in 1926 tying up the door of the automobile of the unidentified person at left. Newton helped his brother Sumner Newton build Newton's Garage in 1923. Dick Newton's parents were E. Hollis Newton (1847–1928) and Mattie W. Newton (1847–1935). Dick Newton also had a sister named Lulu E. Newton.

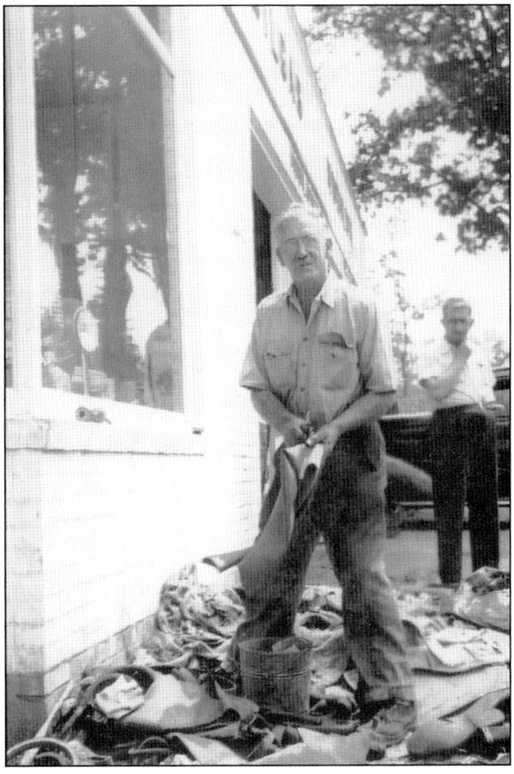

This is Sumner Newton (1887–1955) in front of Newton's Garage around 1942. In 1923, Newton, with the help of his brother Dick, established Newton's Garage. Sumner was also handy in wiring electricity in people's homes around town. In his free time, he enjoyed going deer hunting upstate with friends.

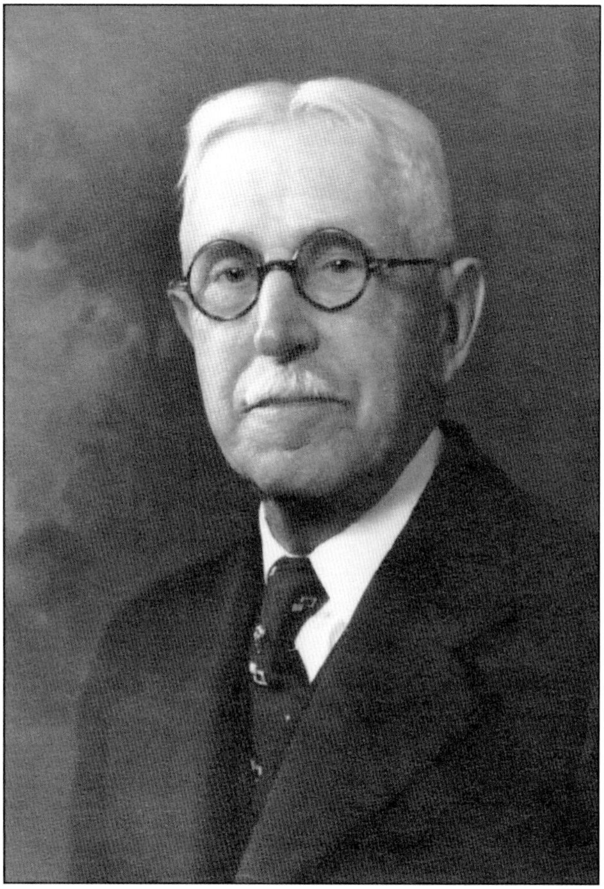

George C. Raynor (1868–1950) was born and raised in Lake Ronkonkoma. Raynor taught school at Millersville State Normal School at Millersville, Pennsylvania, and Polytechnic Institute in Brooklyn. In 1914, he retired from the educational field and went into the real estate business. Raynor was president and treasurer of W.N. Hallock Company. In 1921, he established Raynor's Beach. In 1927, he was one of the founders and the first president of the National Bank of Lake Ronkonkoma. Raynor was a trustee of the Lake Ronkonkoma school district and a district school commissioner of Suffolk County. He was also a member of the Brookhaven Town Planning Board. Raynor's wife, Lottie Havens Raynor, died in 1947. The photograph at left was taken c. 1940. The photograph below was taken c. 1910.

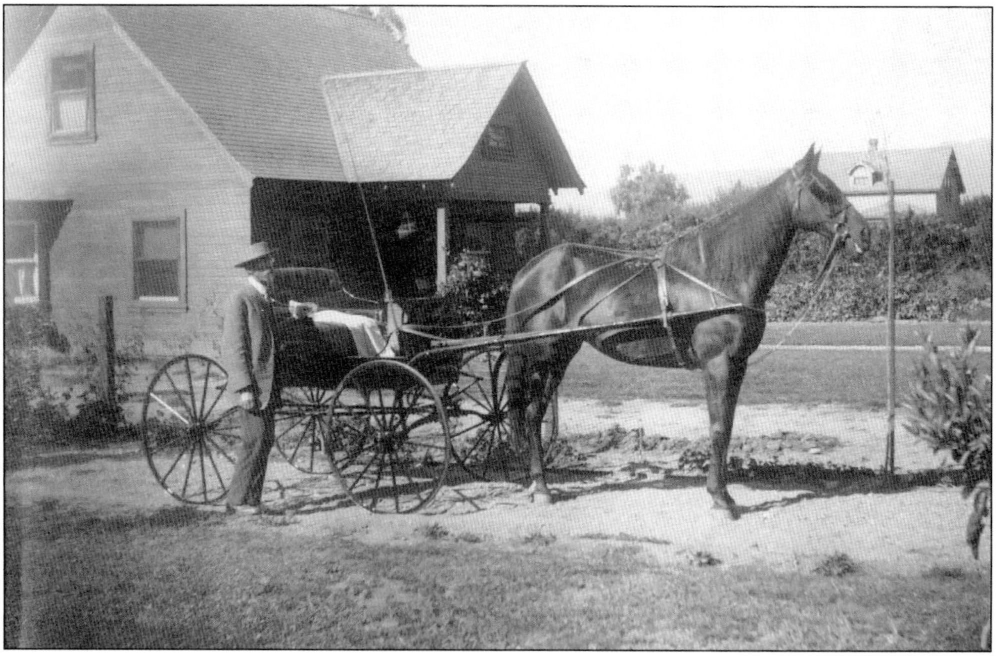

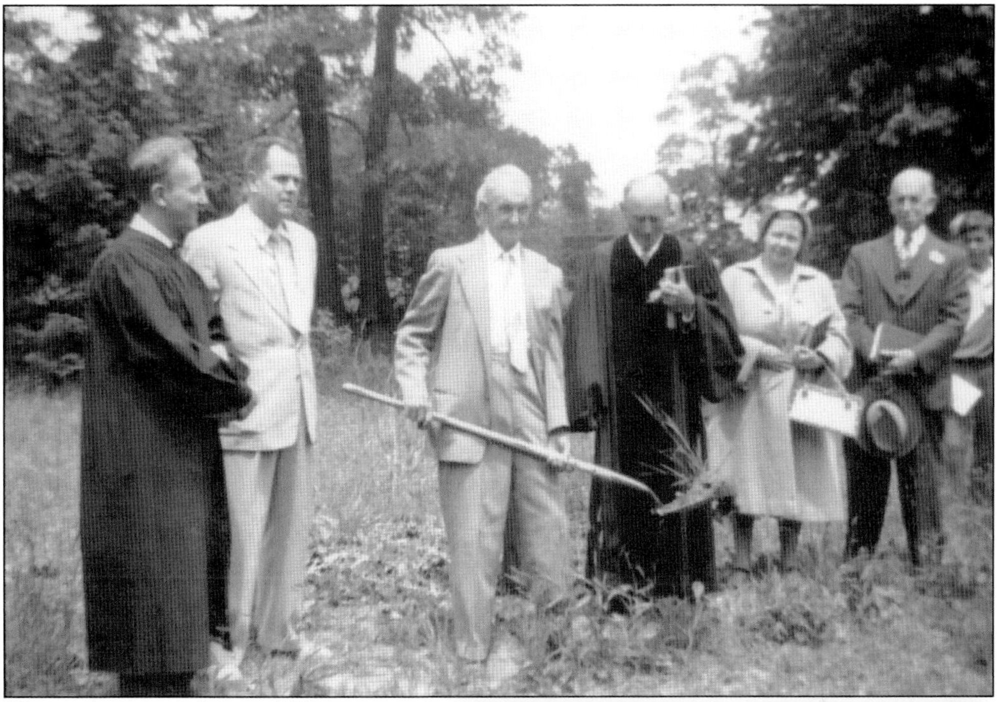

This picture was taken c. 1956. Pictured are, from left to right, Francis Terry, William Miller, Morris M. Hawkins, Rev. Harold Sobin, Bertha Horvath, and Louis Hertlin. Hawkins is breaking new ground for a new Methodist Church at Five Corners on the border of Lake Ronkonkoma and Lake Grove. Hawkins was the Lake Ronkonkoma Methodist Church treasurer for 60 years.

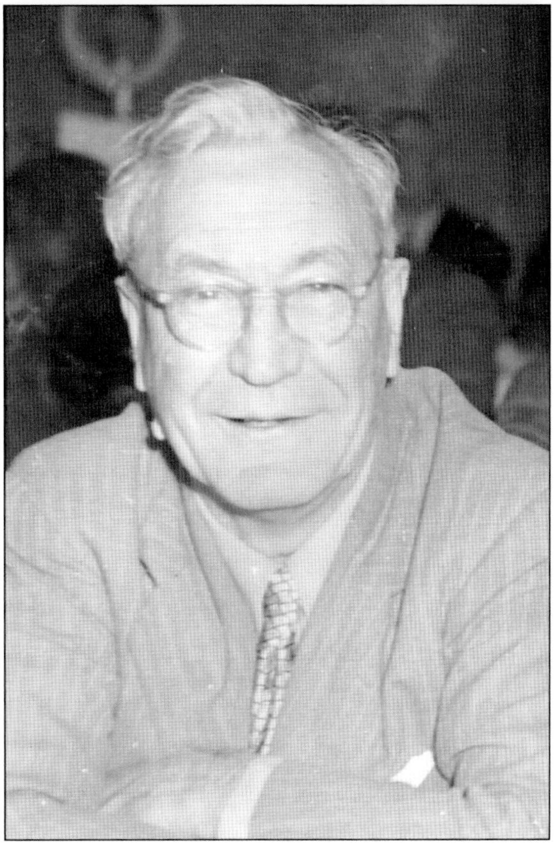

Clarence A. "Cad" Duffield (1882–1966) moved to Lake Ronkonkoma in 1912 and became a building contractor. In 1919, Duffield and Kirk established a well drilling firm, which became known throughout the country. Duffield was also the fire chief for Lake Ronkonkoma Fire Department in 1941. Duffield was the first president of the Lions Club of the Ronkonkomas in 1948. This picture was taken c. 1960.

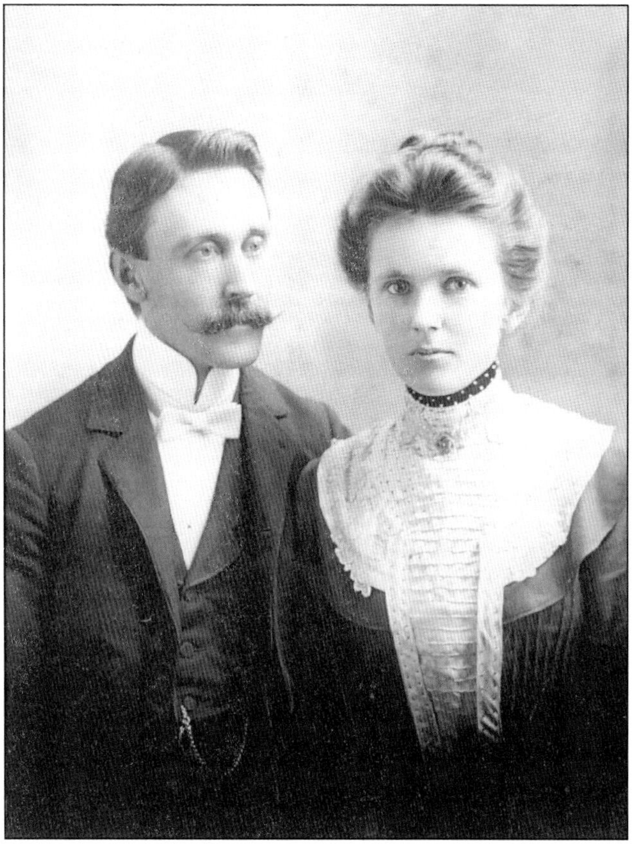

Willis N. (1876–1920) and Nettie N. Hallock (1877–1969) ran a general store that became Agnew and Taylor. They had two children, Ruth Natalie Hallock and Willis Francis Hallock. Willis N. Hallock and his cousin George C. Raynor were partners in a real estate business. Willis N. Hallock succumbed to the flu epidemic of 1918, and Nettie believed that his death was due to the aftereffects of the illness.

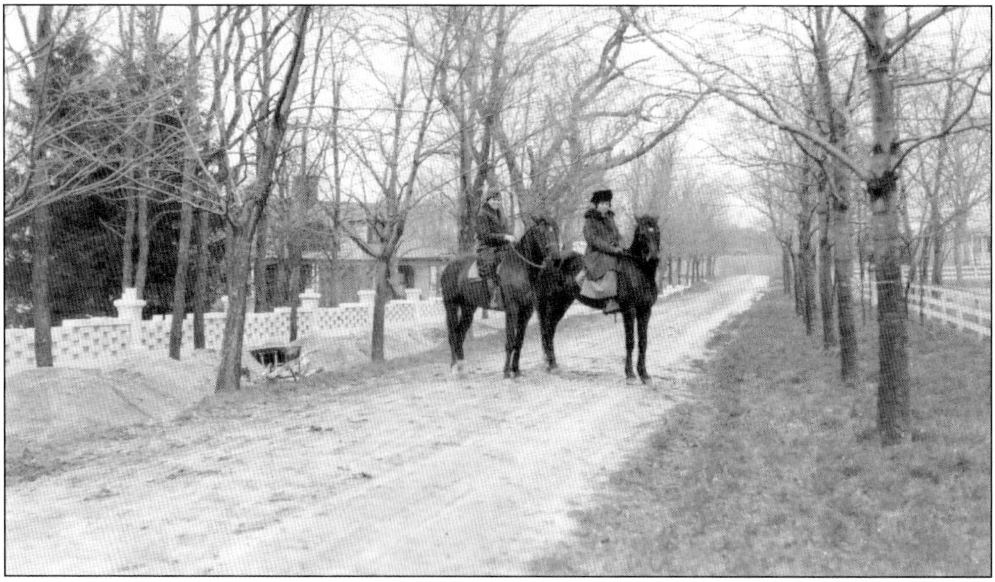

Two women are pictured on horses in front of the Metzner house c. 1920. The dirt road is Parsnip Pond Road in Lake Grove. During the winter months, the Metzners utilized this home. During summers, they would pack up and travel south to Lake Ronkonkoma. It is unknown who these two women are. They might be two of the Metzner girls, Alma, Rose, or Magie.

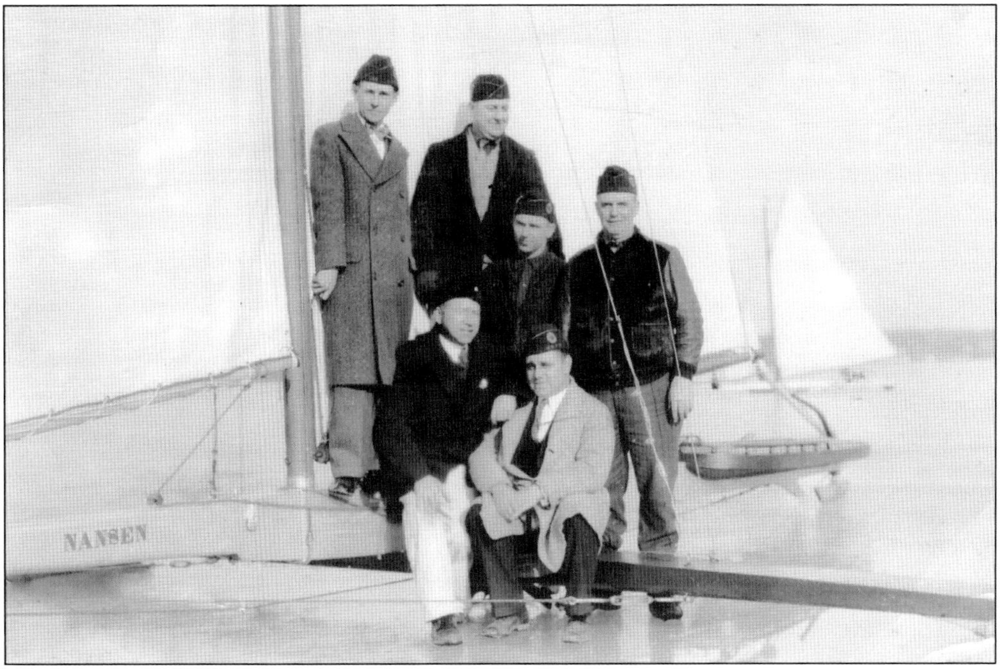

This photograph was taken in March 1929 on Lake Ronkonkoma. In 1923, the Lake Ronkonkoma Yacht Club and Ice Boat Club were founded. The founders were "Bunny" Gubner, Tom Fish, Joe Kirk, Sumner Newton, J. Eberhardt, Anton Pedisich, and Louis C. Heilman. Pictured are, from left to right, (first row) Bunny Goobner and Harold Sorenson; (second row) Ray Duffield, Joe Kirk, Dick Newton, and Jack Milan.

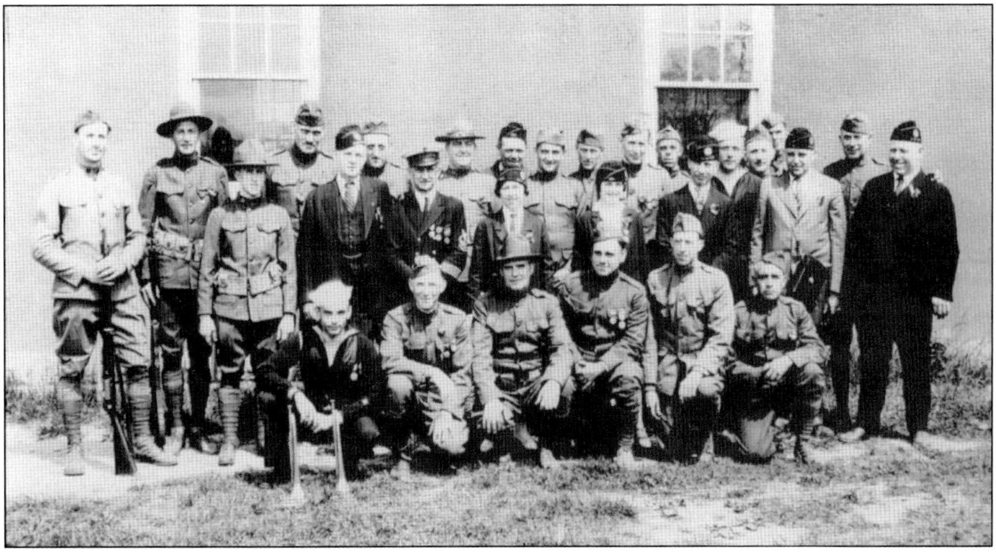

This photograph was taken in front of the William Merritt Hallock American Legion Post. Pictured are, from left to right, (first row) Ben Woodward, Van Wein, Jack Millan, Harold Sorenson, Harold Gould, and unidentified; (second row) Malcolm Hawkins, Dr. Guy McLean, H. Cruise, unidentified, Lew Terry, and Joe Jedlicka; (third row) Tom Fish, Chas Davis, first commander LeRoy Vollgraff, ? Steigerwald, Joe Kirk, Bill Mars, Van Wyen, George Weaver, Henry Tuthill, William Pinchen, and six unidentified.

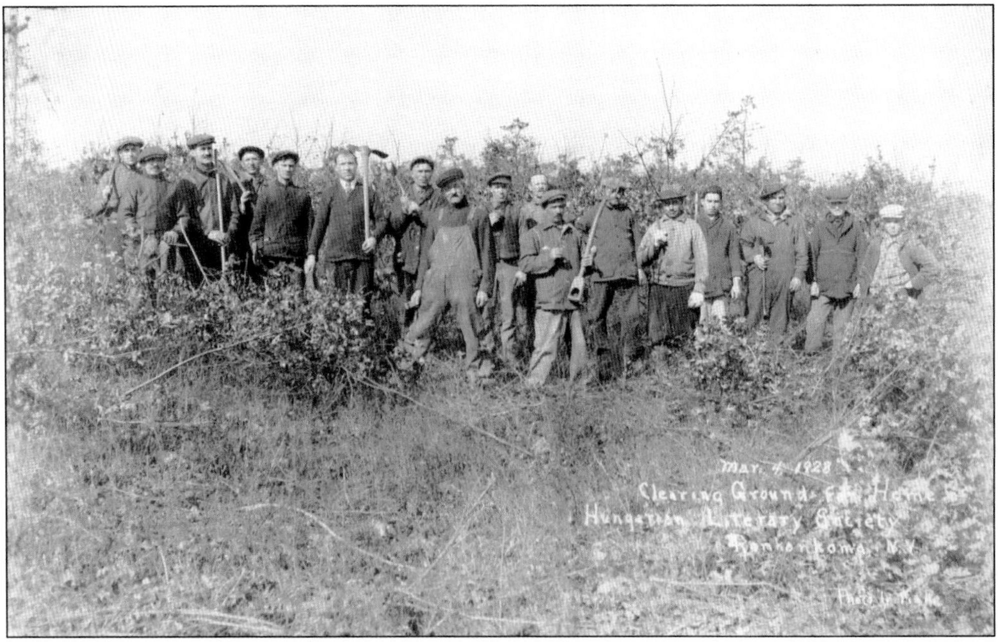

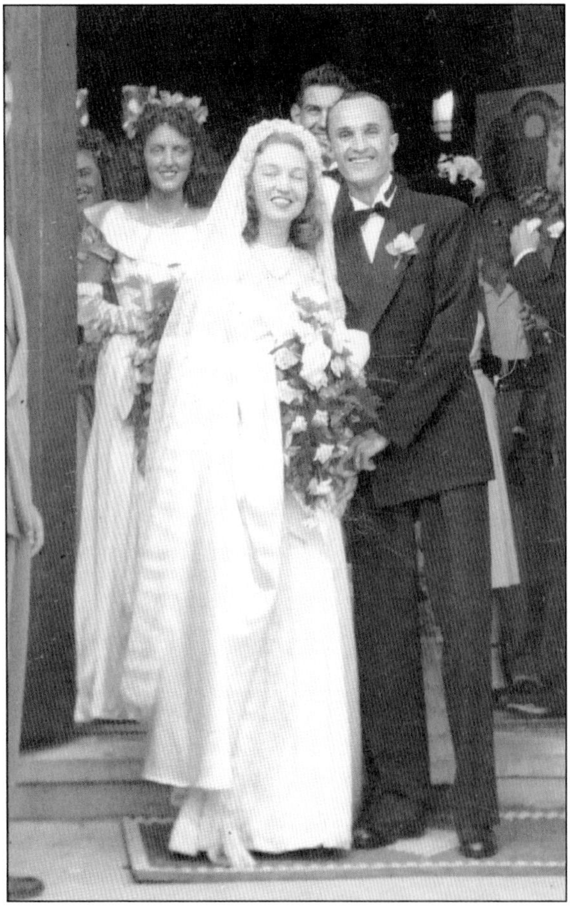

In March 1928, these men cleared the ground off Ocean Avenue to construct the American-Hungarian Literary Society. Pictured are, from left to right, George Quentz, Frank Becker, Joseph Buchler, John Tangel, George Rosch, Richard Schrammel, Fred Kraics, Joseph Zsemberi, Steve Bucsak, Joseph Huszar, Michael Pfeiffer, John Knobloch, John Vigh, Michael Rosch, James Fenyak, Steve Sipos, and Alexander Sipos.

Lawrence Holzapfel (1922–) and Dolores Holzapfel (1924–) were married on September 14, 1947. The Holzapfels have lived in Lake Ronkonkoma all their lives. Lawrence is the first generation to live in Lake Ronkonkoma; Dolores is the fourth generation. He worked for Grumman's for 35 years and owned the Book House for over 25 years. (Courtesy of Lawrence and Dolores Holzapfel.)

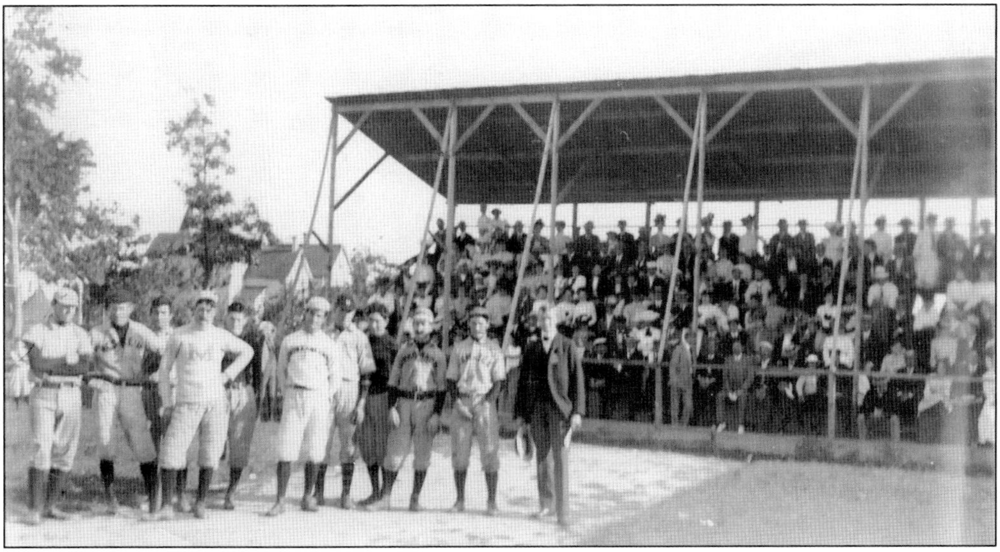

This page shows two images of the Ronkonkoma baseball team. The team achieved considerable fame between the years of 1885 and 1935 and played all the leading teams of Long Island and Eastern New Jersey. The photograph above shows the entire team at a game on August 16, 1902. Baseball was already a very popular sport, and games such as this were an important social event. Notice the full grandstand. The photograph below, taken on July 1, 1905, shows the starting lineup. Manager Charles W. Hawkins is in the second row at far right. This team included six of the Hawkins brothers. Around 1912, the governors of the league asked the Hawkins brothers to create an all-Hawkins team. The six Hawkins brothers and their sons became the Hawkins Nine. The other team members became known as the Lake Grove Athletic Club.

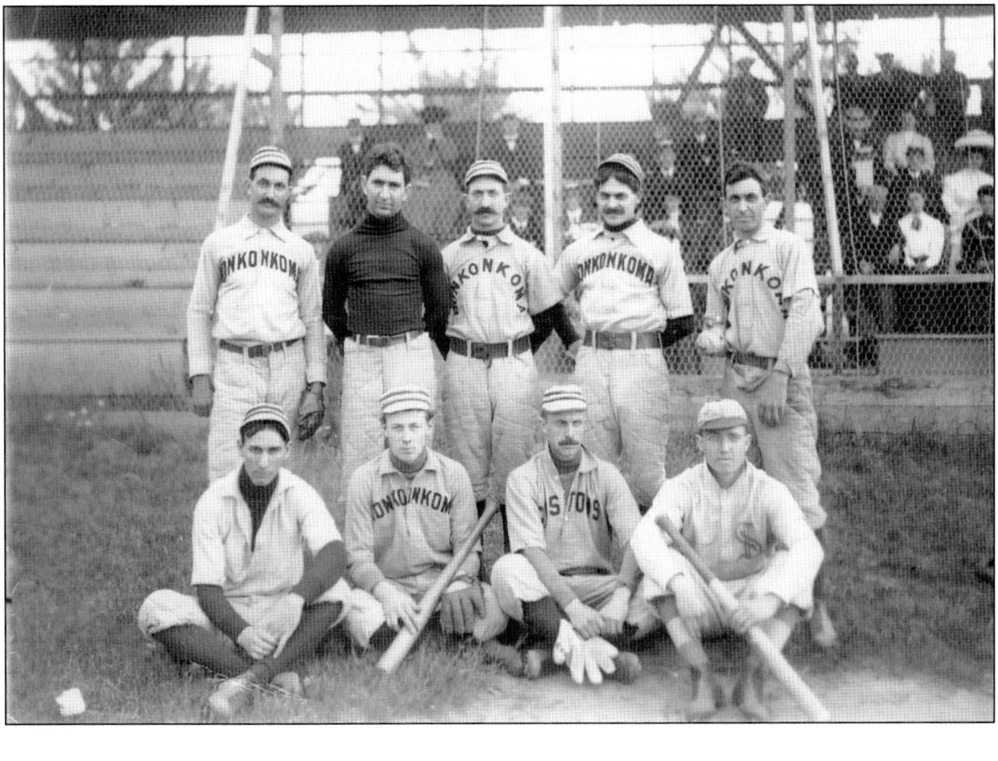

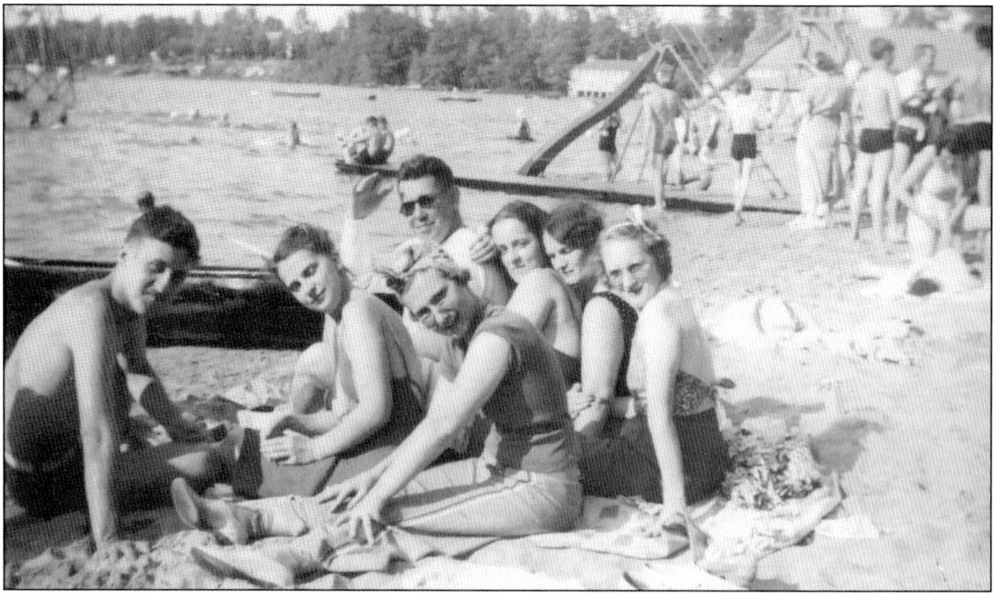

Pictured are, from left to right, unidentified, Eva Korocz, Walter Zoltan Hethy, Irene Binder, Yolanda Korocz, Bertha Majthenyi, and Ann Korocz enjoying a summer day at the Hollywood Beach in 1939. Pictured behind the slides are the Mayfair, Raynor's, and the Green Pavilions. (Courtesy of Helen Hethy Mulvihill.)

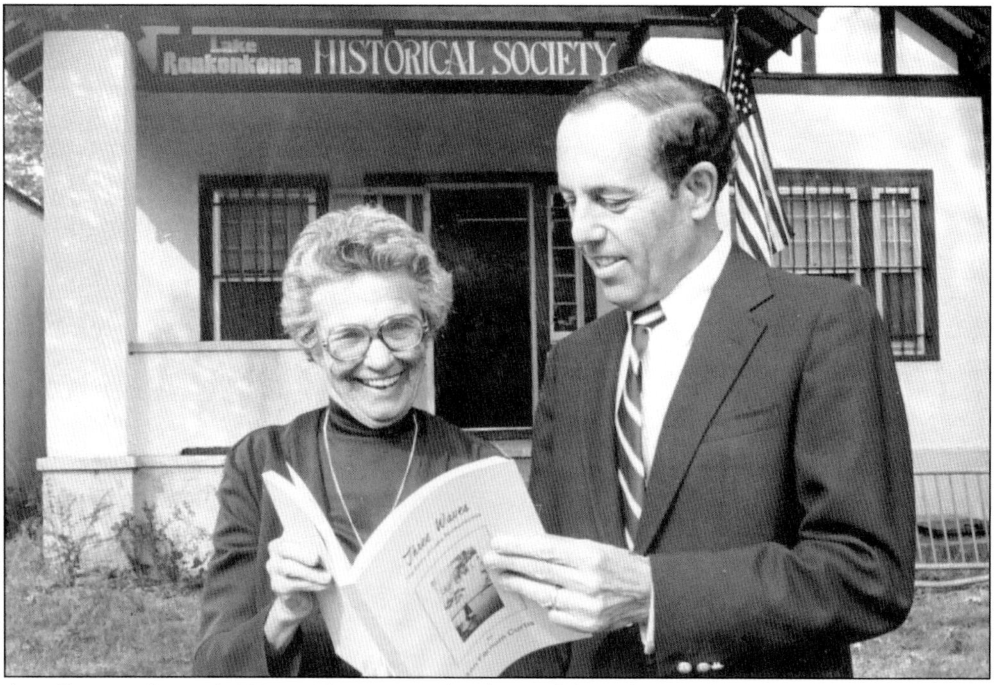

Ann Farnum Curtis (1908–1982) is pictured in front of the Lake Ronkonkoma Historical Society on November 8, 1980. Curtis was the founder of the historical society. She devoted years of her life to preserving the history of the Lake Ronkonkoma area and was instrumental in the effort to preserve land around the lakeshore as parkland in the early 1970s; she later wrote the definitive history of the area.

Five

Fire Department, Churches, Schools, and Railroad

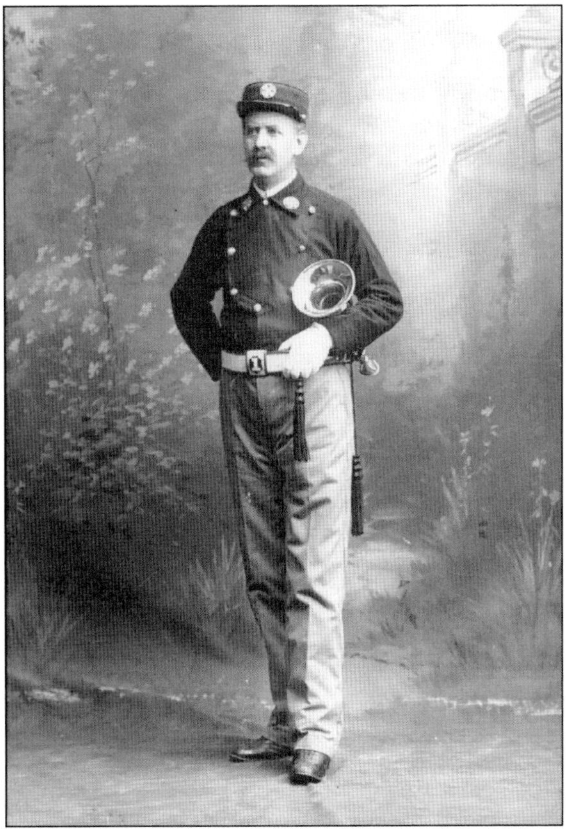

This 1904 photograph shows John W. Cleary, first chief of the Ronkonkoma Fire Department. After a fire at the Lake Front Hotel injured 14 people and caused one death, Cleary and 23 other locals organized a volunteer force. On June 15, 1904, the Ronkonkoma Hook & Ladder Company No. 1 was officially organized. Townspeople raised money for the first fire truck, which was a horse-drawn vehicle.

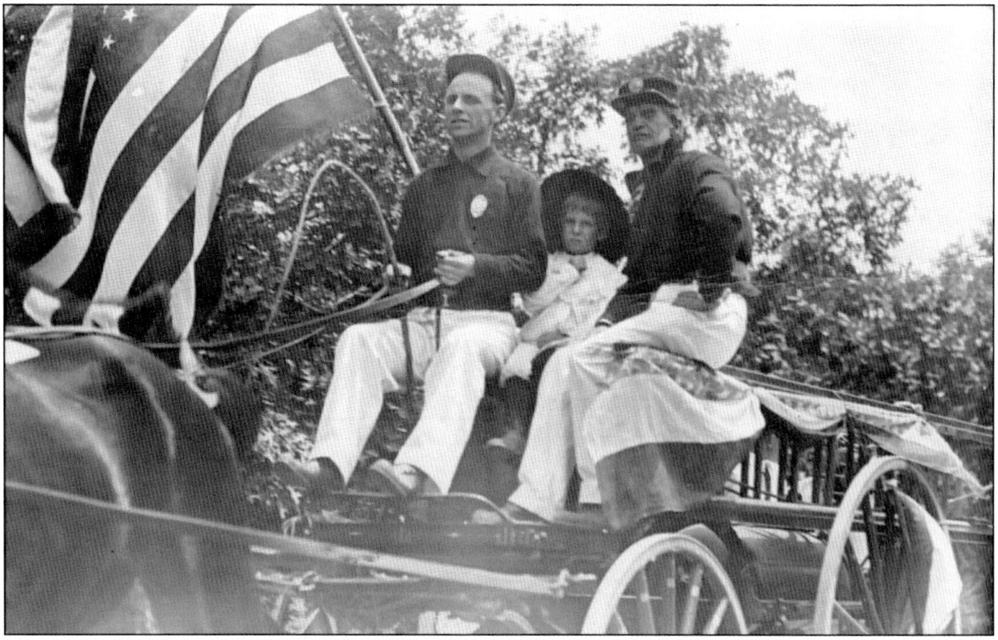

The photograph shows the horse-drawn fire wagon in the Fireman's Fair Parade in 1907. Fred Wilkison is driving, and Gustavus Devere is seated next to him. The Fireman's Fair was the most successful form of fundraising for the fire department. The fair was held at the field at the corner of Portion Road and Hawkins Avenue and was very popular with the local residents.

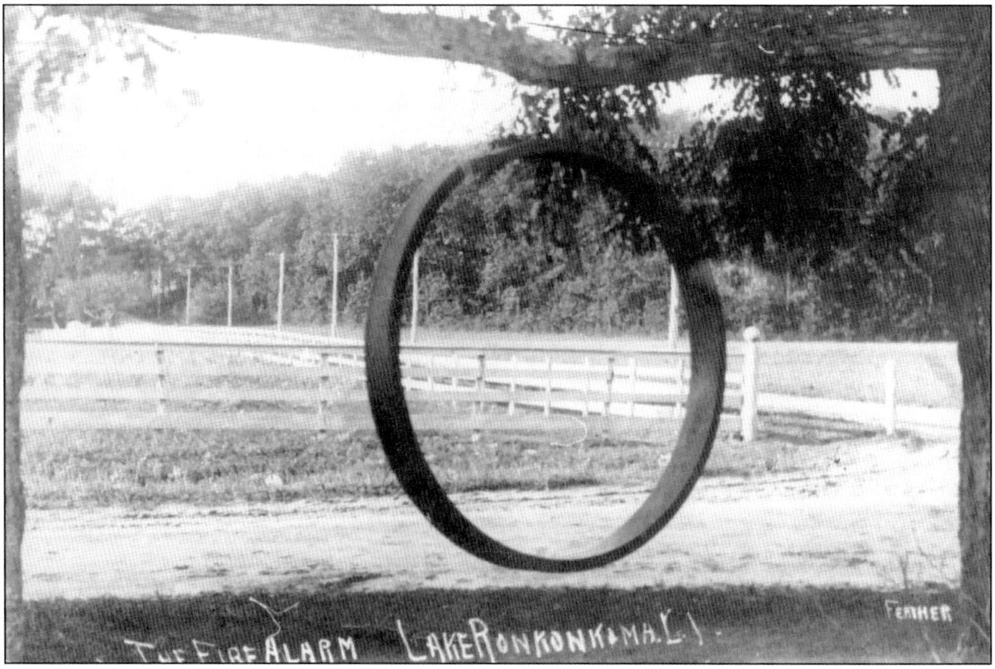

The original fire bell, shown here in 1904, was made from a locomotive tire hung from a locust tree. It stood at the corner of Hawkins Avenue and Portion Road. When struck with a hammer, it made a distinctive sound that could be heard for miles around. The original bell is now on display in front of the current firehouse on Portion Road.

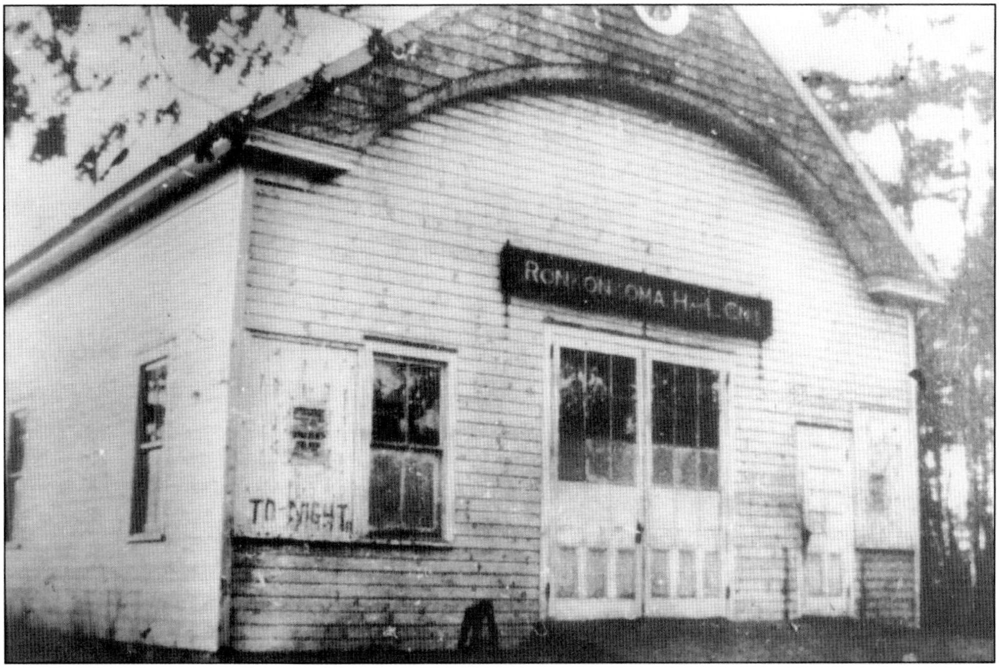

The first firehouse, shown here, was built on Hawkins Avenue and dedicated on July 4, 1906. Funds to build the firehouse were raised by donations and by dues paid by the firefighters themselves. The building was rented out to various local groups, including town churches; events such as dances and movie showings were held there. This firehouse remained in service until 1924.

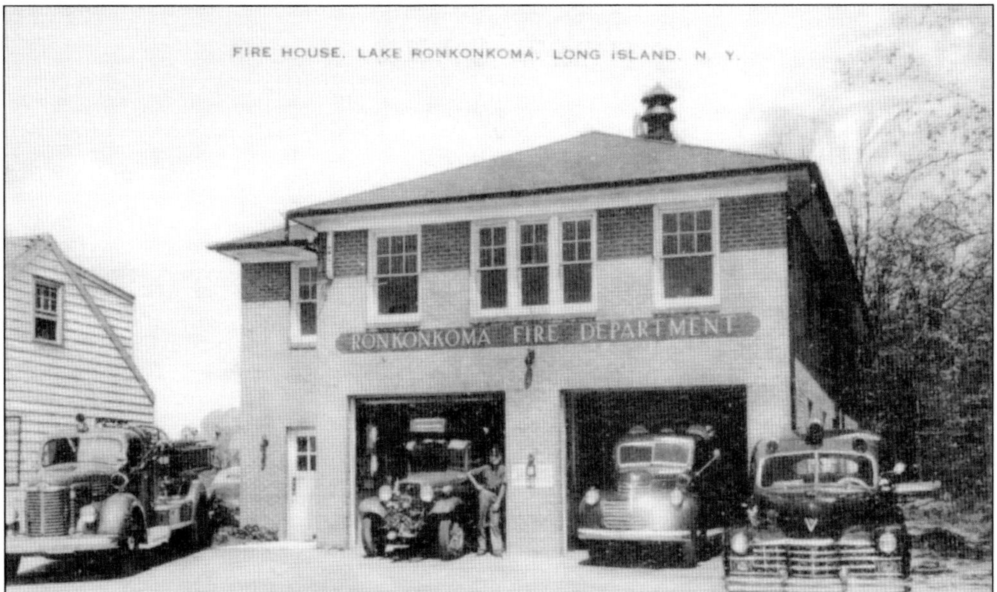

The new fire department building, shown here in the 1940s, opened on August 4, 1924, on Portion Road, just east of Hawkins Avenue. The area was growing rapidly, and the fire department building was expanded numerous times over the next five decades. In 1977, the fire department constructed a new building. The original firehouse on Hawkins Avenue was demolished in September 1978.

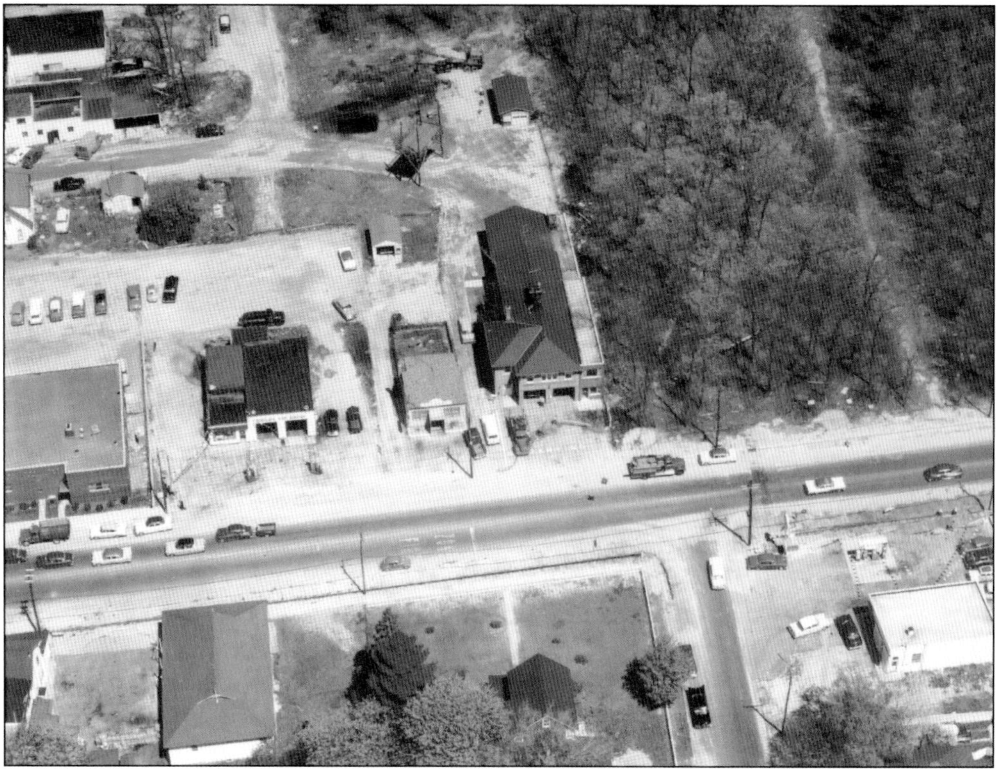

This photograph, taken May 4, 1959, shows the many additions made to the original 1924 building over three decades. The fire department's equipment and training methods were state of the art and remain so to this day. The rescue unit purchased the first Jaws of Life machine in 1972. The Ronkonkoma Fire Department was the farthest east in Suffolk County to have this equipment. (Courtesy of James Mooney.)

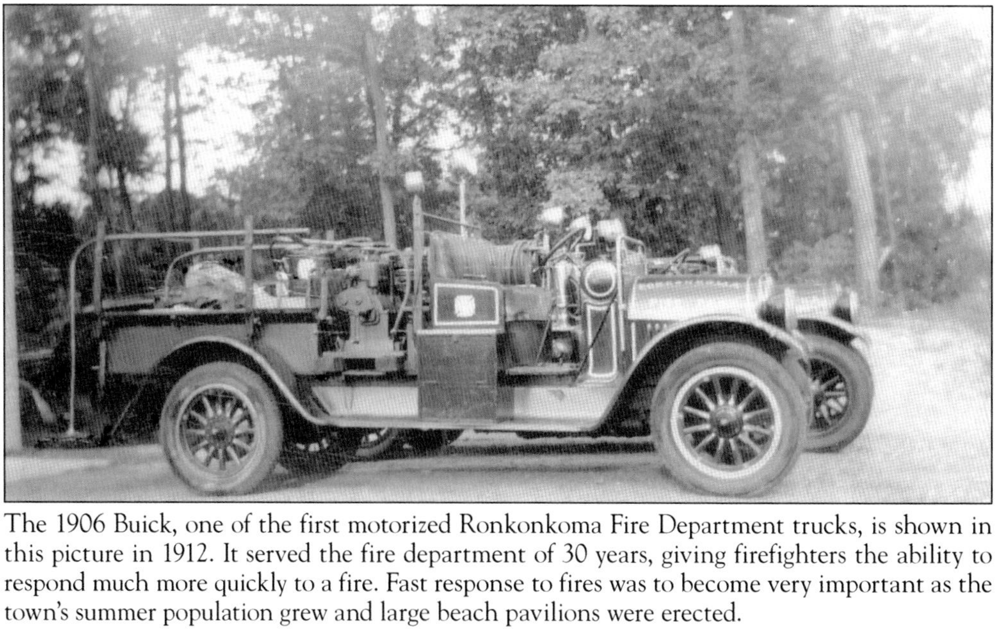

The 1906 Buick, one of the first motorized Ronkonkoma Fire Department trucks, is shown in this picture in 1912. It served the fire department of 30 years, giving firefighters the ability to respond much more quickly to a fire. Fast response to fires was to become very important as the town's summer population grew and large beach pavilions were erected.

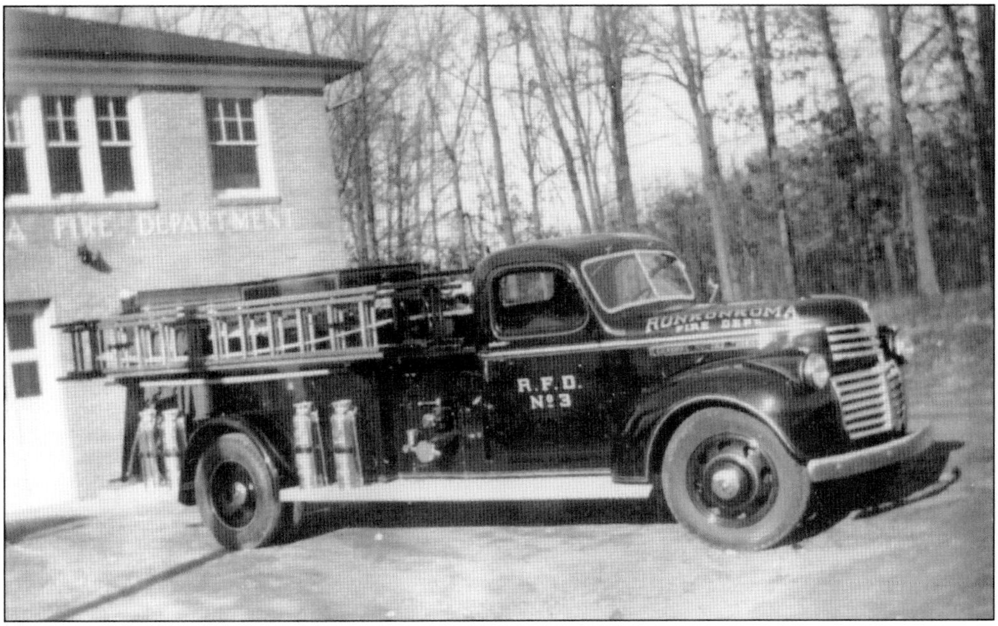

This photograph shows the 1941 GMC Pumper, one of the many new pieces of firefighting equipment purchased by the Ronkonkoma Fire Department. With thousands of extra residents in the summertime, firefighting in Ronkonkoma became a more vital service. Financial support from the townspeople assured that the firefighters would have the best training and equipment.

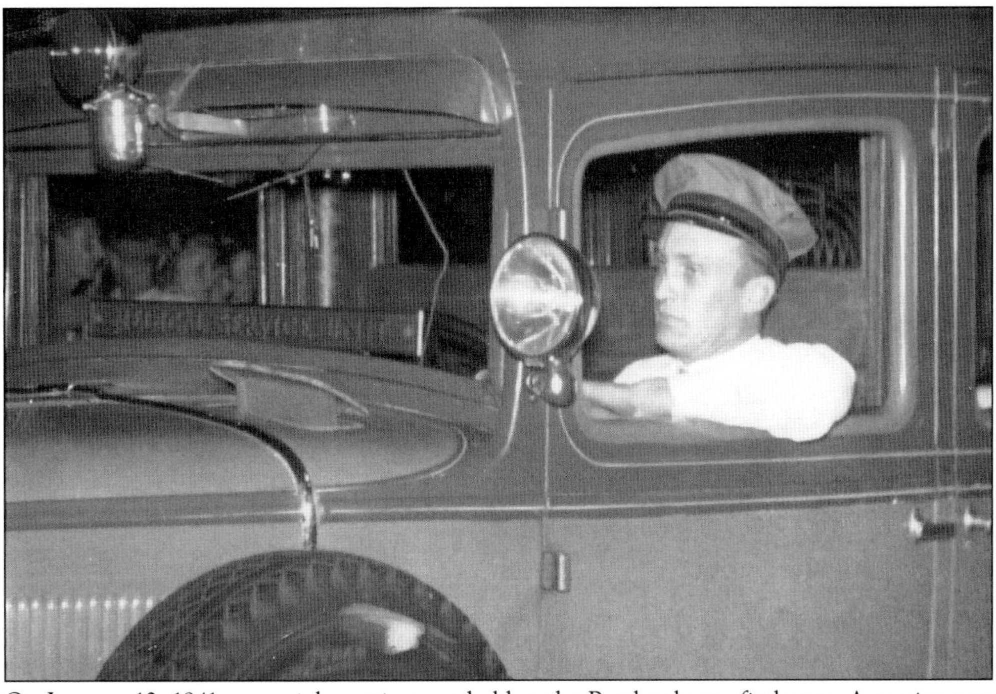

On January 10, 1941, a special meeting was held at the Ronkonkoma firehouse. A motion was made to form a medical unit and purchase an ambulance. After the sum of $150 was raised, the first ambulance was purchased—a used 1934 Nash. This 1941 photograph shows Francis Pfeifer, the first medical unit president, behind the wheel.

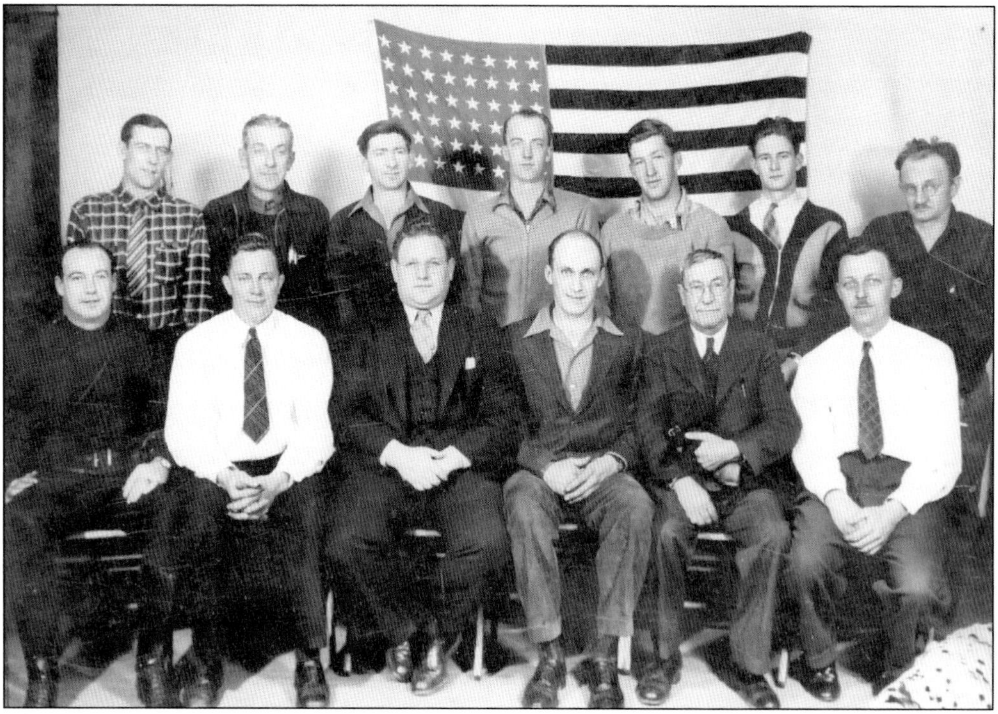

This 1941 photograph shows the charter members of the Ronkonkoma Medical Unit. The medical unit was self-supporting from its formation in 1941. The unit was absorbed into the Ronkonkoma Fire District in 1948. Dr. Walter Roettinger, shown first row, third from left, trained unit members in first-aid procedures.

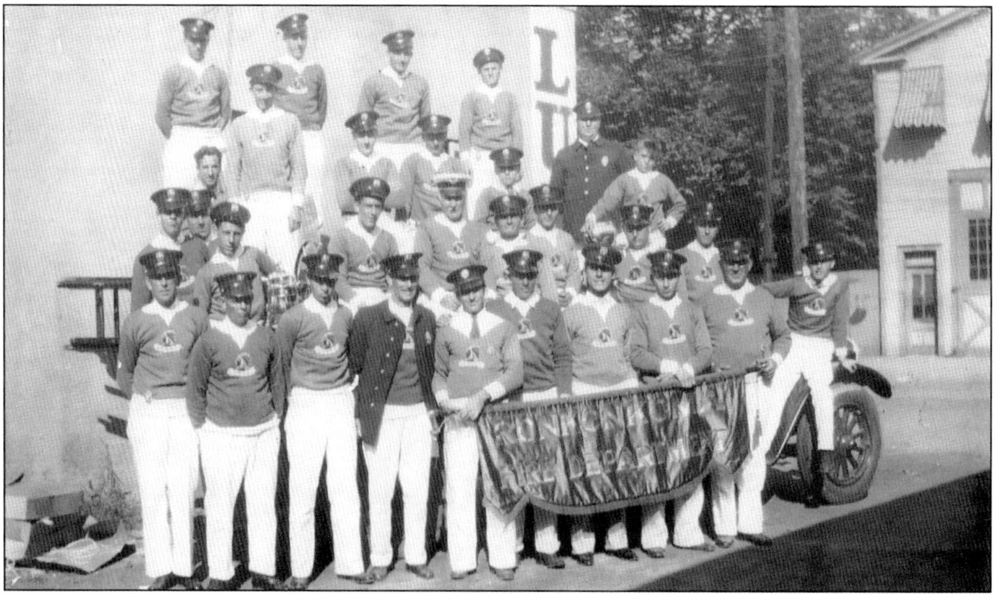

Members of the Ronkonkoma Fire Department proudly pose by their fire truck in this photograph taken September 12, 1933. The occasion was the second annual outing to the Coney Island Mardi Gras. Outings like this were one of the rewards for the hard work and risks volunteer firefighters faced.

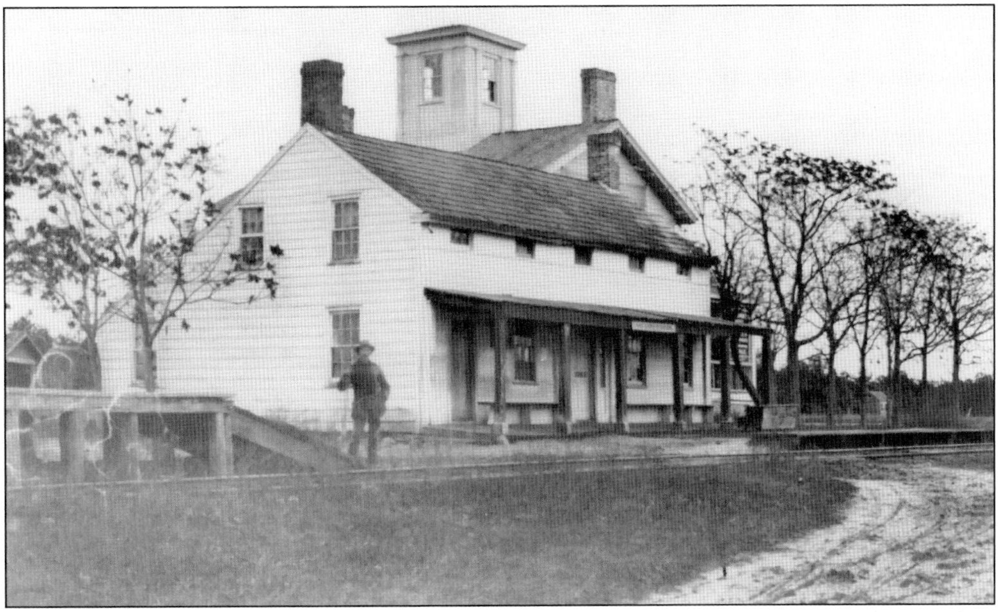

As the Long Island Rail Road extended east in 1844 to Greenport, a farmhouse on a flat plain was converted into a station house. This was called the Lake Road Station, or Lakeland Station, located at the southwest corner of Lakeland Avenue. This railroad stop helped to expose travelers to Lake Ronkonkoma, and it slowly developed into a vacation spot for wealthy New Yorkers. (Courtesy of Ron Ziel.)

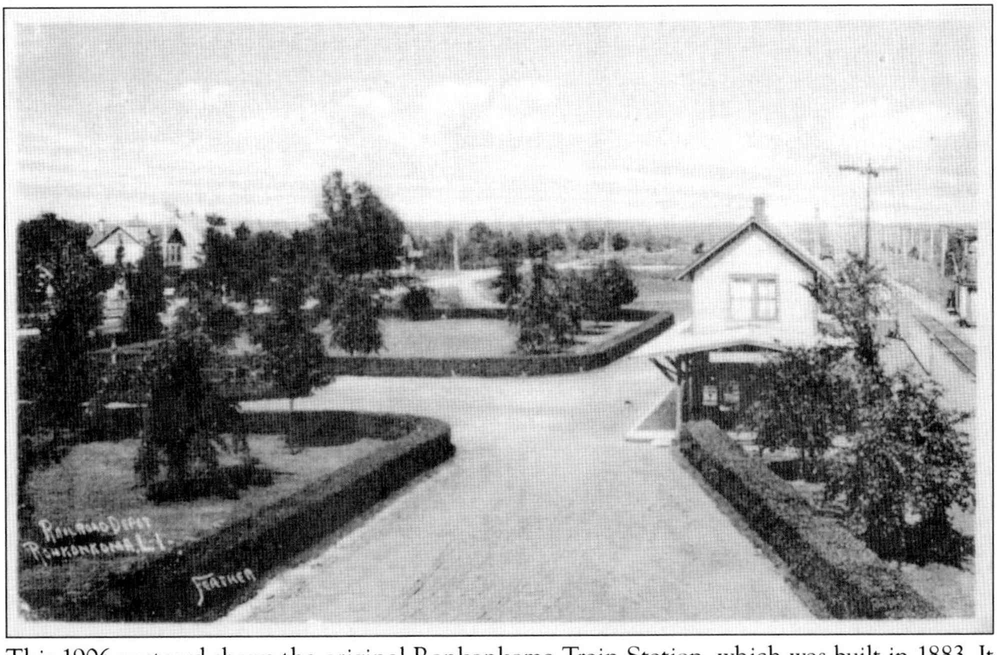

This 1906 postcard shows the original Ronkonkoma Train Station, which was built in 1883. It replaced the Lakeland Station, one mile west on Lakeland Avenue. Around 1900, the famed Broadway actress Maude Adams donated funds to landscape the property. With hedges, elm trees, and spacious lawns, its beauty would impress visitors to the town. A fire destroyed the station house on February 6, 1933.

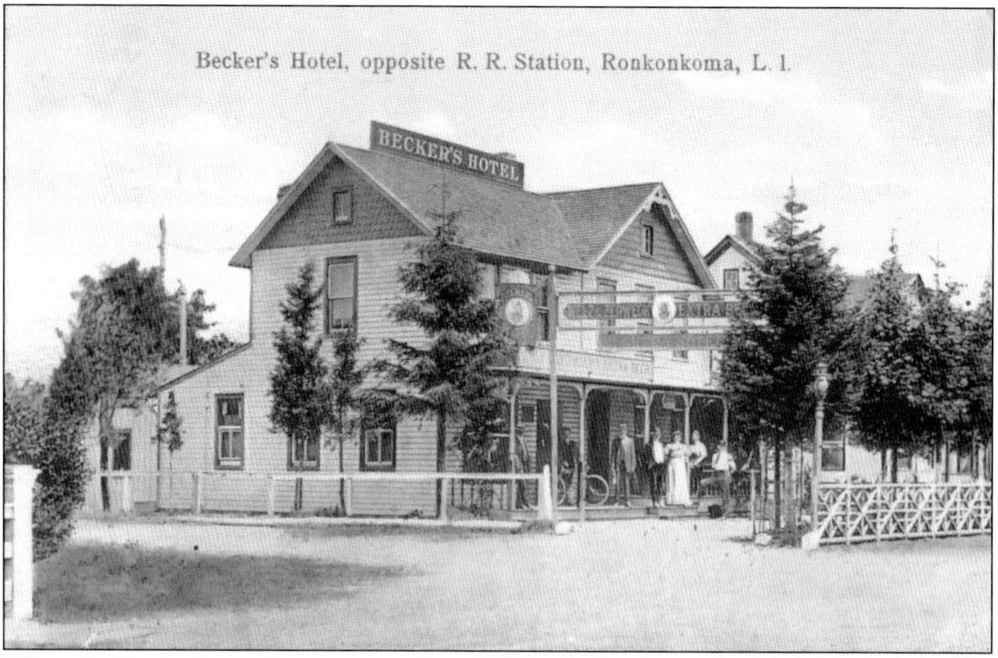

When the Ronkonkoma Station opened in 1885, hotels began to appear around it on Railroad Avenue. This lovely 1910 postcard depicts Becker's Hotel, located at the corner of Railroad Avenue and Gerrity Street. It featured comfortable rooms, fine dining, and a selection of beer, wine, and brandies for wealthy travelers visiting Lake Ronkonkoma. The corner of Ronkonkoma Avenue and Railroad Avenue became known as Union Square.

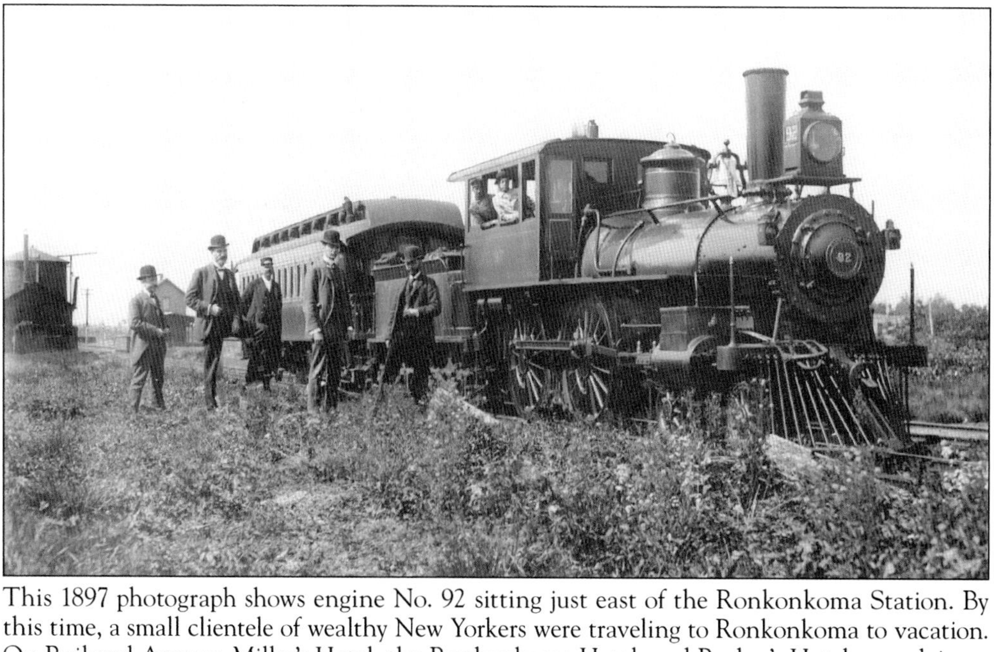

This 1897 photograph shows engine No. 92 sitting just east of the Ronkonkoma Station. By this time, a small clientele of wealthy New Yorkers were traveling to Ronkonkoma to vacation. On Railroad Avenue, Miller's Hotel, the Ronkonkoma Hotel, and Becker's Hotel were doing a booming business. Over on the lake shoreline, the large Lake Front Hotel Complex with its many buildings was flourishing. (Courtesy of Ron Ziel.)

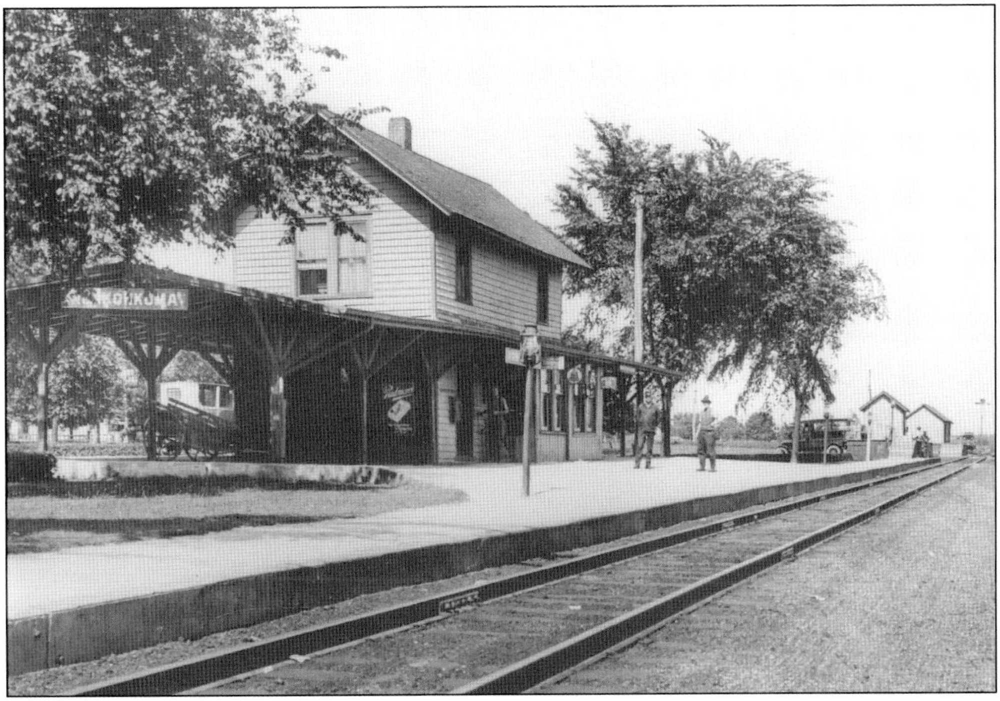

This 1922 photograph shows the platform at the Ronkonkoma Station. Gas lanterns provided lighting on the platform at night. A public telephone was available, and telegrams could be sent inside the station. The two buildings to the right in the background were to handle freight, a growing business for the railroad. (Courtesy of Ron Ziel.)

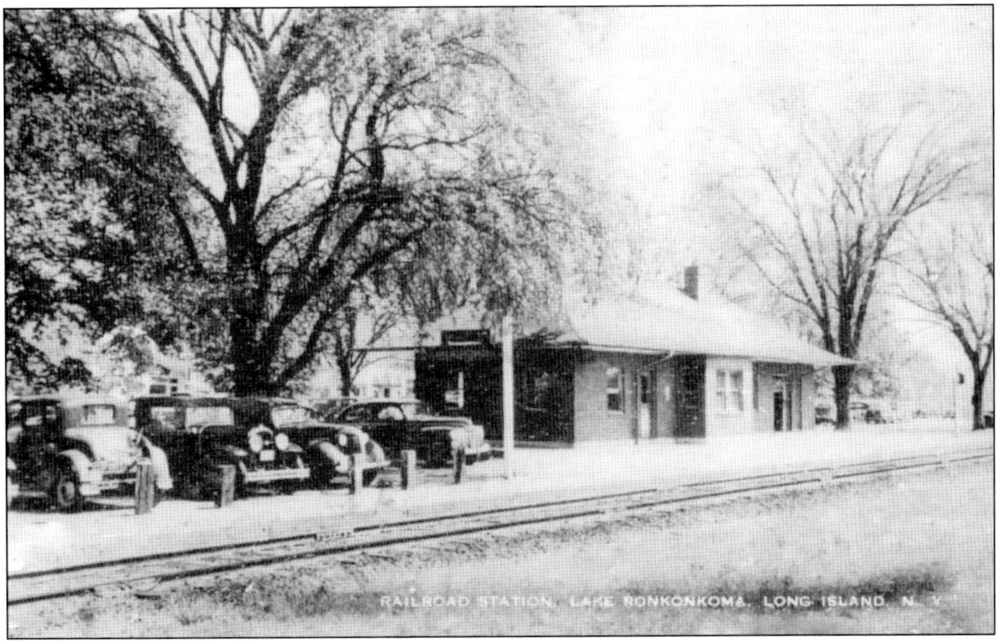

After the original train station burned down in 1933, funds were raised to build a new one. It took over three years to raise the funds and complete the work, but on August 21, 1937, the new Ronkonkoma Station was dedicated with a gala celebration at the Max Greis Parkway Inn.

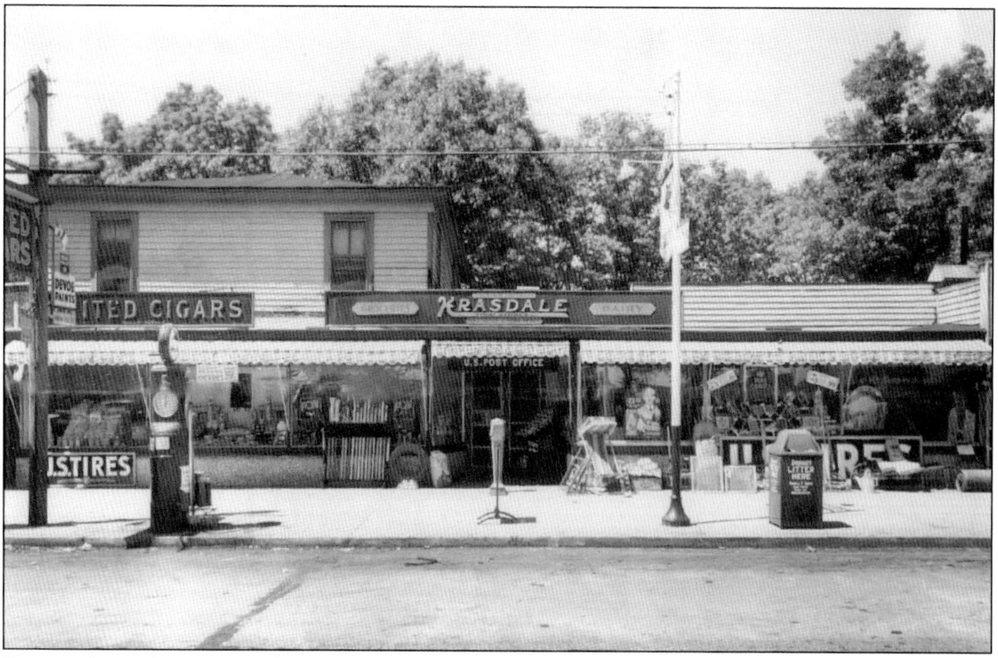

During the early 1900s, as the town grew and the railroad station became busier, a business district developed on Railroad Avenue, catering to summer visitors as well as townspeople. This 1932 photograph shows the Krasdale Food Store. Other items sold were lawn mowers, rakes, shovels, screens, watering cans, gasoline, tires, bicycles, beach chairs, paints, and toys.

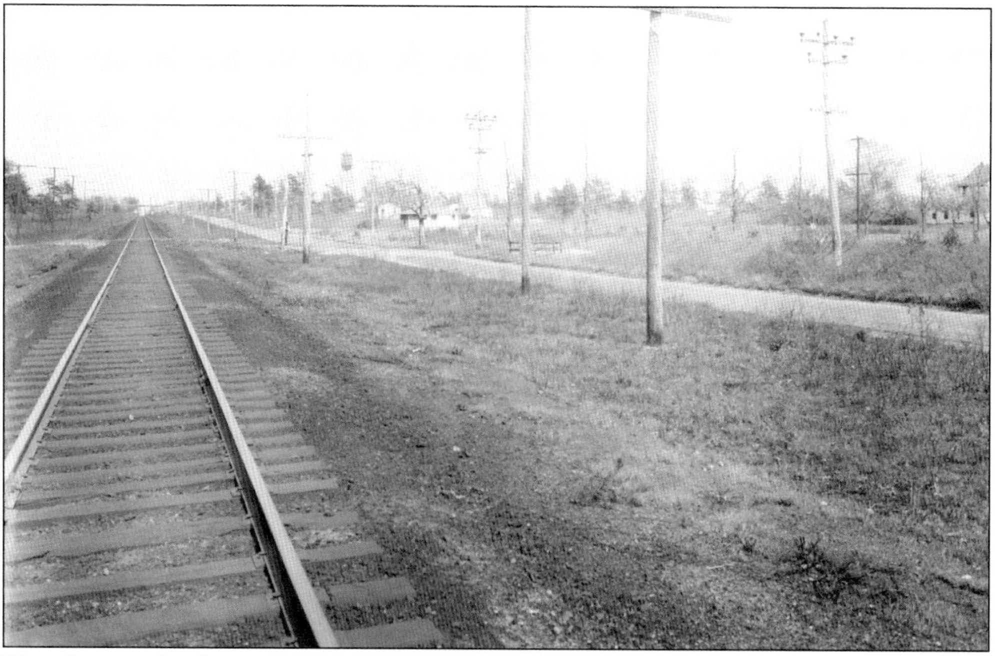

This photograph taken on May 11, 1936, shows the railroad crossing at Pond Road, looking east. In the distance, the Ronkonkoma Avenue Bridge can be seen crossing the tracks. This photograph illustrates that Ronkonkoma was still a country town, despite the booming summer tourist trade. (Courtesy of Ron Ziel.)

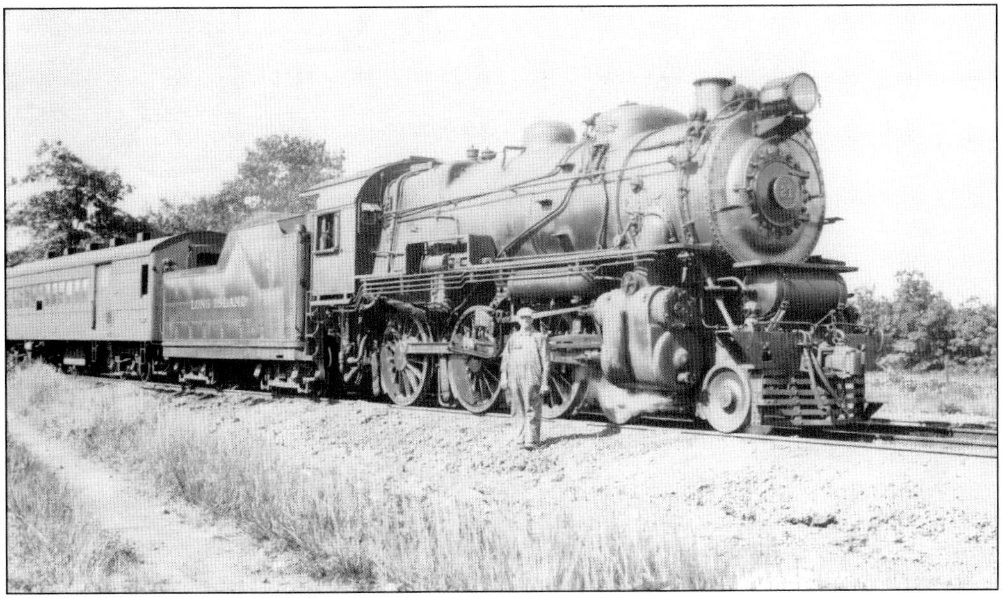

In this photograph taken on July 28, 1935, engineer and Lake Ronkonkoma resident Charles Benjamin poses next to engine No. 21, just west of the Ronkonkoma Station. When Benjamin was promoted to full engineer in 1912, he was given a Long Island Rail Road oiling can with his name embossed on it. He proudly carried it with him for the rest of his long career.

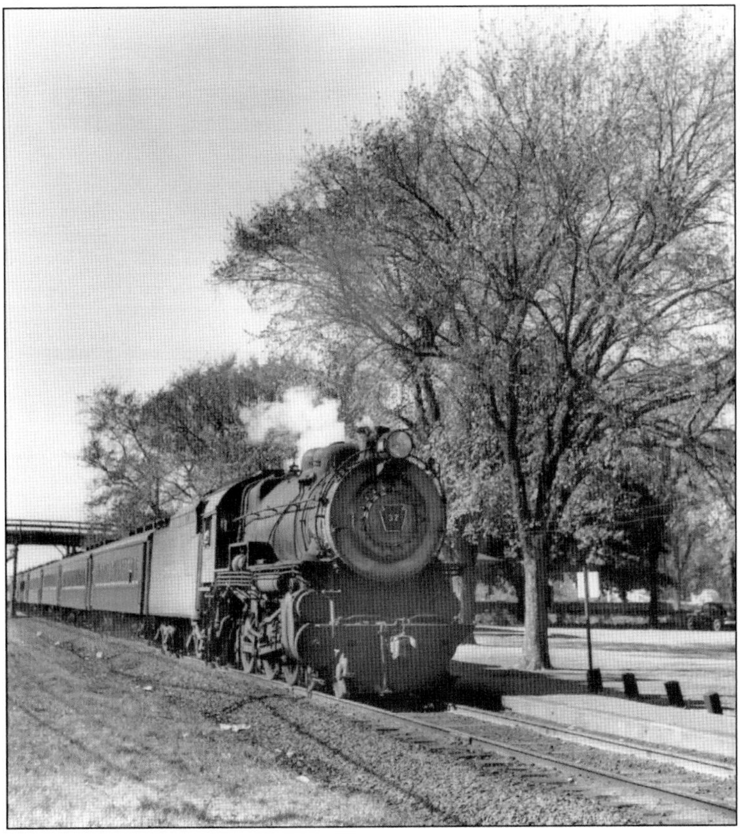

In the period following World War II, Lake Ronkonkoma underwent many changes. As soldiers returned from the war, the number of permanent residents in town grew. In this photograph from October 23, 1949, engine No. 37 crosses eastbound under the Ronkonkoma Avenue Bridge into the train station. The railroad was now a commuter line, taking workers to and from New York City. (Courtesy of Ron Ziel.)

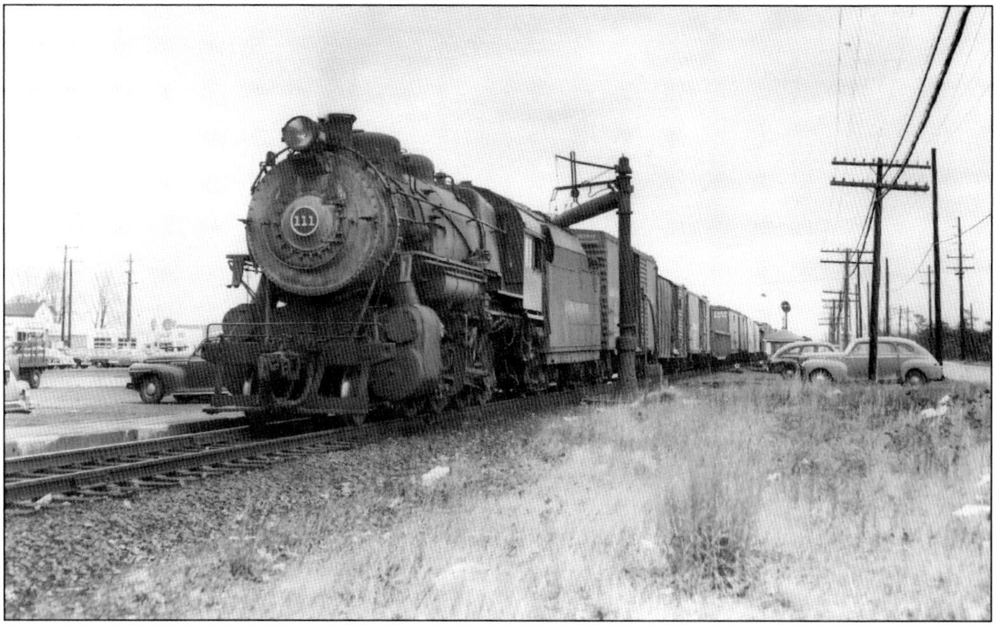

In this c. 1954 photograph, engine No. 111, with freight cars attached, takes on water at the Ronkonkoma Station. The tender of this steam engine held almost 10,000 gallons of water. The era of steam engines was ending, and by October 1955, the Long Island Rail Road replaced them with diesel locomotives. (Courtesy of Ron Ziel.)

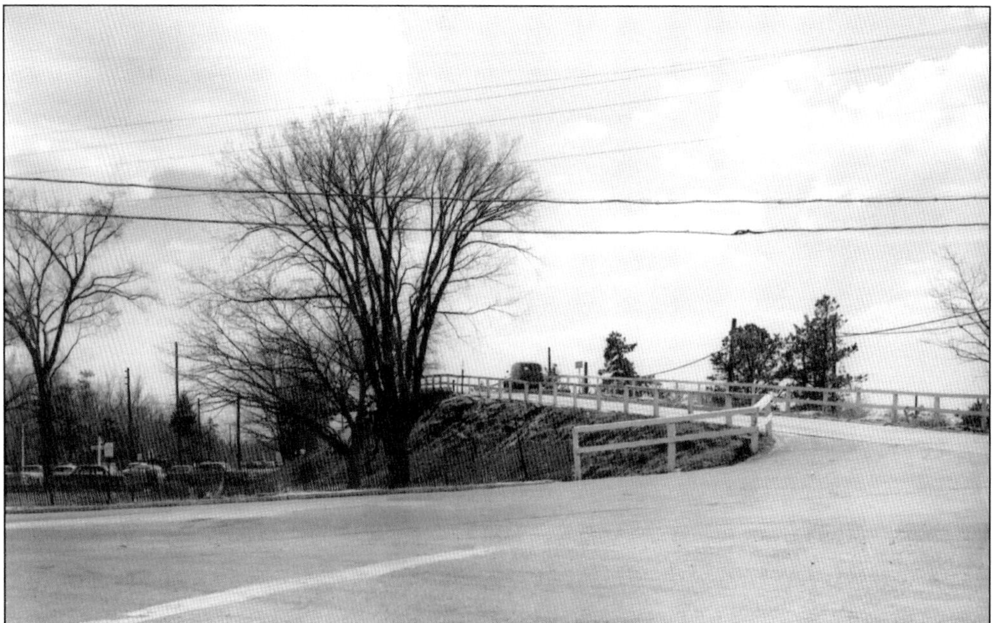

This image, dated April 4, 1961, shows the original bridge (built in 1912) over the railroad at Ronkonkoma Avenue. This bridge, which was privately built, served the community for almost a century. The steep incline of the bridge and its two narrow lanes (one lane each way) made careful navigation of the bridge a must. The bridge was replaced with a modern bridge in the 1990s. (Courtesy of James Mooney.)

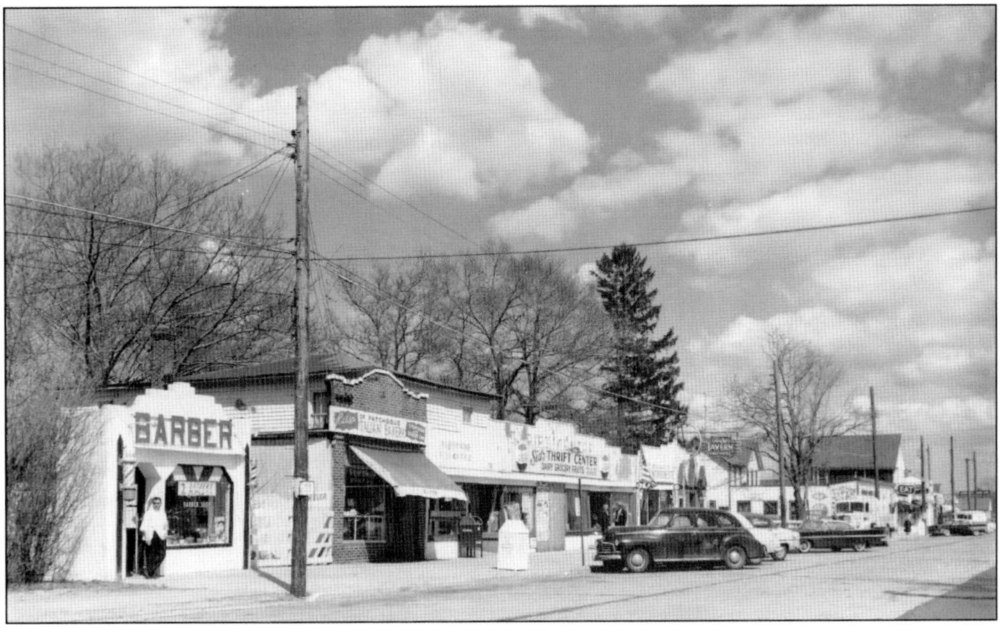

By the time these two April 1961 pictures of Railroad Avenue were taken, the Railroad Avenue business district had changed. The fancy hotels that once lined the street were now apartment buildings housing year-round residents. The fine landscaping of the Railroad Station had given way to huge parking areas to hold the many hundreds of commuters who now took the railroad to New York City to work every day. The last of the stately elm trees were cut down in early 1962 for more parking. The stores on Railroad Avenue now catered to commuters and year-round residents. The street now contained three barbershops, two luncheonettes, a bakery, and a drugstore. (Courtesy of James Mooney.)

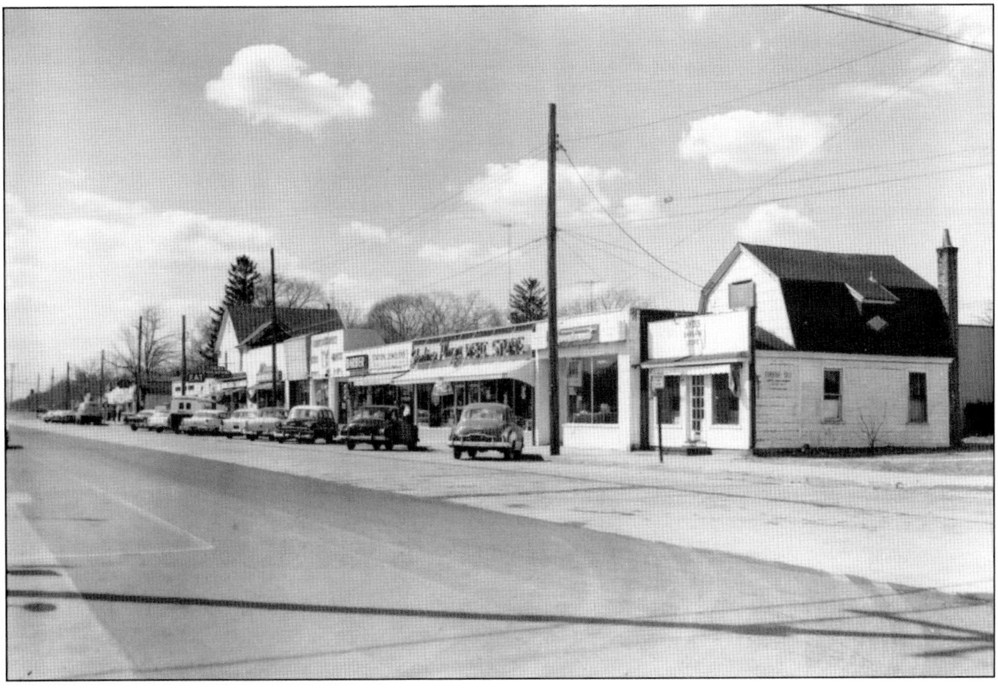

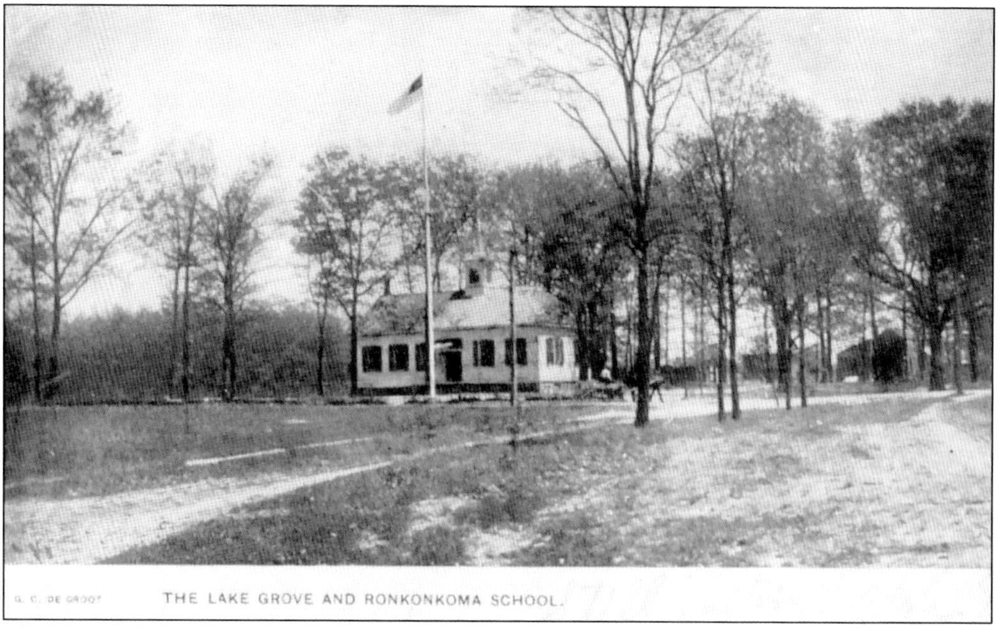

This postcard, taken c. 1911, shows the Lakeville School. The school, also called the Lake Grove and Ronkonkoma School, was located on the northeast corner of Hawkins Avenue and Smith Street. It was built in 1812 and served the area for 100 years. In 1834, it was expanded and used for meetings and prayer by the local Methodist group for the next 19 years.

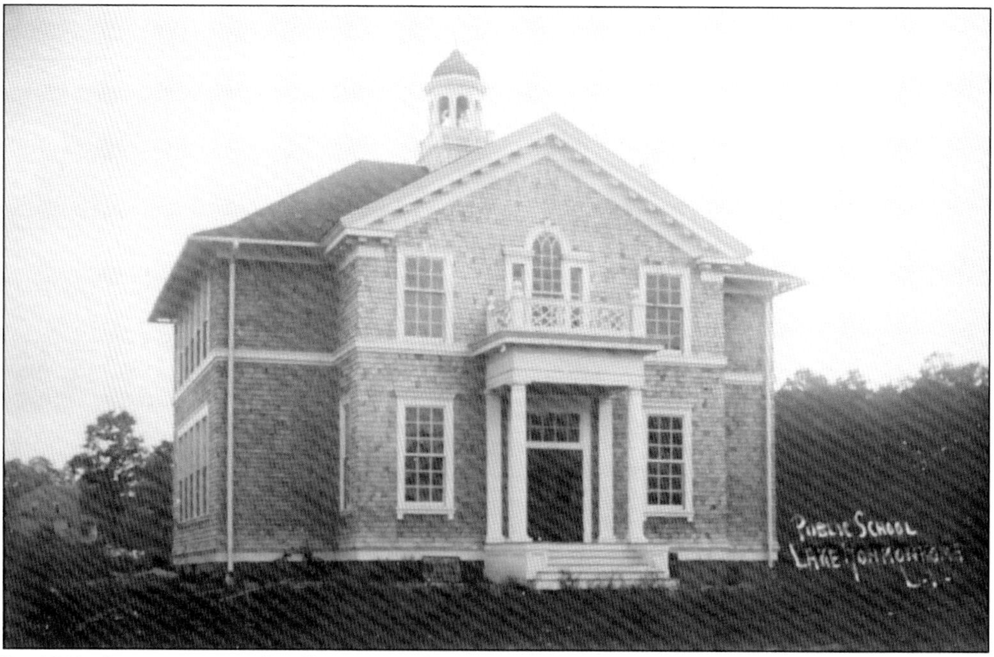

By 1911, the one-room schoolhouse was becoming too crowded. The townspeople raised funds and a new schoolhouse was built. It is shown in this c. 1912 photograph. The new school was located at the northeast corner of Hawkins Avenue and School Street. It served the area until a fire destroyed it on January 4, 1946. It was replaced by the Gatelot Avenue School, which is still used today.

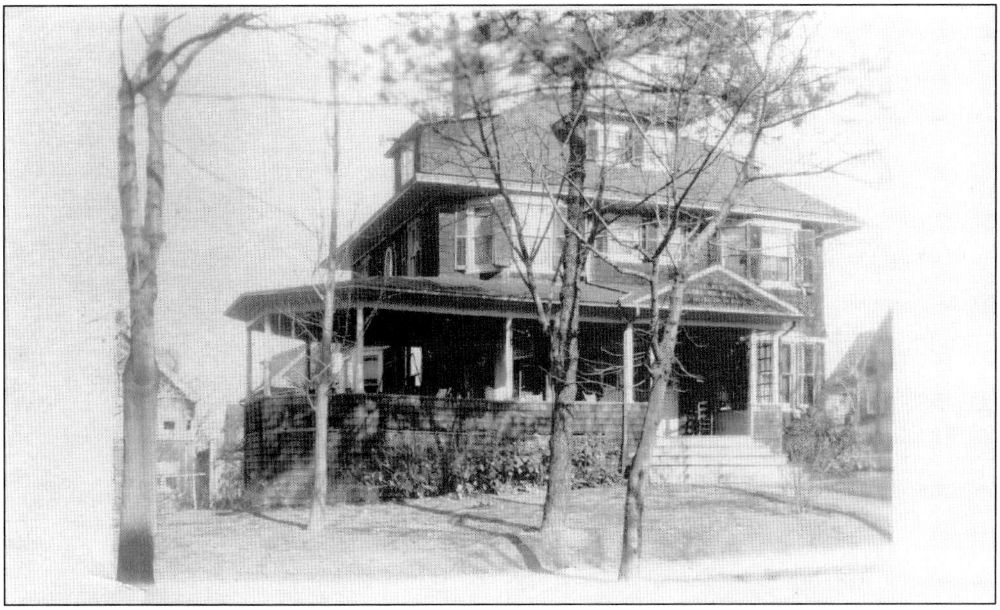

This 1931 photograph shows the Cleary School for the Deaf, which was founded in 1926 by Genevieve Cleary and her sister Rosemary Cleary at their summer home at Lake Ronkonkoma. The school is located on the north side of Smithtown Boulevard, west of Gibbs Pond Road. The Cleary sisters also operated the Peter Pan Camp at the same location.

On March 31, 1945, Fr. Francis H. Liller was granted permission to make plans for a new school and auditorium at St. Joseph's Parish. The finished school and auditorium were officially dedicated on June 18, 1950. This aerial view from February 11, 1959, shows the school on the left and the auditorium to its right, located on Church Street, east of Pond Road. (Courtesy of James Mooney.)

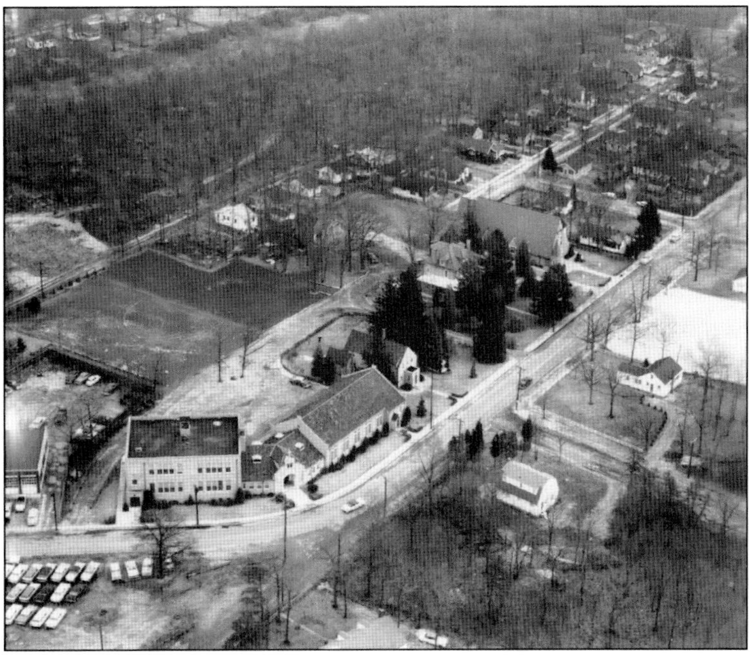

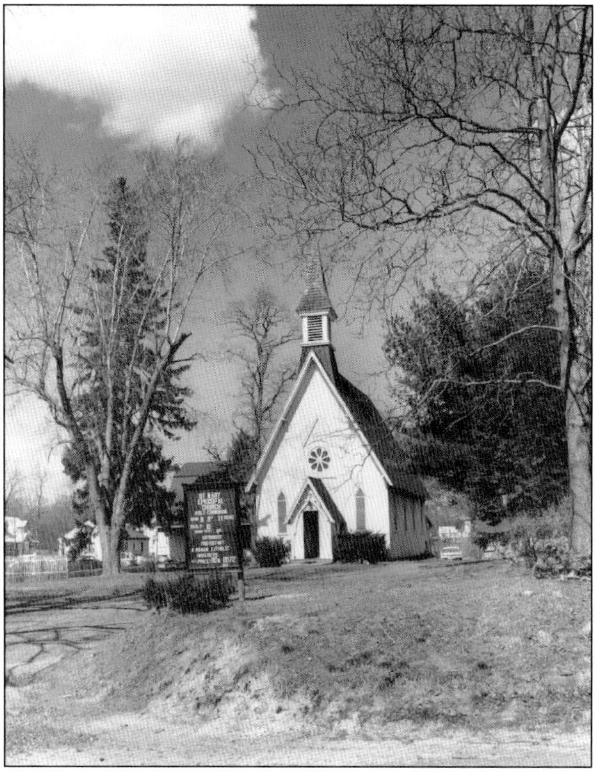

St. Mary's Episcopal Church, dedicated on December 24, 1867, is shown in an April 5, 1961, photograph. The church was built on the north side of Lake Shore Road on land donated by John Henry Puleston. He was a former member of the British Parliament. The church served the community until 1971, when it was deconsecrated and demolished to make way for a new building. (Courtesy of James Mooney.)

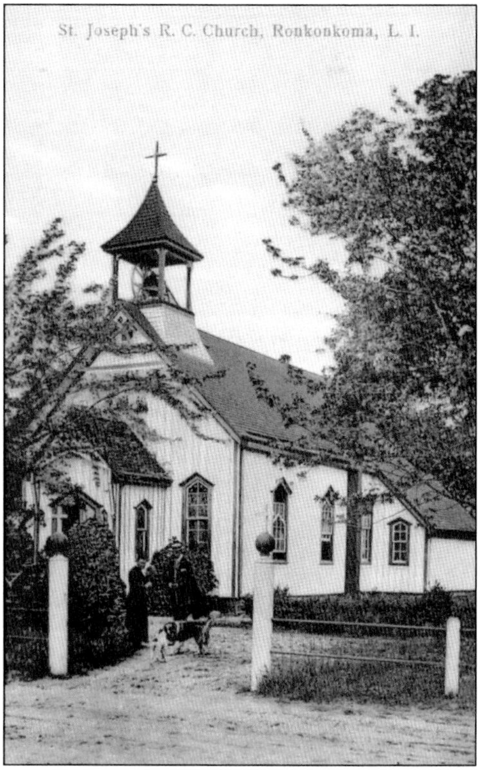

This beautiful 1912 postcard shows the original St. Joseph's Church located on Church Street, east of Portion Road. The church was dedicated on June 22, 1884, and operated as a mission until 1901, when it became a full-fledged parish. The congregation could not support the church, and after three months, it again became a mission. After nine years, in 1910 it permanently became a full-fledged parish.

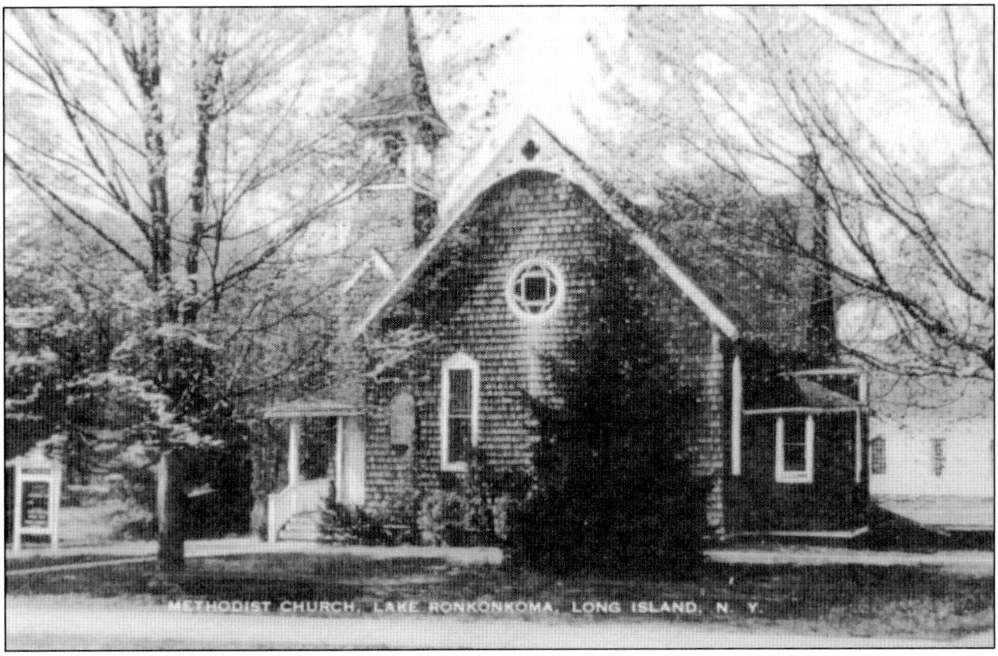

This postcard from 1948 shows the Methodist Church of Lake Ronkonkoma. Opening day was on October 20, 1907, and it was located on the northwest corner of Hawkins Avenue and Smith Street. By 1954, the growing congregation made it necessary to enlarge the church. The consecration of the enlarged church was held on April 24, 1955.

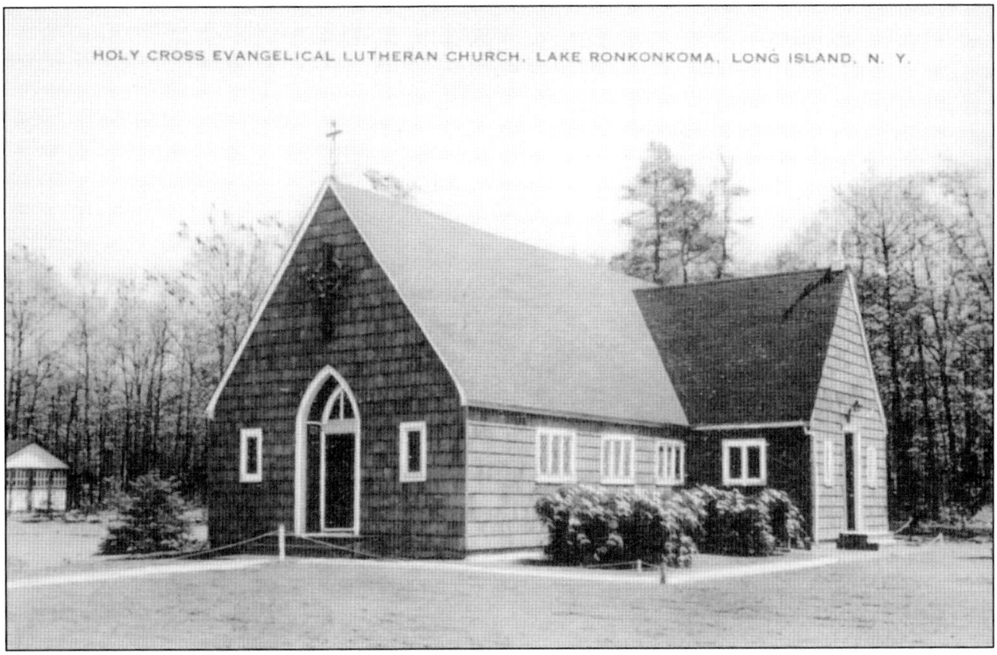

The Holy Cross Lutheran Church, located on the southeast corner of Hawkins Avenue and Lakewood Road, was dedicated on February 6, 1949. This 1950 postcard shows the original church. The congregation grew rapidly, and by 1954, a fund drive was under way to expand the facility. The new wing was dedicated on September 8, 1957.

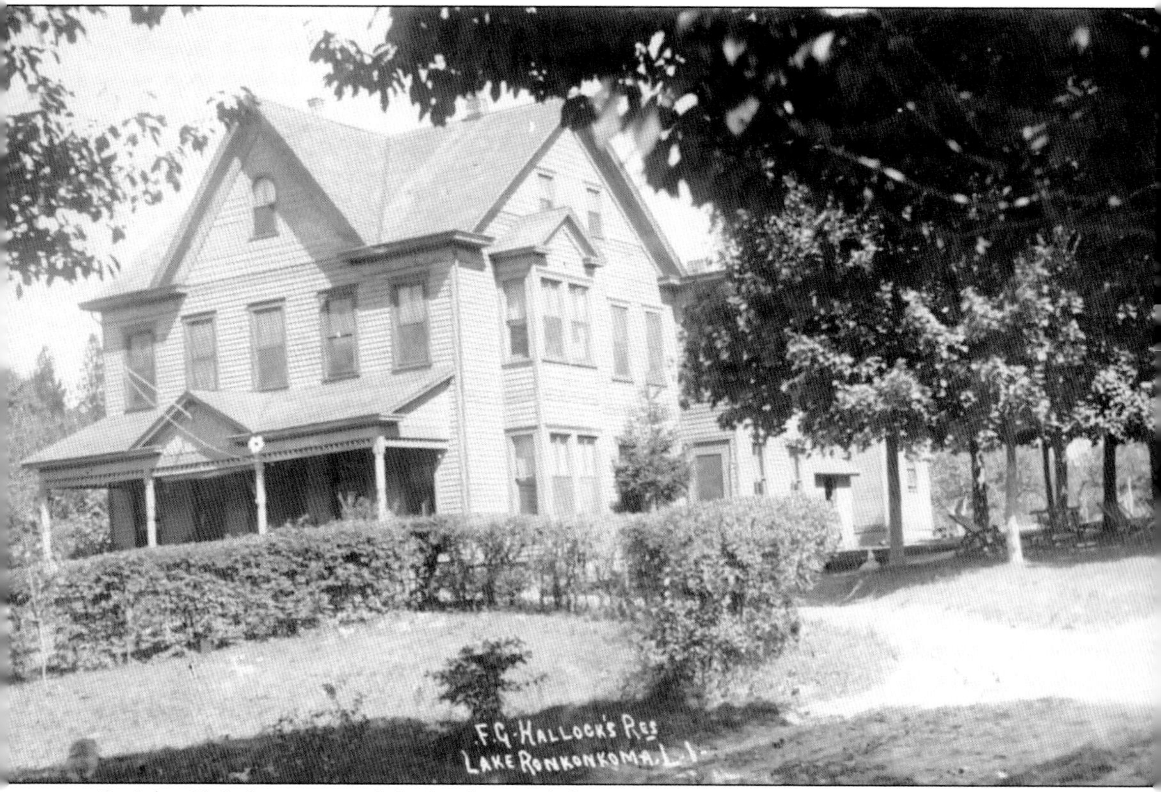

Sir John H. Puleston owned the land around the 1870s–1880s. He was called back to Parliament in England. He then sold the land to a lady from London who came and had an octagonal house built. In a few years, there was a fire, rendering it useless. She then sold the home to Fitz-Greene Hallock in 1887. Hallock used the ruins and incorporated it into a barn. The home was built north of the barn in 1888, on seven acres of land. The home was modeled after a Hallock house built in Orient, New York. Hallock was married to Cassie Rolston in 1882. They had four daughters and one son, William Merritt Hallock, who died in World War I. On the property there is the main house, a water tank shed, and a chicken coop. Katherine Hallock, the last surviving daughter, donated the house to the Lake Ronkonkoma Historical Society in 1995.

Six

Present-Day Lake Ronkonkoma

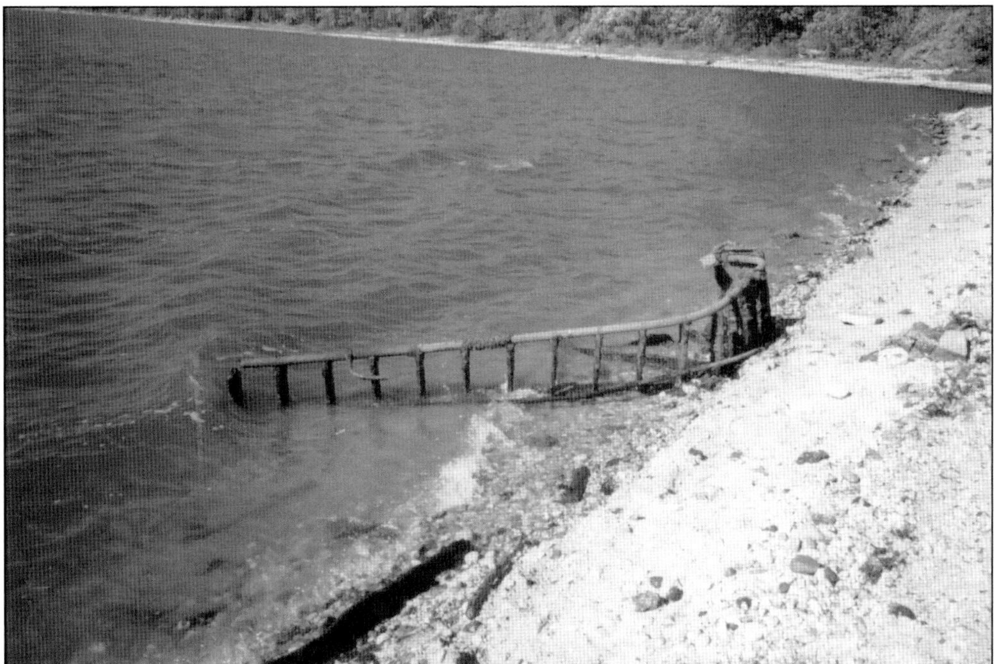

From the 1970s into the 1980s, more families were moving into the area. There were problems with an increase in pollution and bacteria levels in the lake. This picture shows a ladder that would have been used for a waterslide at the Lake View Inn during the 1960s. Recently, there have been major cleanups in and around the lake.

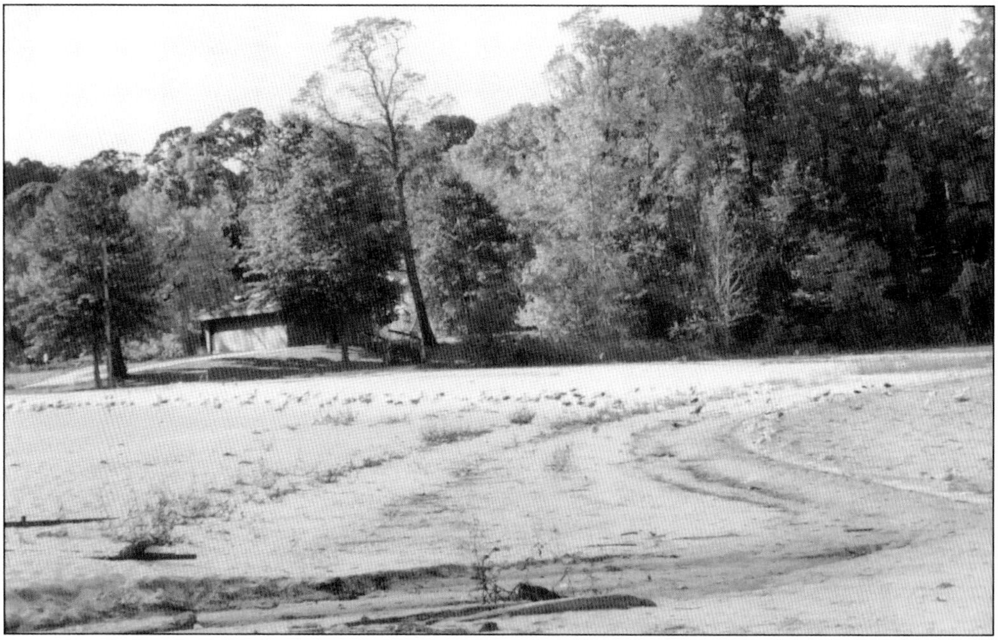

This photograph shows a cool autumn morning in October 2002, looking at the southernmost tip of the lake. At this time, there was plenty of beach to enjoy. The water was much lower than in recent years. The Hollywood Pavilion would have been located in the back center of the picture. The Green Pavilion would have been situated in the foreground to the left. (Courtesy of Keith Oswald.)

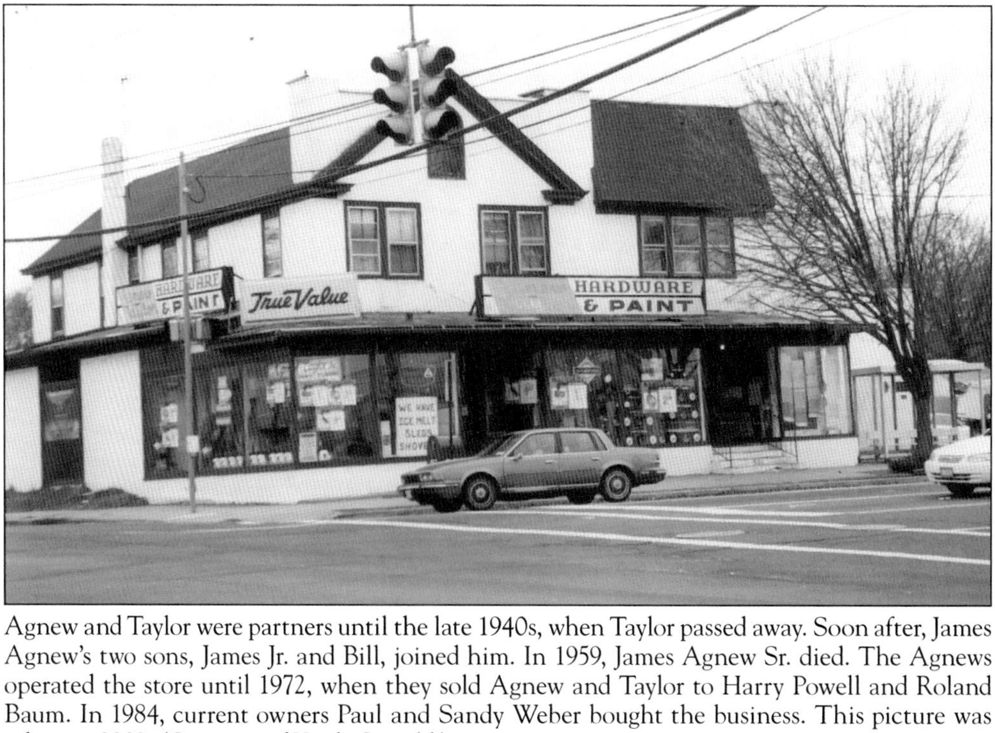

Agnew and Taylor were partners until the late 1940s, when Taylor passed away. Soon after, James Agnew's two sons, James Jr. and Bill, joined him. In 1959, James Agnew Sr. died. The Agnews operated the store until 1972, when they sold Agnew and Taylor to Harry Powell and Roland Baum. In 1984, current owners Paul and Sandy Weber bought the business. This picture was taken in 2002. (Courtesy of Keith Oswald.)

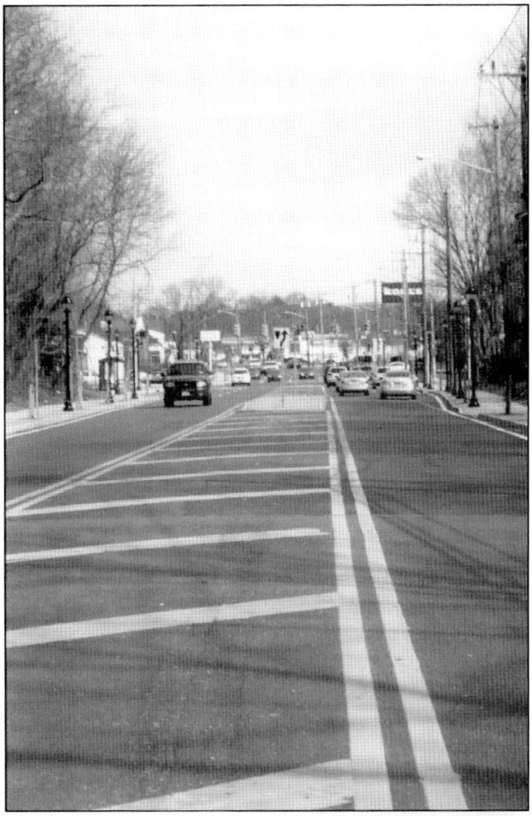

This is Portion Road (CR16) looking east in March 2011. Now that construction is complete, the new features included are a new bike lane, continuous sidewalks on both sides of the road, brick paving between the curb and the sidewalk, street trees adjacent to the curb, new bus shelters, pedestrian crossing signals, several median islands, and decorative streetlights. (Courtesy of Keith Oswald.)

This photograph looks east towards the Rosevale Avenue and Motor Parkway (CR 67) intersection. The road behind the traffic lights is Lake Drive. The Petit Trianon would have been at the end of Lake Drive and on the shoreline of the lake. Behind this photograph is the Lake Hills Community. This picture was taken on June 18, 2011. (Courtesy of Keith Oswald.)

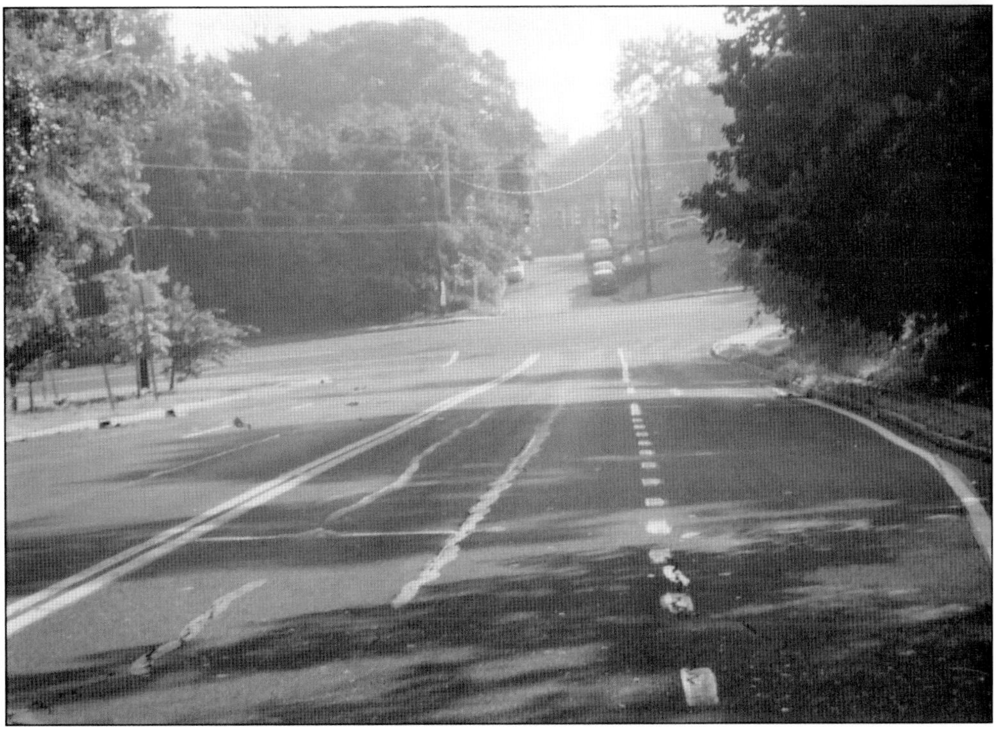

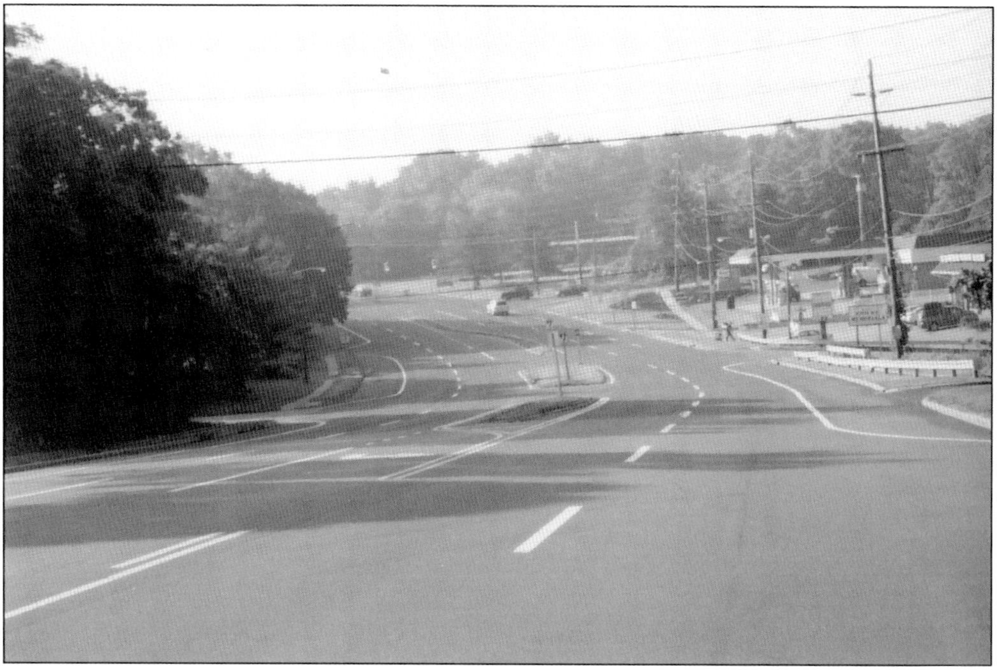

This is a view from the middle of Rosevale Avenue (CR 93) on June 18, 2011, facing south. Lake Ronkonkoma is through the trees on the left. Rosevale Avenue and Motor Parkway are at the intersection in the background. Continue driving southeast on CR 93, and Rosevale Avenue becomes Ocean Avenue. (Courtesy of Keith Oswald.)

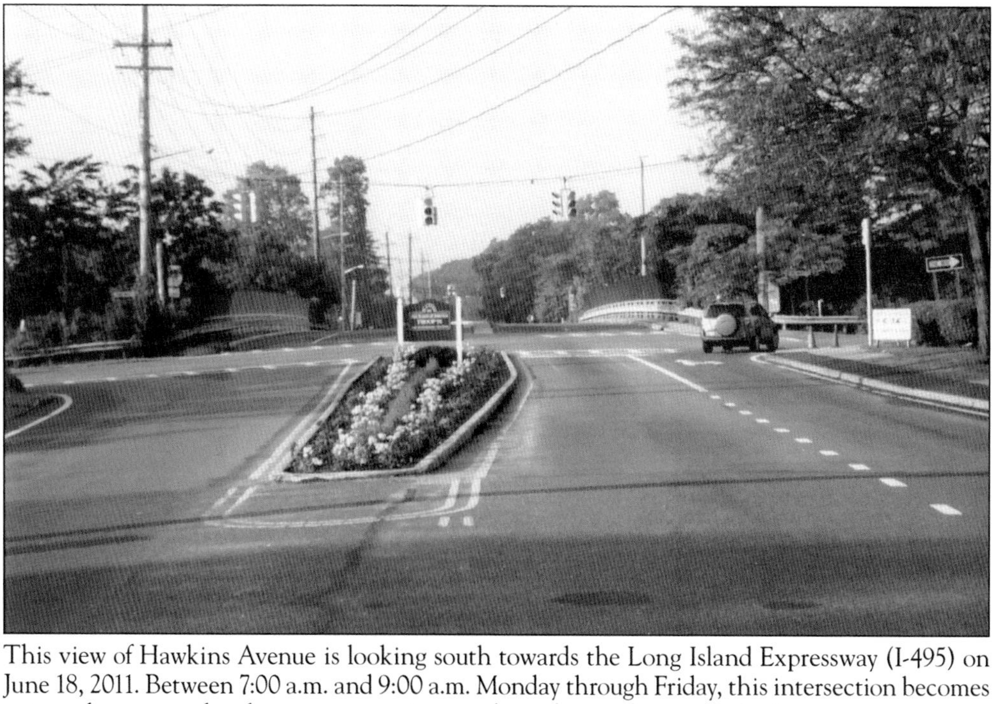

This view of Hawkins Avenue is looking south towards the Long Island Expressway (I-495) on June 18, 2011. Between 7:00 a.m. and 9:00 a.m. Monday through Friday, this intersection becomes extremely congested with commuters going westbound towards New York City. The photographs on page 74 show the same view 46 years earlier. (Courtesy of Keith Oswald.)

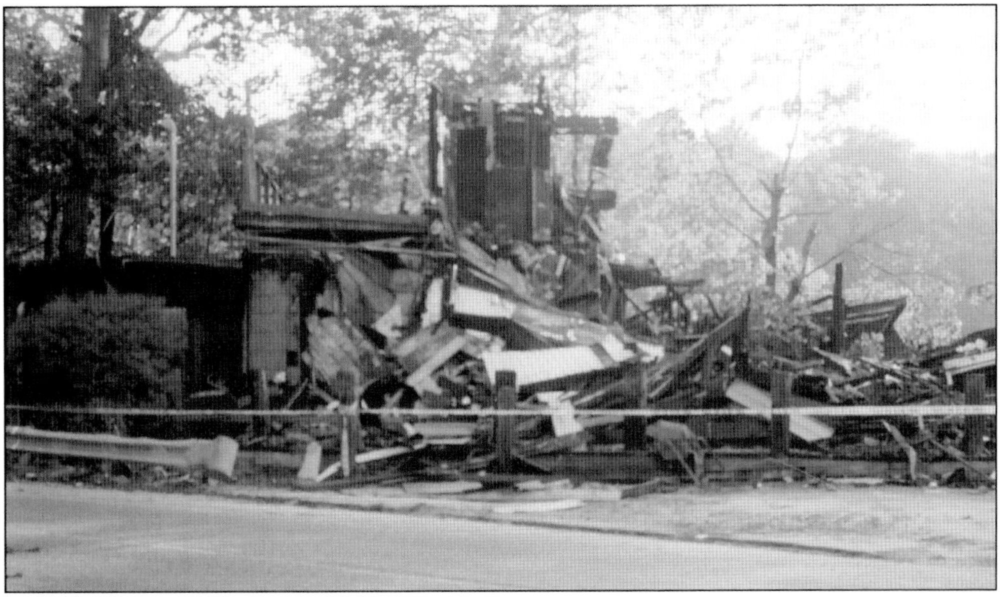

One of the last landmarks to disappear around the lake was Rugen's, also known as Indian Hill Café and Hoyt's Casino, on Lake Shore Road. In 1974, a club named Jack's opened; it was renamed in 1978 as KISS. In the mid-1980s, a club named Sand Pebbles came into existence. This photograph on June 18, 1994, shows the remains of Sand Pebbles after a mysterious fire. (Courtesy of Helen Hethy Mulvihill.)

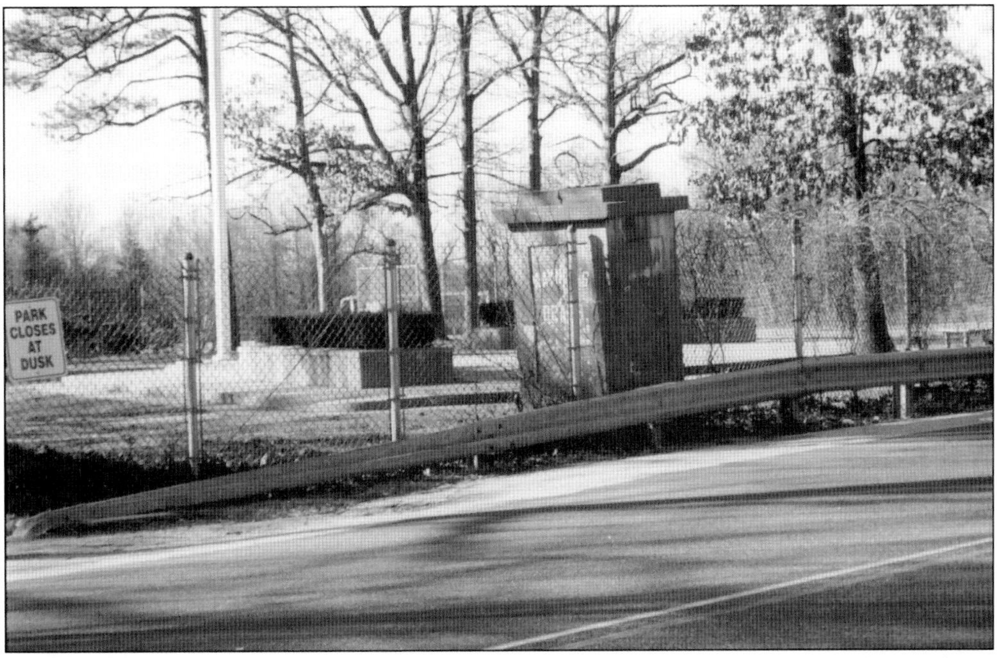

In 2002, plans were in the making to revitalize Raynor's Park. Up until this time, graffiti, garbage, and vandalism have taken their toll on the area. This picture was taken from the Ronkonkoma Avenue entrance in October 2002. The large pillar says "Raynor's Beach" and dates back to the 1930s. Since then, the park has improved dramatically. The pillar though was destroyed. (Courtesy of Keith Oswald.)

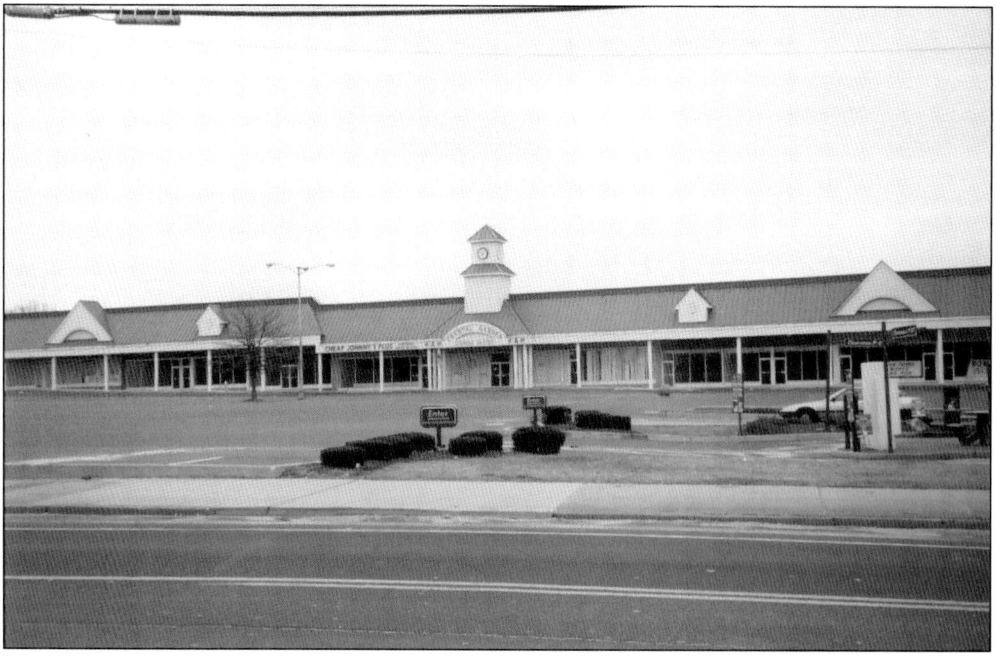

This is the Lake Shore Commons shopping center on the south side of Portion Road in October 2002. In 1959, this was the first shopping center in Lake Ronkonkoma. Some of the original stores were as follows: Grand Union, a movie theater (with a bowling alley downstairs); Woolworths; LILCO Office; a post office; dry cleaners; Buy Rite Liquors; a stationery store; and a jeweler to the left of the post office. (Courtesy of Keith Oswald.)

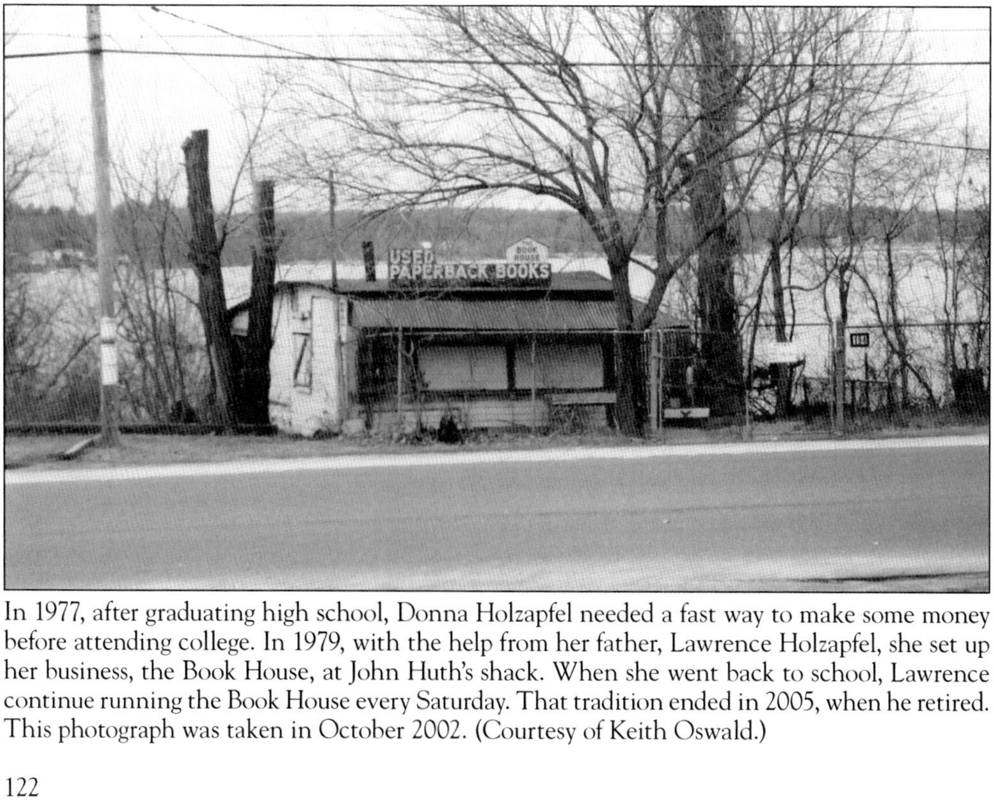

In 1977, after graduating high school, Donna Holzapfel needed a fast way to make some money before attending college. In 1979, with the help from her father, Lawrence Holzapfel, she set up her business, the Book House, at John Huth's shack. When she went back to school, Lawrence continue running the Book House every Saturday. That tradition ended in 2005, when he retired. This photograph was taken in October 2002. (Courtesy of Keith Oswald.)

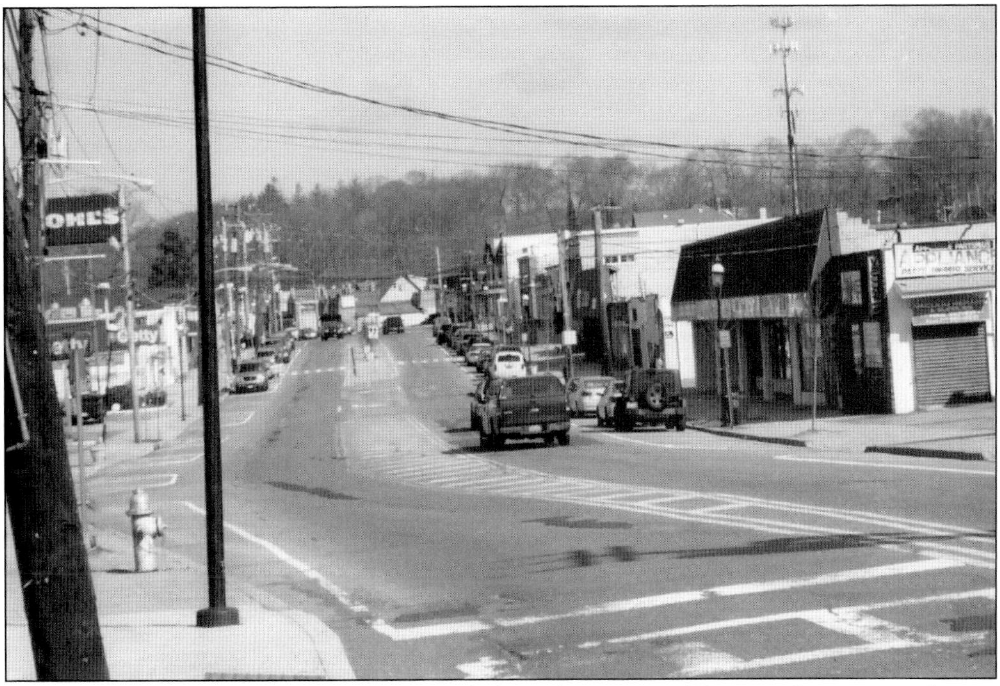

This view of Hawkins Avenue looking north from the corner of Division Street was taken in March 2011. The intersection in the background is Hawkins Avenue and Portion Road. To the left is one of the entrances to the Kohl's shopping center. Across the street is Bruno's Village restaurant and bar. (Courtesy of Keith Oswald.)

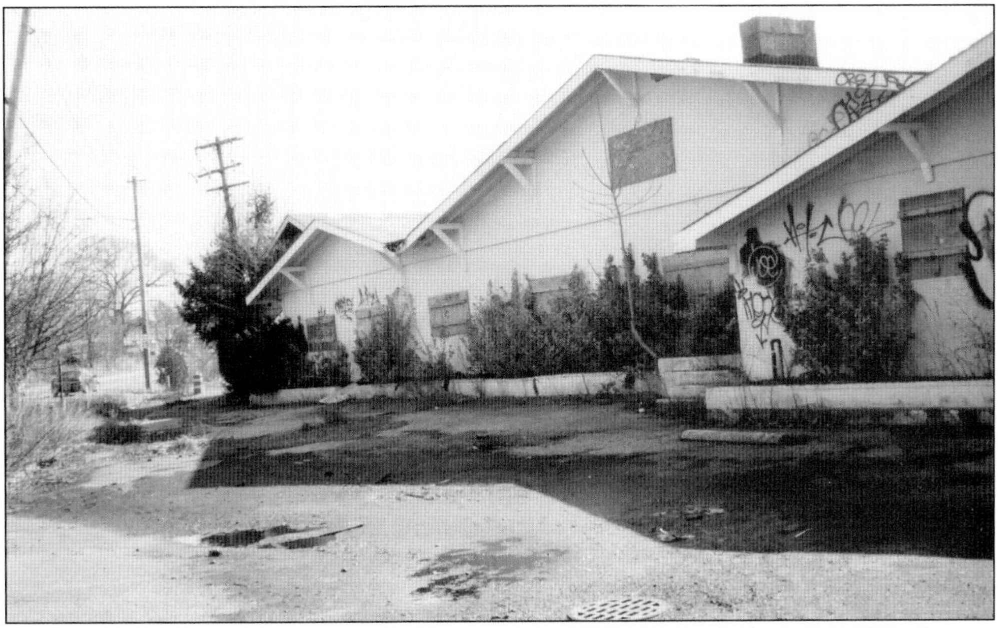

The Bavarian Inn is seen here in March 2011. Currently, the 12th district Suffolk County legislator, John M. Kennedy Jr., has been working to obtain funding and seek out a plan for a county purchase of the land. Kennedy wants to transform the area into a county park. (Courtesy of Keith Oswald.)

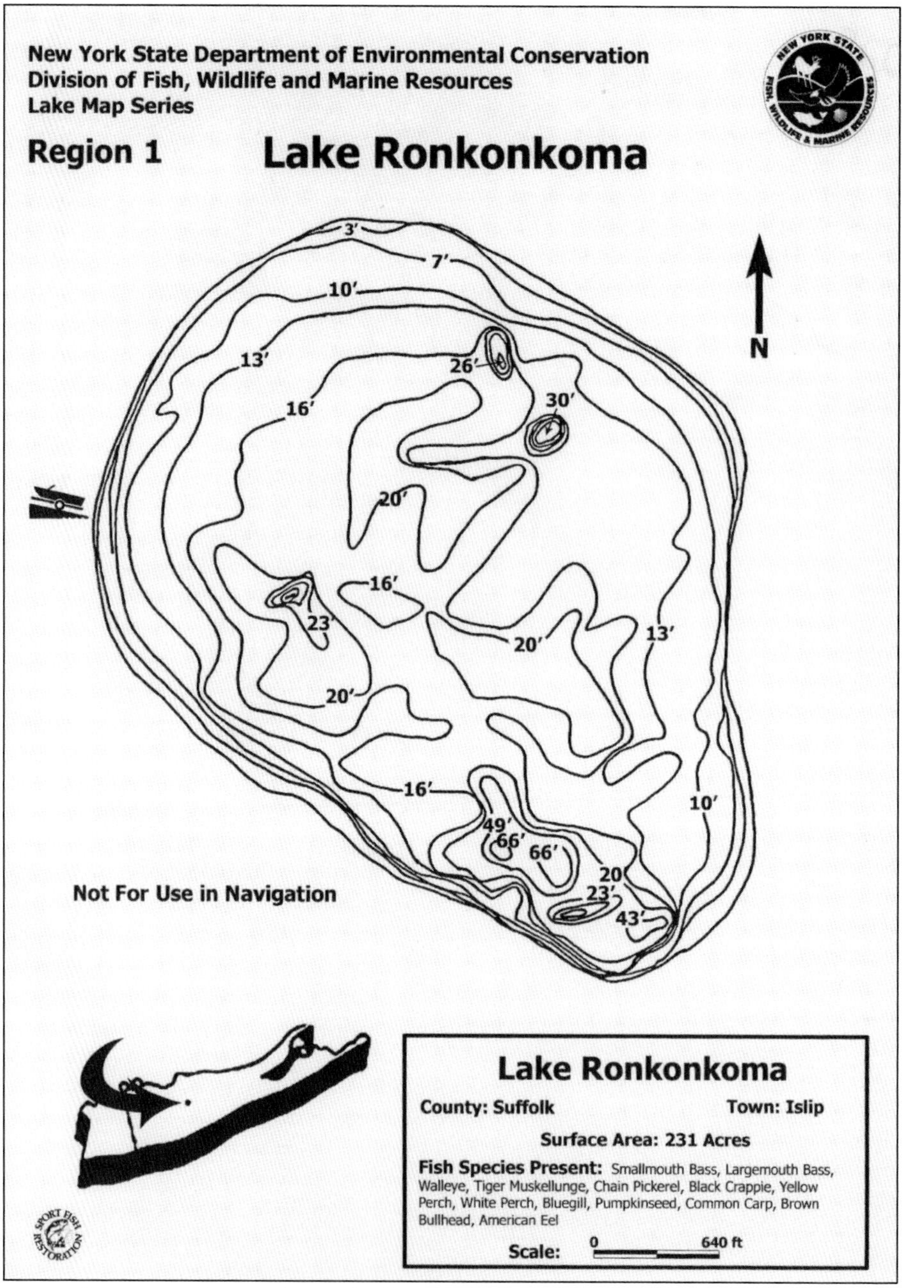

There was always speculation that Lake Ronkonkoma was bottomless. Stories circulated from the 1700s and 1800s that men would drop as much as 1,000 feet of heavily weighted fishing line into the deep holes of the southwestern section of the lake. There was a story about a wagon that disappeared into one of the holes and was later discovered in the Great South Bay. Another rumor was that a whirlpool would form in the middle of the lake and drag people down into the bottomless hole, never to be seen again. In the early 20th century, diving expeditions were made to determine how deep the lake actually is. The New York State Department of Environmental Conservation put together this map of Lake Ronkonkoma in 2010. The map shows the depth of the lake. The southwest corner of the lake depicts the deepest section of Lake Ronkonkoma.

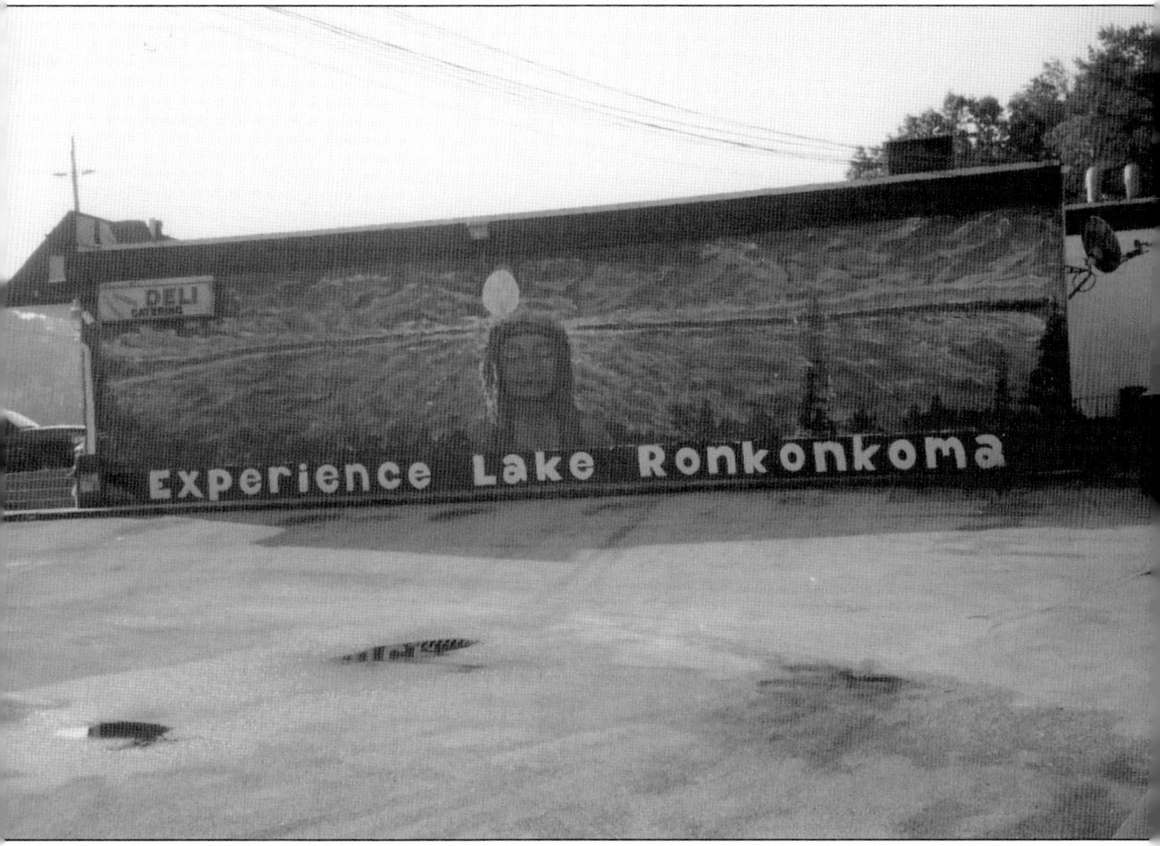

The photograph was taken in June 2011. Many people are intrigued with the myth and folklore of Princess Ronkonkoma, who belonged to the Setauket Indian tribe. During the mid-1600s, Ronkonkoma fell in love with a settler named Hugh Birdsall. He lived in a log cabin near the Connetquot River. On moonlit nights, Ronkonkoma would make her way through the forest and watch Birdsall through the trees. One night, Birdsall could not sleep and paced back and forth in front of his cabin. The beads in Ronkonkoma's hair caught the light of the full moon and revealed her presence. Birdsall saw her and fell in love with Ronkonkoma immediately. Her father, though, forbade the marriage and told his daughter never to see Birdsall again. For seven years, the two lovers continued their affair. Ronkonkoma would paddle her canoe to the middle of the lake and float back a piece of birch bark, embedded with a note of longing. Birdsall would wait at the edge of the water for the piece of bark. (Courtesy of Janet Rischbieter.)

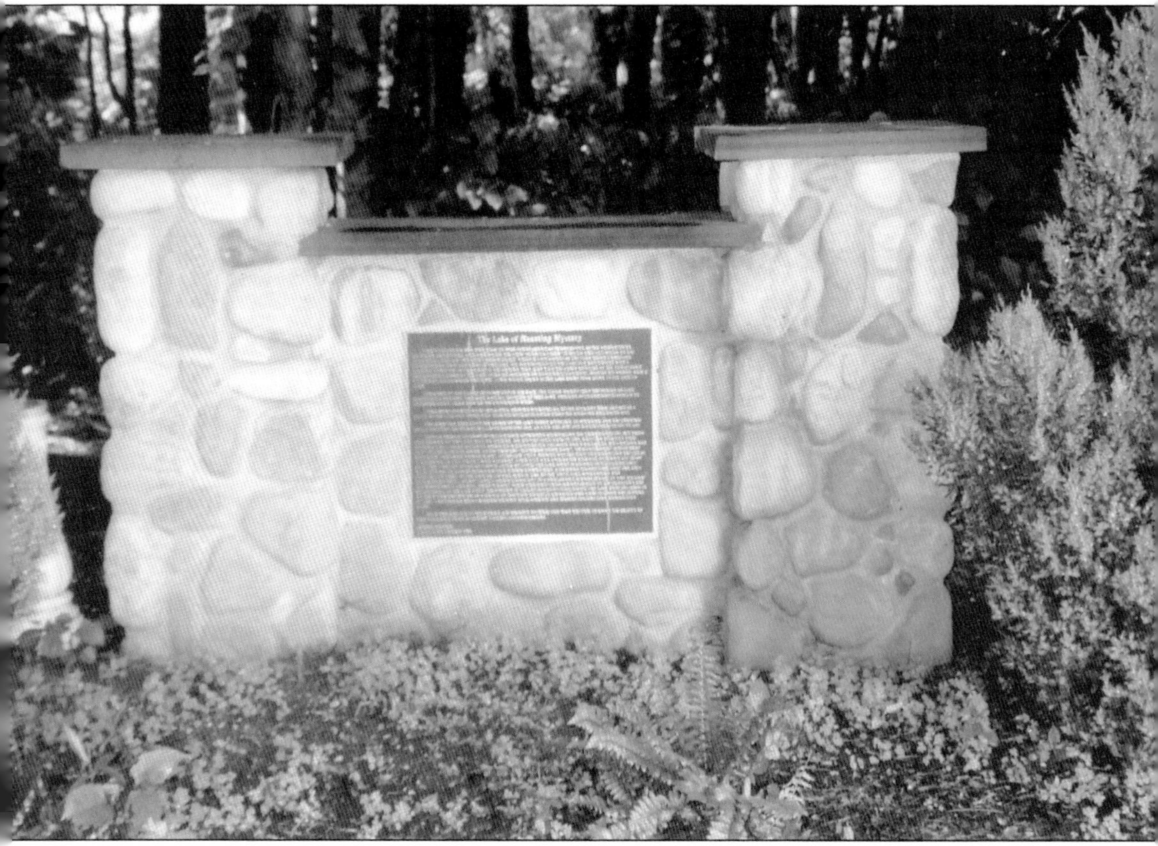

During the last month of the seventh year, Ronkonkoma could not break the pain and solitude she had for Birdsall. She sent a cryptic message to her lover, saying that she would join him in the morn. As dawn broke, Birdsall, waiting by the riverside, saw a canoe rise from the depths of the lake. Inside was his princess with a knife piercing her heart. Birdsall leaped into the canoe and held her lifeless form as the two were carried out to a life beyond the grave. Some eyewitnesses say they have seen the princess revisit the lake and walk on water. Many people feel that the princess takes the life of a man each year in search of her forbidden love. The thought is considered the basis for the curse that at least one person shall drown in the waters of Lake Ronkonkoma each year. (Courtesy of Keith Oswald.)

ABOUT THE ORGANIZATION

Ann Farnum Curtis and a group of dedicated volunteers created the Lake Ronkonkoma Historical Society to preserve the history of the Lake Ronkonkoma area. Ann wrote a history of Lake Ronkonkoma called the *Three Waves* and decreed that all the revenue from the book be used to support the organization. She convinced the Sachem Library to donate the vacant 1916 Ronkonkoma Free Library. Ann and her group of volunteers renovated the building, turning it into a small museum. They then convinced local residents to donate artifacts and share their family's histories. Ann's legacy lives on through the continued work of the society.

For more information, contact:
Lake Ronkonkoma Historical Society
PO Box 2716
Lake Ronkonkoma, New York 11779
(631) 467-3152